SPATIALIZING LAW

Spatializing Law: An Anthropological Geography of Law in Society focuses on law and its location, exploring how spaces are constructed on the terrestrial and marine surface of the earth with legal means in a rich variety of socio-political, legal and ecological settings. The contributors explore the interrelations between social spaces and physical space, highlighting the ways in which legal rules may localise people's rights and obligations in social space that may be mapped onto physical space. This volume also demonstrates how different notions of space and place become resources that can be mobilised in social, political and economic interaction, paying specific attention to the contradictory ways in which space may be configured and involved in social interaction under conditions of plural legal orders. *Spatializing Law* makes a significant contribution to the anthropological geography of law and will be useful to scholars across a broad array of disciplines.

Spatializing Law
An Anthropological Geography of Law in Society

Edited by

FRANZ VON BENDA-BECKMANN
Max Planck Institute for Social Anthropology, Germany

KEEBET VON BENDA-BECKMANN
Max Planck Institute for Social Anthropology, Germany

ANNE GRIFFITHS
University of Edinburgh, UK

ASHGATE

Published by

Ashgate Publishing Limited
Wey Court East
Union Road
Farnham
Surrey, GU9 7PT
England

Ashgate Publishing Company
Suite 420
101 Cherry Street
Burlington
VT 05401-4405
USA

www.ashgate.com

British Library Cataloguing in Publication Data
Spatializing law : an anthropological geography of law in
society. - (Law, justice and power series)
1. Law and geography 2. Sociological jurisprudence
I. Benda-Beckmann, Franz von II. Benda-Beckmann, Keebet von
III. Griffiths, Anne M. O.
340.1'15

Library of Congress Cataloging-in-Publication Data
Spatializing law : an anthropological geography of law in society / [edited] by Franz von Benda-Beckmann, Keebet von Benda-Beckmann and Anne Griffiths.
p. cm. -- (Law, justice and power)
Includes bibliographical references and index.
ISBN 978-0-7546-7291-3 -- ISBN 978-0-7546-9053-5 (ebook)
1. Law and geography. 2. Boundaries--Social aspects. 3. Spatial behavior--Political aspects. 4. Law and anthropology. 5. Sociological jurisprudence. I. Benda-Beckmann, Franz von. II. Benda-Beckmann, Keebet von. III. Griffiths, Anne M. O.

K487.G45S68 2009
340'.115--dc22

2008050199

ISBN 978 0 7546 7291 3
eISBN 978 0 7546 9053 5 (ebook)

Mixed Sources
Product group from well-managed forests and other controlled sources
www.fsc.org Cert no. SA-COC-1565
© 1996 Forest Stewardship Council
FSC

Printed and bound in Great Britain by
MPG Books Ltd, Bodmin, Cornwall.

Contents

List of Maps

List of Contributors

Gerhard Anders is Senior Lecturer at the Institute of Social and Cultural Anthropology, University of Zurich. His research focuses on the anthropology of law, political anthropology, global governance and the anthropology of development. He has conducted fieldwork in Malawi, Sierra Leone and Liberia. Recent publications include 'Normativity of Numbers: World Bank and IMF Conditionality' (*PoLAR: Political and Legal Anthropology Review* 31(2), 2008) and 'Follow the Trial: Some Notes on the Ethnography of International Criminal Justice' (*Anthropology Today* 23(3), 2007). He co-edited with Monique Nuijten *Corruption and the Secret of Law: A Legal Anthropological Perspective* (Ashgate 2007). A monograph titled *In the Shadow of Good Governance: An Ethnography of Civil Service Reform in Africa* is forthcoming.

Laurens Bakker is a Researcher and Lecturer at the Radboud University in Nijmegen. His main interests are the crossovers between anthropology and law, authority and power, and normativism in anthropological research on such issues as art and tourism. Laurens has carried out extensive field research in Indonesia (Nias, Mentawai and East Kalimantan) and on specialized courts of law in the Netherlands. Recent (2007) publications include 'Land Administration and hak ulayat. A Comparison of Policies in the East Kalimantan Districts of Pasir and Nunukan' in Hans de Iongh, Gerard Persoon and Wawan Kustiawan (eds) *Options for Biodiversity Conservation and Sustainable Use in Lowland Forests of Southeast Borneo*, Institute of Environmental Sciences, Leiden University, pp. 153–70, and 'Foreign Images in Mentawai. Authenticity and the Exotic' in: *Bijdragen tot de Taal-, Land-, en Volkenkunde* 163(2–3) 263–88.

Maarten Bavinck is a Human Geographer attached to the University of Amsterdam, the Netherlands. He completed his PhD in 1998 with a dissertation on legal pluralism in the marine fisheries of South India, and now heads the social science Centre for Maritime Research (MARE) at this university (www.marecentre.nl). His current work is on legal pluralism and governance of marine fisheries and involves intensive collaboration with representatives of natural science disciplines. Recent publications include: *Marine Resource Management – Conflict and Regulation in the Marine Fisheries of the Coromandel Coast* (Sage Publications 2001) and *Fish for Life – Interactive Governance for Fisheries* (ed.) (University of Amsterdam Press 2005).

Franz von Benda-Beckmann is head of the Project Group 'Legal Pluralism' at the Max Planck Institute for Social Anthropology in Halle/Saale, Germany, since 2002 Honorary Professor for Legal Anthropology at the University of Leipzig and since 2004 Honorary Professor for Legal Pluralism at the University of Halle/Saale. He holds a PhD in law (1970) and obtained his habilitation in anthropology at the University of Zurich (1979). Before 2000 he was professor for law in developing countries at the Agricultural University Wageningen. He has done fieldwork and supervised research in Malawi, West Sumatra, the Moluccas and Nepal. He has written and co-edited several books and published widely on issues of property rights, social (in)security and legal pluralism in developing countries and on legal anthropological theory. He co-edited together with Keebet von Benda-Beckmann and Anne Griffiths *Mobile People, Mobile Law. Expanding Legal Relations in a Contracting World* (Ashgate 2005) and with Keebet von Benda-Beckmann and Melanie G. Wiber *Changing Properties of Property* (Berghahn 2006). He published jointly with Keebet von Benda-Beckmann *Social Security between Past and Future: Ambonese Networks of Care and Support* (LIT Verlag 2007).

Keebet von Benda-Beckmann is head of the Project Group 'Legal Pluralism' at the Max Planck Institute for Social Anthropology in Halle/Saale, Germany, since 2003 Honorary Professor for Legal Anthropology at the University of Leipzig, and since 2004 Honorary Professor for Legal Pluralism at the University of Halle/Saale. She has carried out research in West Sumatra and on the Moluccan Island of Ambon, Indonesia and among Moluccan women in the Netherlands. She has published extensively on dispute resolution, social security in developing countries, property and water rights, decentralization, and on theoretical issues in the anthropology of law. She co-edited together with Franz von Benda-Beckmann and Anne Griffiths *Mobile People, Mobile Law. Expanding Legal Relations in a Contracting World* (Ashgate 2005) and with Franz von Benda-Beckmann and Melanie G. Wiber *Changing Properties of Property* (Berghahn 2006). She published jointly with Franz von Benda-Beckmann *Social Security between Past and Future: Ambonese Networks of Care and Support* (LIT Verlag 2007).

Anne Griffiths holds a personal chair in the Anthropology of Law at the School of Law at Edinburgh University, Scotland. Her research focuses on anthropology of law, comparative and family law, African law, gender, culture and rights. Her most recent project involves a UN Study on Informal Justice. Over the years, she has held visiting appointments at various institutions including Distinguished Visiting Professor, Faculty of Law, University of Toronto, the Max Planck Institute for Social Anthropology in Halle/Saale, Germany, The International Institute for the Sociology of Law Oñati – Gipuzkoa, Spain, The University of Texas at Austin, School of Law and the Southern and Eastern African Regional Centre for Women's Law at the University of Zimbabwe. She is currently President of the Commission on Folk Law and Legal Pluralism, a branch of the International Union of Anthropological and Ethnological Sciences.

Randy F. Kandel is an Adjunct Associate Professor at John Jay College of Criminal Justice, City University of New York. She has written many recent chapters and articles on children and the law, with her co-researcher/writer Anne Griffiths. They include 'Children's Confidentiality at the Cross Roads: Challenges for the Scottish Children's Hearings System', *Journal of Social Welfare and Family Law* 28(2), 2006; 'Half-Told Truth and Partial Silence: Managing Communication in the Scottish Children's Hearings' in *The Power of Law in a Transnational World: Anthropological Enquires* (eds) Franz and Keebet von Benda-Beckmann and Anne Griffiths (in press); and 'Custody and Coming of Age: Three American Cases' in *Reframing Parenthood and Childhood: Global Trends, Institutional Transformations, and Local Responses* (eds) T. Thelen and H. Haukanes (in press).

Davíd Lorenzo Rodríguez is a PhD candidate at the Department of Society and Globalization of Roskilde University, Denmark. He has conducted extensive research in Mexico and Peru on communal land tenure institutions. His current research in Andean communities focuses on a variety of topics that altogether try to shed more light on processes of territorialization in stateless places.

Monique Nuijten is Associate Professor at the rural Sociology Group of Wageningen University, the Netherlands. In Mexico and Peru she conducted extensive research on state–peasant relations, agrarian reform and communal land tenure institutions. At present she directs a research project about social organization and the construction of space in urban slums in Recife, Brazil. She is author of the book *Power, Community and the State; the Political Anthropology of Organisation in Mexico* (Pluto Press 2003), editor together with G. Anders of the book *Corruption and the Secret of Law: a Legal Anthropological Perspective* (Ashgate 2007) and numerous articles, including 'Between Fear and Fantasy: Governmentality and the Working of Power in Mexico' (*Critique of Anthropology* 2004) and 'External Interventions and Rituals of Resistance: The Implementation of Participatory Approaches in Rural Mexico' (*Journal of Peasant Studies* 2004).

Richard W. Whitecross is an Honorary Fellow of Social Anthropology at the School of Social and Political Studies, University of Edinburgh, he is also a qualified lawyer and anthropologist. His doctoral research on law and legal change in Bhutan was the first anthropological research on law to be conducted in Bhutan. He was awarded an Economic and Social Research Postdoctoral Fellowship (2003). After conducting research on tribunals in Britain, Richard was appointed as Senior Researcher in the Justice Directorate of the Scottish Government. He is currently writing the chapter on 'Constitutionalism' for a volume on Law and Buddhism and on Political Change in Bhutan for *Resurgent Democracies: Experiences of South and Southeast Asia*. Recent publications include 'Transgressing the Law: Karma, Theft and its Punishment' (*Revues d'Etudes Tibétaines* 2008) and 'Separation of Religion and Law?: Buddhism, Secularism and the Constitution of Bhutan' (*Buffalo Law Review* 2007).

Melanie G. Wiber is Professor of Anthropology at the University of New Brunswick, Canada. Her primary focus is natural resource management with research on irrigation, dairy and fishery quota, and community-based management. Her publications include *Politics, Property and Law in the Philippine Uplands* (Wilfrid Laurier Press 1993); *The Role of Law in Resource Management* (co-edited with Joep Spiertz, Vuga 1996) and *The Changing Properties of Property* (co-edited with Franz and Keebet von Benda-Beckmann, Berghahn 2006). With Chris Milley, she recently co-edited a special issue of the *Journal of Legal Pluralism*: 'After Recognition: Implementing Special Rights in Natural Resource Management' (2007).

Edwin N. Wilmsen received his PhD in Anthropology from the University of Arizona in 1967 after teaching and practicing architecture subsequent to receiving a Master of Architecture degree from MIT in 1959 with a thesis on community development at Shiprock on the Navaho Reservation. Since 1973, he has worked with Zhu, Herero and Tswana peoples in Botswana and has represented them in petitions to District and Ministry agencies. In 1975–1976, he served as consultant to the Rural Income Distribution Survey and, in 1981, wrote an analysis of 'Remote Area' peoples for the National Migration Study which served as a source for the subsequent sixth National Development Plan of Botswana. His book *Land Filled with Flies: A Political Economy of the Kalahari* (University of Chicago Press 1989) was awarded the 1990 Herskovits Prize of the African Studies Association (USA) and the 1992 Graham Prize of the School of Oriental and African Studies (London); its companion, *Journeys with Flies* was published in 1995 by University of Chicago Press. He has edited *The Kalahari Ethnographies of Siegfried Passarge (1896–1898): Nineteenth Century Khoisan- and Bantu-speaking Peoples* (Rüdiger Köppe Verlag 1997) and co-edited *The Politics of Difference: Ethnic Premises in a World of Power* (the University of Chicago Press 1996).

Gordon R. Woodman is Emeritus Professor of Comparative Law at the University of Birmingham, Britain, where he has been based since 1976. Previously he worked in University Law Faculties in Ghana and Nigeria for 15 years. He has made a study of customary laws generally in the modern world, and especially in Africa and related issues in legal theory concerning the nature of customary law and the theory of legal pluralism. He has been Editor-in-Chief of the *Journal of Legal Pluralism and Unofficial Law* since 1994. His recent publications include: *Local Land Law and Globalization: A Comparative Study of Peri-urban Areas in Benin, Ghana and Tanzania* (LIT 2004, edited with Ulrike Wanitzek and Harald Sippel) and *Law and Religion in Multicultural Societies* (DJØF Publishing 2008, edited with Rubya Mehdi and others).

Acknowledgements

This volume is the third publication that has resulted from a series of conferences organized by the School of Law, Edinburgh University and the Max Planck Institute for Social Anthropology in Halle/Saale, Germany, on the development of the anthropology of law. The first volume *Mobile People, Mobile Law: Expanding Legal Relations in a Contracting World* appeared in 2005 with Ashgate. The second volume *The Power of Law in a Transnational World: Anthropological Enquiries* will appear with Berghahn 2009. We thank the Max Planck Institute for Social Anthropology; the Economic and Social Research Council (UK); the British Academy (UK); and the Wenner-Gren Foundation for Anthropological Research (US) for their financial support. We are deeply indebted to Margaret Beechey and Myra Reid for their work when organizing the conference and to Gesine Koch, Philipp Humpert and Titus Rebhann for preparing the manuscript.

Chapter 1

Space and Legal Pluralism: An Introduction

Franz von Benda-Beckmann, Keebet von Benda-Beckmann
and Anne Griffiths

Since the spatial turn in the social sciences, impressive advances have been made in analysing the interrelations between social organization and processes and space, place and boundaries.[1] This spatialization of social theory has been prompted by a critical social geography and a heightened interest in the effects of globalization and the challenges it has posed to notions of state-based territoriality.[2] Studies addressing space usually focus on urban studies, where issues of households and gender, identity, public and private spaces, and inequality are discussed, but legal issues are marginally discussed at best.[3] While some studies of political and economic organization have touched on law in their examination of territoriality and land tenure, they rarely investigate the specific ways in which law features in any detail.[4] In general the relationship between law and space still seems to be considered marginal to social sciences in general, relegated to a specialization within geography.[5]

In recent years, however, the relationship between law and space has drawn broader interest. There is a growing body of geographic studies of law by authors

---

1 Since Giddens' statement: 'Most forms of social theory have failed to take seriously enough not only the temporality of social conduct but also its spatial attributes' (1979, 202), there have been quite dynamic developments. See among others Giddens (1984; 1985); Appadurai (1990); Lash and Urry (1994, 223); and Harvey (1996, 264). See also Marcus (1992, 316) on the significance of the spatial and the temporal for ethnography.

2 Low and Lawrence-Zuniga (2003, 25). Robertson (1990) speaks of 'mapping' the global condition. Featherstone and Lash (1995). See also Appadurai's (1990) discussion of scapes and territorialization and deterritorialization; Appadurai (2003); Perry and Maurer (2003); Benda-Beckmann et al. (2005); Tsing (2005); and Benda-Beckmann and Benda-Beckmann (2007).

3 For example, Tickamyer's (2000) plea for an analysis of inequality that takes space seriously only in passing refer to some legal issues.

4 Ingold (1986, 136); Wilmsen (1989b); Dijk (1996); Rösler and Wendl (1999); Abramson and Theodossopoulos (2000); Hagberg and Tengan (2000); and Saltman (2002).

5 Blomley (1994, 107) notes that the spatiality of law is widely ignored in legal theory. In his view, this 'geographical silence is not a function of the geographical imagination but of its constitutional exclusion' (Blomley 1994, 25).

such as Blomley (1994; 2006) and Taylor (2006).[6] Blomley (1994, 107) noted in the mid-1990s that the spatiality of law was widely ignored in legal theory. In his view, this 'geographical silence is not a function of the geographical imagination but of its constitutional exclusion' (Blomley 1994, 25). By now, there is also a substantial amount of critical legal literature on the discursive references to space within legal discourse. Delaney (2006, 69) points out that 'liberal legal discourse is an embarrassingly rich source of spatial tropes and metaphors'. He calls this Space-in-Law, to be distinguished from Law-in-Space, which inquires into 'the way in which situated legal practices … contribute to the spatialities of social life' (2006, 68).[7] Delaney argues that these discursive metaphors are inextricably intertwined with the material spatial arrangements created by law. These studies document how law is being used to 'shape a landscape of "social apartheid, inequitable distribution of public resources and political disenfranchisement"', as Kedar (2006, 405) suggests.

In legal anthropology space is discussed in a number of ways. There is an emerging interest for issues of a cartography and geography of law and rights.[8] More recently the interest in space in the anthropology of law has been extended to transnational movements of legal models and their appropriation or rejection at different levels of state organization and by local actors.[9] A number of authors have used spatial metaphors to characterize social spaces in order to delineate the places where law is being made and put into practice.[10] Their analyses, however, do not examine how these social spaces are grounded in physical space in any systematic way, with the danger that the two become conflated. This makes it difficult to examine the interrelations between social, legal and physical space.[11]

With this volume, we want to contribute to the emerging anthropological geography of law, building upon theoretical and methodological insights that have been developed in spatialization theory in geography, sociology, anthropology and critical legal studies, but putting legal complexity at centre stage. The notion of space

6 *Stanford Law Review* (Vol. 48/5) published a special issue on law and geography in 1996. Blomley et al. published a reader on the Geographies of Law in 2001, and the volume Law and Geography of 2006, edited by Holder and Harrison, attempts to bring insights from geography and law together. Together these volumes provide a good overview of the state of the art on the relationship between law and space.

7 Kedar (2006, 412) also argues that 'while law plays an important role in creating and organizing spaces of inequalities, it simultaneously conceals and legitimizes these inequalities beneath a neutral and professional discourse'.

8 Santos (1987); Benda-Beckmann and Benda-Beckmann (1991; 1998); and Benda-Beckmann, F. von (1999; 2001).

9 See Merry (1997; 2005; 2006); and Benda-Beckmann and Benda-Beckmann (2007).

10 Moore (1973); Kidder (1978); Galanter (1981); and Santos (1985).

11 Such conflation of spaces may also be used to map the cultural self-legitimation of nation states (Greenhouse 1998). See also Gupta and Ferguson's critique of 'spatially territorialized notions of culture' (1997, 6).

provides an important lens through which to view law. This is because it provides both a grounded, physical setting, as well as a more intangible universe, in which to locate the varying ways in which social relationships are created and regulated with differing effects. Such investigation is critical, for as Blomley (1994, preface) observes 'within legal thought and legal practice are a number of representations or "geographies" of the spaces of political, social and economic life'. Conversely, law is a crucial way of constructing, organizing and legitimating spaces, places and boundaries. Law is crucial because it not only 'serves to produce space yet in turn is shaped by a socio-spatial context' (Blomley 1994, 51). For in struggling to make sense of the complexity and ambiguity of social life 'legal agents – whether judges, legal theorists, administrative officers or ordinary people – represent and evaluate space in various ways' (Blomley 1994, xi). Thus the legal representation of space must be seen 'as constituted by – and in turn, constitutive of – complex, normatively charged and often competing visions of social and political life under law' (Blomley 1994, xi). This does not imply a deterministic and homogeneous influence of legal notions of space for people's actual interactions, but that it is likely that they will have some influence on social interactions.

All social and legal institutions, relations and practices are located and distributed in space. Following Giddens (1984; 1985) we conceive of space, time and place as constituent elements of social life and organization that help to individuate people, interactions and relationships in time and space.[12] This includes the processes of giving meaning to space and bounding it. It involves taking account of the ways places are carved out, and people, relationships and objects are located and bounded in space. At the same time, spatial structures are, like other structures, involved in the duality of structuration processes, as Löw et al. (2007, 63), following Giddens, have argued. They form the environment, medium and outcome of social interactions.[13] As a result, the interrelationships between law and space become open to investigation, for just as space in this context is viewed as a social product that embodies social relationships (Lefebvre 1991), so law represents an arena in which the politics of space is enacted and negotiated, one that requires an understanding of the extent to which legal spaces are embedded in broader social and political claims (Blomley 1994, xi). Spatial constructions as embodied in legal categories and regulation provide sets of resources that become part of the repertoire for 'spatial idiom shopping' and that can be mobilized against each other by a variety of actors in the pursuit of their economic and political objectives.[14] Thus, space not only serves 'as a means of production but also as a means of control and hence of domination, of power'

12 See also Lash and Urry (1994, 223).

13 Manderson (2005, 1) points out that '[T]he law both structures our understanding of certain spaces, while at the same time those spaces themselves radically transform the experience, application, and effect of the law'. See also Werlen (1988, 181).

14 See Giddens (1979; 1984); Orlove (1991); Benda-Beckmann, F. von (1992); and Benda-Beckmann and Taale (1996). For a particularly vivid illustration from Costa Rica,

(Lefebvre 1991, 26). The relationship between these domains is multifaceted, for as Lefebvre (1991, 33) observes they embrace 'spatial practice' that highlights lived-in space, and 'representations of space' that reflect state-centred conceptions and ordering of space, as well as 'representational spaces' that embody the ways in which space is perceived from citizens' perspectives. For this reason, focusing on space reveals the extent to which law is a powerful tool that is constantly in the making and that is used in a variety of ways by different social actors to create frameworks for the exercise of power and control over people and resources on varying scales.[15]

The relations between law and space are particularly interesting under conditions of legal pluralism. The emerging literature about law and space pays relatively little attention to the complexities of the relations between law and space that arise from the coexistence of legal orders. So far, most work in the geography of law and in legal studies has mainly focused on law and space in the context of state law in industrialized states in Europe and America, with an urban bias. However, many people live under plural legal constellations. For example, they negotiate one set of rules relating to personal law, such as customary law, with another such as religious or international human rights law (reflecting a more transnational dimension), along with state law that also reflects a degree of heterogeneity (Benda-Beckmann et al. 2005). We argue that legal pluralism deserves a central position in the analysis of law in space. For it highlights the ways in which legal constructions of space in state and international law, religious and traditional law operate with their own spatial claims for validity. Under plural legal conditions, often a result of colonial rule, diverse and often contradictory notions of spaces and boundaries and their legal relevances come to coexist. The ways in which physical spaces, boundaries or borderlands are conceived and made legally relevant varies considerably within and across legal orders. Relations between space and social organization, the temporality of constructions of space and place, the scale on which they operate, and the political loading and moral connotations pertaining to specific spaces may all differ. Thus multiple legal constructions of space open up multiple arenas for the exercise of political authority, the localization of rights and obligations, as well as the creation of social relationships and institutions that are characterized by different degrees of abstraction, different temporalities and moral connotations. We suggest that research on law as a crucial factor in the ways space, place and boundaries are shaping social behaviour under conditions of legal pluralism requires more theoretical reflection and empirical scrutiny. Understanding how law operates, or is mobilized, in these contexts requires a recalibration of the relationship that exists between law and social space. With this emphasis, this volume contributes to an understanding of the implications of law's location for social inequality.

---

see Brooijmans (1997). See also Spiertz (1989) on idiom shopping and Geisler and Bedford (1996) for the United States.

15 See Anderson (1991); and Harvey (1996, 44, 266).

This volume focuses on the interrelations between social spaces and boundaries and physical space, highlighting the contradictory ways in which space may be configured and involved in social interaction under conditions of plural legal orders. Contributions explore how spaces are constructed and mapped with legal means on the terrestrial and marine surface of the earth (and below) in a rich variety of socio-political, legal and ecological settings, ranging from micro-spaces such as the rooms in which child hearings are conducted in Scotland to much larger geographical and political regions in Canada, Latin America, African and Asian states. The contributions address the significance of legal constructions of space and boundaries as a means of governance and the conflicts between different legal constructions of spaces of political and economic authority. They also highlight how legal rules localize people's rights and obligations in physical and social space and explore the interrelationship between physical, legal and other social spaces. Moreover, they examine the different scales on which legal orders are projected and operate. Finally, some authors explore the mapping of law and its ramifications.

Conflicting Constructions of Space

Legal systems define their own claim to validity in social and physical space. Law defines the boundaries and the territory within which it claims validity and which becomes the, or one of the, relevant criteria for citizenship and nationality. Most of these spaces brought into being by law have clearly defined boundaries, as is the case with nation states where their territory and its borders mark the limit of their jurisdiction. However, laws may also claim validity as 'mobile law' and rights, by inscribing their validity into the status of persons, animals or movables detached from a specific place irrespective of where they live. On a larger scale, spaces extending beyond state boundaries may acquire legal validity through multinational agreements created by transnational entities, such as the European Union. Indeed, for some types of law, such as human rights law, global or cosmopolitan validity is claimed, while traditional legal and religious legal orders often define the validity of their law independently from any spatial demarcation, as is the case, for instance, with Islamic law.

Law is also used for creating spaces for more specific purposes with special legal regimes that are superimposed on this general geographical political and administrative grid, such as economic zones, zones for urban planning, 'problem' or 'safety' zones, zones related to resource management, such as village commons, forests, agricultural regions, nature reservations and fishery grounds, or plots of property demarcated in a cadastral registration system. Within one legal system there may be a multiplicity of different constructions of legally relevant space that may coexist and compete, such as nature reserves and residential building plans or UNESCO world heritage site versus new traffic infrastructure. The measure of abstraction largely depends on the consequences lawmakers aim at when selecting specific characteristics while abstracting from and leaving other characteristics legally irrelevant.[16] For some purposes, for example citizenship, law may define legally relevant space in a very general way. But for other purposes it may select or attribute specific ecological or economic characteristics to certain spaces in order to create nature reserves, tourist regions or economic zones. Legal rules also localize people's rights and obligations in space, whether this is for purposes of acquiring state citizenship, exercising voting rights, providing and using legal services such as courts and police, organizing tax obligations or residence rights and duties of married spouses.[17] The localization and material embodiment of such rights in resources and people in physical space and bounding are important attributes for the definition of objects, events and relationships (Harvey 1996, 264). Through such location and bounding, 'places' are constructed in space.[18]

Legal systems differ greatly in the degree of abstraction and temporality that frames their major spatial categories and spatially grounded rights and obligations. Rights and obligations attached to space have varying degrees of permanence. In anthropology, Bohannan (1967) has been one of the first to point to the relevance of these differences in perceiving space in his discussion of land tenure in Africa. He pointed to the need of understanding the different 'folk geographies', of people's representations of the country in which they live and their ways of correlating man and society with the physical environment (1967, 54–5). The Tiv described by Bohannan (1967) provide a good example. In the process of shifting cultivation, the Tiv genealogical map and the segmentary social organization based upon it 'moves' over the surface of the earth, creating only temporary connections between people and their places in the physical world. Similarly, Wilmsen (1989a; 1989b) drawing on some of Gluckman's (1965; 1971) insights, demonstrates how ascribed and acquired kinship and affinal relations among San, Tswana, and Herero define a person's rights to allowing tenurial relations to remain intact, when land actually occupied is changed due to ecological and political conditions.

While contemporary states maintain a stability of territorial and administrative boundaries, other (local) political and economic structures have been far less preoccupied with permanence of space and boundaries. Several authors in this volume address the implications of confrontations between property regimes that construct property relations to natural resources differently each with a degree of permanence (see Bakker; von Benda-Beckmanns; Nuijten; and Wiber and Wilmsen in this volume). Ownership in Western legal systems, for instance, tends to be treated as a timeless concept but categories of property derived from these systems often have a built-in restricted time horizon. Some of the new property

16 See Scott (1998); and Blomley's (1994) on strategic abstractions and simplifications.

17 See Benda-Beckmann and Benda-Beckmann (1978); and Economides et al. (1986).

18 Such 'permanences – no matter how solid they seem – are not eternal: They are always subject to time as "perpetual perishing", and contingent on the processes that create, sustain and dissolve them' (Harvey 1996, 261, 264, 294).

categories such as cultural heritage are defined by reference to the past, while others, such as nature reserves, explicitly refer to future generations.[19]

Under conditions of legal pluralism the overlap between different spaces imbued with different political and economic, moral or religious meaning becomes more complex. They carry with them diverging claims to legitimacy, political and economic authority. Moreover, different functions may be inscribed in space and resources. For example, religiously defined (sacred sites) and ecological defined spaces (nature reservations) may, but often do not coincide and are in different ways linked or opposed to other spaces that involve different authority structures (see Fisiy 1997). These do not necessarily lead to conflicts but can also coexist peacefully side by side or develop forms of hybridity. However, the juxtaposition of differently defined and legitimated political and economic authority spaces in practice regularly leads to serious conflicts. This is especially evident in the case of colonial and post-colonial political organization where the introduction of European notions of bounded space led to a situation of legal pluralism. Here, the state law may, under the legal construction of recognition, provide enclaves for the validity of customary or religious law, confined to specific territorial administrative spaces and to specific sectors of social life. These spaces have different authority structures and differ in constellations of political and economic power.[20] Different notions of space and spatially grounded rights and obligations become pitted against one another in strategic interactions over contested forms of political authority in the (sometimes violent) fight for control over resources, as most chapters in this volume illustrate.

However, transformations of space in plural legal orders have not always been mere top-down impositions by colonial rulers; they could also be consciously and strategically manipulated by local actors as well, as Bohannan (1967, 58) showed for the Osage Indians in North America and the Yoruba in Nigeria. Today, many indigenous peoples engage in mapping their territory and claiming demarcated resource zones although in former times they had no fixed boundaries. Thus Scott's statement that 'backed by state power through records, courts and ultimately coercion, these state fictions transformed the reality they presumed to observe, although never so thoroughly as to precisely fit the grid' (1998, 23) must be treated with caution, as the chapters by the von Benda-Beckmanns and Bakker in this volume demonstrate. States' attempts to impose their own property regimes over the years had varying degrees of success as many failed land law reforms have shown. Such conflicting notions of political and economic resource spaces, moreover, are not restricted to the opposition between state and customary

19 For a comparative analysis of the spatial and temporal dimension of Minangkabau and Ambonese law, see Benda-Beckmann and Benda-Beckmann (1994); and this volume. See also Benda-Beckmann et al. (2006).

20 Assignment of place within some socio-spatial structure indicates distinctive roles, capacities for action and access to power. As Gupta and Ferguson (1997, 8) note, 'the making of spaces into places is always implicated in hegemonic configurations of power'.

laws. Such contradictions also obtain between different versions of customary law which actors mobilize against each other in their claims to land and trees as the von Benda-Beckmanns show (Chapter 6). Indeed, the insertion of clearly demarcated spatial boundaries into traditional and customary notions of political and economic spaces was an important aspect in what has been called the 'creation' of customary law (see Clammer 1973; and Chanock 1985). As the case of Ambon described by the von Benda-Beckmanns (Chapter 6) illustrates, such transformed versions of ethnic law do not necessarily supersede the earlier forms but may coexist with them. Thus historically older regulations and the spaces they have defined may continue to be of social and political significance long after the state has replaced them by new legislation, or, as in the Ambonese case, with a new version of customary law. The more radical reinterpretations of past categories usually occur when the political constellation is undergoing fundamental change, as Nuijten, Bakker and the von Benda-Beckmanns demonstrate. Under such circumstances, these reinterpretations are usually hotly contested. The political dynamics in the post-Suharto Indonesia provide many illustrations.[21]

Spaces and places often have a moral or religious value attached to them. Nature sanctuaries, village or lineage land, burial places, but also commercial fisheries are not only social or economic but at the same time moral categories. Within legal spaces, we also find constructions of 'dangerous' spaces as opposed to 'good' or sanctioned spaces for action of urban youth, that either in social or legal terms point at radically different perceptions and moral evaluations of the moral spaces where they hang out (A. Griffiths and R.F. Kandel in Chapter 8). Wiber shows how within a political setting of large-scale commercial fishery and scientific resource management, local fishing communities are considered the odd case, being backward, traditional, unwilling to move to find work elsewhere if the fishing industry takes away their living. Their attachment to place rather than the exclusion from fishing grounds is seen as the source of the social problems within the community.[22] A well known instance of contrasting economic moralities is visible in the legal treatment of natural resource environments not maximally exploited in the short term. In the expanding capitalist agriculture in the nineteenth-century colonies, such unproductive land was deemed 'waste' since it was not cultivated in an efficient economic sense.[23] By contrast, in many village laws such land and forest are morally assessed as taking care of future generations. The same holds true for resources held as morally valued inalienable linage property which is 'not yet' accessible by 'the market' and therefore 'backwards'.[24] The moral significance of

21 See Benda-Beckmann and Benda-Beckmann (2007); and Schulte Nordholt and Klinken (2007).

22 See also Peters (1997, 80); and Tsing (2005).

23 See for example for West Sumatra, Benda-Beckmann and Benda-Beckmann (2006).

24 Malkki (1997) has pointed out that people not linked to a particular territoriality are seen as 'uprooted', 'cultureless', 'not ordinary' and 'a problem' (Malkki 1997, 62).

space and places may be also given legal relevance through respectful recognition of this value, for example, through exemptions from certain economic or political obligations. Where such legal recognition is not given but the moral value is shared by most people, conflicts are likely to occur. This contestation often entails more than a conflict over specific space as it embodies a more general challenge to dominant legal norms. The moral value of space thus exacerbates the intensity of conflicts about resources within contested resource spaces.

Space as a Governance Resource

Legal constructions of space are used as an instrument to control people and resources. Especially state governments use constructions of space in order to effectively transform their imagined community into a well controlled and bounded space.[25] In contemporary state systems, such validity spaces tend to be represented as rather homogeneous maps, as consequences of what Blomley calls the centralization narrative, 'in which the geography of legal evolution has been one of a continued disembedding of legal practice and knowledge from the locality, and a centralization of legal authority, in step with the formation of national state structure' (1994, 107). One concept of space for which this is particularly true and that has been vexing for social anthropologists is the notion of community. The abstraction from characteristics of people placed together, for instance in constructions of 'community' often suggest a politically intended 'equivalence' while masking important social differentials. As Gupta and Ferguson (1997, 13) say, the notion of a space representing a community is primarily 'a categorical identity that is premised on various forms of exclusion and constructions of otherness'. As a result 'the legal understanding of local communities can reveal themselves as very different from the formalized legalities of the judiciary' (Blomley 1994, xii). This may give rise to a situation where 'legal obligations and rights are understood in radically different ways by groups at different social and spatial locations' (Blomley 1994, 42).[26] Thongchai Winichakul (1988) and Anderson (1991) have shown for Thailand, in Blomley's words (1994, 53), a process in which an a-spatial and individualized modern grid of legal interpretation was forcibly imposed upon a traditionally variegated, contextual and deeply local legal map.

Several chapters in this volume highlight the ways in which the legal constructions of spaces interrelate with social, ethnic and economic spaces that are

---

See also Hatcher (2006, 456). As Fitzpatrick (1992, 81) has argued, the law of modern states is premised on the opposition of state and savagery.

25 For the imposition of spatially demarcated village community in Southeast Asian countries, see Breman (1987); Kemp (1988); Benda-Beckmann, F. von (1999); and this volume. See Gooding (1994) for North American Indians; Mertz (1994). Blomley (1994, 52, 54) for Aborigines in Australia.

26 See also Rosen-Zvi 2005 on the denial of spatial segregation in Israel. See also Kelly (forthcoming).

used as a means of controlling population and a means of inclusion and exclusion. In Chapter 2, Nuijten and Lorenzo Rodríguez explore the ways in which 'lived space', as experienced by people in their daily lives, relates to 'abstract space' created and imposed by the state in the context of peasant communities in the Andean highlands of Peru. They examine how territorial struggles over land between local communities and the state represent mechanisms for controlling populations through the classification of space that was used to delimit categories of person who were to be included or excluded from the process of land distribution. Under the Spanish this was achieved by establishing a *hacienda* system. This involved assigning large tracts of land to a *hacienda* owner that required substantial labour by the indigenous population. Instead of mandating the indigenous population to provide this labour by law, territorial means were created to induce them to provide the necessary low paid labour. By allotting very large tracts of land to the *hacienda*, they created artificial land scarcity for the indigenous population, forcing them to perform agricultural labour on the *haciendas* in exchange for land. This land, however, could only be used for subsistence and not for commercial purposes. Thus, under colonial rule, the land was carved up in territories assigned for different use which in fact created an intricate system of control over the indigenous population.

Under the Peruvian state similar territorial strategies have been employed to control the indigenous population up until the present. Nuijten and Lorenzo Rodríguez demonstrate how Indian villages in the Andean highlands were forced to exist 'in silence' because of their lack of official and legal recognition. This was achieved through regulating access to territory by creating a system of ethnic categorization that operated to exclude those who did not fall within its remit. By representing these laws in terms of the neutral administration of land, processes of exclusion were impersonalized and obscured. In this process a patronage system in relation to land became established that led to indigenous communities being inserted into a larger economy and system of domination. Members of these communities resisted in various ways, demonstrating the internal divisions that existed among members of the *communidad*, based on power and inequality. The fact that some members sought to utilize state law for their own ends, in conflict with other members of the community, highlights the complexities of the overlapping and conflicting claims to rights embodied in places and people. This leads Nuijten and Lorenzo Rodríguez to conclude, in their analysis of the intended and unintended consequences of land tenure reform over the years, that the relations between state and civil society cannot be viewed in strictly oppositional terms for the effects of such reforms have proved somewhat double sided.

Whitecross addresses the relationship between physical, social and legal space in the context of citizenship, borders and the notion of 'belonging' in Bhutan. In Chapter 3 he examines how the Bhutanese state, through recourse to law, has promoted the concept of citizenship to construct a particular vision of the nation state in a changing landscape of political and economic vulnerability posed by external and internal factors. Such a project presents a challenge given the porous nature of the physical borders that mark Bhutan and the fear of encroachment (both physically and culturally) by powerful, territorial neighbours like China and India. Whitecross traces the changing criteria of citizenship with its attendant effects through three main sources of legislation, the Nationality Act 1958, the Citizenship Act 1977 and the Citizenship Act 1985, along with the newly drafted Constitution published in 2005 and enacted in 2008. He demonstrates how processes of inclusion and exclusion, associated with the status of citizenship, have varied over time according to the exigencies of different historical periods.

Such developments represent an attempt to deal with what is perceived as a threat to Bhutan's ability to maintain its cultural heritage and political survival. They also underline the complex relationship between notions of social behaviour, 'traditional values', and the various state strategies that have been used to promote and maintain 'Bhutanese' values. The way in which this has been done reflects what Whitecross refers to as an 'imagining' of community that creates spaces for some to gain recognition as citizens but not for others. Law has played an important part in this process, not only through legislation, but also through the courts' upholding of formal legal requirements that endorse important differences in status, involving inclusion and exclusion through the varying levels of legal documentation that are required and that reflect official gradations of belonging. What is imagined and experienced with regard to citizenship has created tensions within the country that not only promote discord among the population through ascriptions in status, such as being Lhotshampa or Bhutanese, but that also, ironically, underpin an increasingly vocalized ethno-nationalism.

Wiber also addresses the relationship between the ways in which space is differentially constructed in terms of political/administrative units and the localization of rights. She discusses these issues in the context of the administration of natural resource management in the Canadian Bay of Fundy. She analyses the ways in which administrative law and management regimes have undermined specific local knowledge bases that are critical for administering natural resources in the area. This is achieved in two ways. First, through regulations that rely on a combination of spatial and temporal management that either excludes locals from physical access to resource stocks or significantly limits times or areas open for access and withdrawal. Second, through management regimes that embody the spatial/temporal expertise emanating from highly technical transnational 'epistemic communities', thereby discounting practice-based knowledge. In Canada, this approach has effectively 'deskilled' members of local fishing communities. This is achieved through the mechanisms by which various levels of government define local variation and specificities as being inconsequential when it comes to scientific resource management. Not only that but moral judgements are made about local knowledge which is presented as static, insular and somewhat backward-looking compared with global management and conceptions of space that are viewed as rational, progressive, forward-looking and cosmopolitan. In this way the struggle for access to natural resources is redefined into a moral problem of lifestyles.

Wiber's analysis highlights the ways in which both livelihoods and their attendant knowledge generation are social processes in which law is implicated. In these processes she demonstrates how international and state law supersede local rights of access and the consequences that ensue. For in the Bay of Fundy longitudinal and place-based fisher knowledge has been devalued in favour of federal bureaucratic and university-based marine research. Her analysis of place is critical of the way social geographers' and political theorists' work has had the effect of making it more 'constructed' than lived-in with the result that how spatial scales are variously used to frame environmental knowledge and to mobilize particular social practices has been largely ignored. As a consequence, discourses of law shape 'place' in ways that often 'misread and mismanage the landscape'. Thus, Wiber argues that since the definition of place and the uses to which it can be put can be so contested, we need to recognize the ways in which multiple layers of law differently define and constrain the uses of legal spaces and to document how local normative orders are negotiated or set aside in the context of political economies that are brought to bear on them. The implications of different perceptions of scale can be far-reaching. As Wiber, in Chapter 4, shows with the example of the Canadian fisheries management, not only do certain categories of actors lose out in the new management structures. Differences in the use of modern statistical analysis and perceptions of the scale at which the problems of fish stocks are perceived and regulated have immediate implications for knowledge structures about these fish stocks. In other words, the scales at which social and ecological issues are perceived and addressed with legal means to a large extent define what the issue is.[27]

Political Authority and Property Spaces

As Chapters 2 and 4, by Nuijten/Lorenzo Rodríguez and Wiber already show, plural legal constructions of political and economic spaces, especially of productive resources, tend to lead to conflicts. Conflicts over resources are nearly always politically loaded, because of the power potential of economic authority and because authority over people and natural resources are often inextricably linked. Contesting natural resources often means contesting the authority structure related to these resources as well and vice versa. Chapters 5 and 6, by Bakker and the von Benda-Beckmanns, focus on claims to land and authority in struggles for political authority and land employing different legal idioms and concomitant resource categories based in different historical periods. They demonstrate that each of these lead to different ways of exclusion and inclusion of diverse local populations.

27 See Street (2006, 326) in his analysis of biodiversity knowledge in agriculture for the importance of seeing local knowledge as embedded in networks of actors that extend beyond localities.

From the perspective of a land dispute in the district of Pasir, East Kalimantan, Bakker discusses the resurgence of sultanates in Indonesia as a result of the post-Suharto political constellation and decentralization policies. He highlights how claims to land by a descendant of a sultanate family, backed by an old map, are not only resisted by another royal descendant but also by the Indonesian state and by a local population all of whom mobilize competing categorizations of space based on different versions of local history, social circumstances and cultural values to substantiate their legal claims. Thus the local hill population, through a non-governmental organization, argue that the sultan is located outside their traditional territory, and thus is categorized as an outsider, a newcomer, who has no original rights to the land under dispute. This enables them to assert their authority over 'their' territory, against the sultan's descendants and the state. One of the sultan's descendants, however, who is a well-educated, middle-range civil servant, challenges this interpretation by positioning himself as a representative of the population living within the total territory of the former sultanate. This interpretation renders him an insider rather than an outsider, one who is entitled to defend the rights of the population including the local hill population who oppose him against an intrusive state.

Bakker clearly demonstrates how various normative systems, including differing versions of local law as well as national Indonesian law, vie with one another on the basis of claims to validity that derive from the specific spatial setting in which they are applied. Such an approach highlights the need for local knowledge for with decentralization considerable powers are now vested in regional authorities which were previously subordinated under central government. As a result there is no longer a dominant discourse but rather a multiplicity of discursive elements that are brought to bear on shaping the local constellation of law. Thus, the spatialization of law in Indonesia has emerged as a potent tool for acquiring and maintaining power at the regional level of government, one that makes for a large and dynamic legal diversity among the country's many regions. In this struggle for authority legal constructions of space are often used as a means of promoting control over people and resources through territorial assertions that reflect both continuity and transformation over time.

The von Benda-Beckmanns analyse historical developments in the legal constructions of property and authority spaces by competing legal orders in two regions of Indonesia, the Minangkabau of West Sumatra and the island of Ambon in the Moluccas, which have been incorporated into the Dutch colonial empire at very different moments in time. In doing so, they show how older categories of space and localizations of property rights have lingered on despite the state's attempts to replace them. They examine the differential impact of colonization on traditional authority and its localization within the village, highlighting the political and administrative spaces related to the various categories of land rights introduced in different historical periods that continue to have relevance today. For on the island of Ambon, the Dutch forced the indigenous hill population to settle at the coast which led to a shift in power between the hill population and the coastal population that had arrived at a later stage in the island's development. At the same time, the Dutch introduced a completely new set of spatial categories that redesigned property relations and authority structures, leading in effect to a new type of customary law. In West Sumatra, however, processes of resettlement and spatial redefinition did not occur in quite the same way during the colonial period. As a result the emerging competition with regard to localization of rights takes on different forms in the two regions. These reflect the conflict between rights based in adat and in state law in West Sumatra, compared with the conflict between two types of adat that is prevalent in Ambon. In both cases localized notions of property compete with one another and are mobilized by the population in an attempt to legitimate claims to land. In the wake of the latest decentralization in Indonesia this competition has obtained a new political and economic impetus.

As the foregoing chapters by Nuijten/Lorenzo Rodríguez (Chapter 2), Whitecross (Chapter 3), Wiber (Chapter 4) and Bakker (Chapter 5) demonstrate, it is important to take account of the social significance of the localization of law and rights in physical space. This is especially pertinent under conditions of legal pluralism where law may be engaged in establishing power differentials that work out spatially in creating centre–periphery relationships (see Butler 2007 on Lefebvre) or in acquiring control over land (Blomley 1994; Forman 2006). Thus, the interrelation between social fields and the relations and interactions between persons or groups and the physical space in which they are actually grounded acquires salience here. For studying the actual location and distribution of people, rights and obligations belonging to the same social field 'enables the researcher to identify patterns of activity that result from the spatial distribution of economic resources, settlements and social classes' (Long and Roberts 1984, 4). Thus, the location in physical space may be an important explanatory factor for variation in social practices.

In exploring how overlapping legal orders create hierarchies of locations within local communities the von Benda-Beckmanns draw attention to the consequences that this differential grounding of rights and physical space has for social stratification and power rations. How a population is localized has important consequences for the ways in which economic and political rights can be negotiated. In both regions it is clear that adat laws distinguish between original settlers and newcomers who are assigned a lower status with less political and economic rights. The effects of this status, however, operate differently depending on whether the population of lower status live interspersed with the higher status population or whether they live in separate locations. The significance of this type of analysis is that it illustrates how crucial it is to look at rights and other social relationships as located in space. The spatial localization of political and economic rights is a valuable factor that helps to explain key differences within the same social field of the 'village' and its internal relationships. This is not self-evident and cannot be based on general, normative claims about law, but requires investigation into the kinds of social processes that are at work with their ensuing consequences. Thus it is necessary to pay close attention to the legal construction of spaces in the physical environment and to the spatial–temporal permanence of political and legal places, however fluid and temporary their boundaries may be.

Scales of Legal Validity

One important way in which law is related to space concerns issues of scale. Wiber, in Chapter 4, draws attention to the detrimental effects of different notions of scale in the assessment of resource bases and the loss of local knowledge. And several authors have pointed at the differences in scale of governance when state institutions are competing with other types of institutions whose range of normative authority varies according to scope of their remit, as for example, in decentralizing African states.[28] Legal regulation also implies questions of scale from another perspective. For the way in which regulations are designed is often related to perceptions about the size and nature of the space to which they are allocated. Thus, the scale at which regulation is made has implications for the scope of issues that are regulated and the perceived actors involved. However, quite often the scale of regulation does not quite fit the space in which the issue is perceived to exist.[29] A number of contributions to the volume examine the relationship that exists between the scale of legal space that is constructed within physical space, where physical space represents a metaphor for what is at stake in local and global relations.

Anders, in Chapter 7, discusses how the disjuncture of scale inherent in the international criminal court in Sierra Leone seriously affects its work. The court was set up to deal with those responsible for crimes against humanity committed during the civil war, but it also represents a symbol of an international global order that is in the making. It is this symbol of global justice that critics and proponents address in their arguments for and against the court, through their attribution of the court as representing a cosmopolitan legal order, or alternatively, a neocolonial, military–humanitarian apparatus. Both positions as Anders demonstrates 'fail to appreciate the local productions of global discourses such as humanitarianism or international justice'. For despite its appearance of being universal and translocal this court is made and instantiated in particular places. Thus, Anders demonstrates how, despite its abstraction, international criminal law is the product of concrete social processes in specific localities. The location of the court on a site previously occupied by government buildings symbolizes the transformation of sovereignty in Sierra Leone. It did not replace functioning state institutions but filled the void

28 Blundo (1996); Bierschenk and Olivier de Sardan (1997); and Engel and Mehler (2005).

29 Tickamyer (2000, 809), for example, discussing the spatial underpinnings of inequality, has remarked that there is a tendency among policymakers to regard the issue of poverty as a national issue and to conflate national with urban poverty. The result is that regulations are designed that overlook the specific needs of poor groups in rural places. On the problems of scale at which issues of resource distribution or human rights to water are concerned, see Benda-Beckmann and Benda-Beckmann (2003).

left by the destruction of state apparatus during the civil war. Through exploring how legal, physical and social spaces intersect Anders's analysis promotes a much more contested and ambivalent depiction of the court than either its critics or proponents acknowledge. For they tend to ignore the subtle ways in which external and internal political influences and power relations are integrated into the court's internal dynamics. Thus the court is more than just a product of US imperialism, while also incorporating local features that belie its abstract, transnational character.

Anders explores the hybrid nature of this institution that acquires its specific form through negotiations involving the major funding governments who wanted to establish a lean and efficient tribunal that would be inexpensive and the government of Sierra Leone that had to establish credibility with its population. Unlike other international forums for justice, such as the International Criminal Tribunal for the former Yugoslavia in The Hague and the International Criminal Tribunal for Rwanda in Arusha, the Special Court for Sierra Leone is not part of the UN structure but has been established as a 'sui generic independent institution' founded on an agreement between the government of Sierra Leone and the UN. As a consequence it has more limited funds and a greater number of staff from within the country, albeit in more junior positions relating to security and administration. Many of these employees have been affiliated with NGOs who have been at the forefront in the struggle for international justice. As a result the court embodies, on the one hand, the product 'of an international debate on the best model for a new global legal order' and, on the other, 'one of the sites where the various actors in the field of international criminal justice compete or collaborate depending on their political agendas and financial resources'. What Anders's analysis highlights are the ways in which the particularity of a constructed space, and thus locality, has a bearing on the construction and implementation of an incipient global governance and global legal order.

Griffiths and Kandel, in Chapter 8, explore legal space in a micro context, that of local children's hearings in Glasgow. These legal proceedings that deal with children under 16 who are in need of compulsory measures of supervision involve local participants who live in the city of Glasgow. For panel members, who reach decisions about what is in the best interests of the child, the table around which such proceedings are located represents a metaphor for transparent, open and participatory decision-making. These values derive from international norms and standards embodied in the United Nations Convention on the Rights of the Child and the European Convention on Human Rights and Fundamental Freedoms that have percolated their way down to the local administration of justice in Scotland. Griffiths and Kandel's analysis of hearings demonstrates how local processes, set up to incorporate international norms and national policies, become invested with meaning in ways that render the process somewhat opaque. This is due to the constraints imposed by the differing institutional and professional demands placed on those involved in the process who speak from different perspectives and with different priorities at hearings. What emerges from their study is the multifaceted nature of power that is not just the product of unequal social relations but that also reflects the dynamics of bureaucratic forms of governance. Their analysis highlights how the realm of the 'local' may constitute a contested terrain, one that engages with different normative orders and that embodies unequal power relations among its participants. For although the actors may be said to be 'local' in that they are located within the bounded space of a city, they nonetheless find themselves situated within very different types of networks that separate them out from one another.

While children and families come from different neighbourhoods all over Glasgow, they generally share the common characteristics of living in areas that have high rates of poverty, deprivation, unemployment, lack of education, drug, alcohol and domestic abuse that set them apart from the more upwardly mobile panel members who deal with them. The different worlds that these actors inhabit have an impact on how they perceive law, creating a form of legal pluralism, for children and families view the local spaces of an 'informal' law of family and neighbourhood as taking precedence over the national law that panel members seek to apply in promoting good citizenship. This is highlighted through participants' approaches to and interpretation of four spaces that represent sites of tension, including the hearing, the home, the streets and school. The last three reflect everyday spaces that embody ambiguous interpretations of danger and safety. For while panel members view young people as putting themselves at risk by hanging about on street corners, this is not how young people view the situation. For them the streets represent a place where they may socialize with others their own age, embodying a positive interactive space for them in circumstances where, given the lack of facilities in the areas in which they live, the streets represent the only form of public space that is available to them. Likewise, when it comes to the home, differing perceptions about what this space encompasses and whether it is limited to actual physical living space, or whether it can be embedded in a larger social matrix, gives rise to contested views among participants as to whether or not it is sufficiently safe for children to remain there. How notions of danger and safety are constructed is important, because reaching a decision about whether or not a young person under 16 should be placed under compulsory measures of supervision involves making an assessment about the risk/danger and/or protection that such spaces represent, when applying the welfare criteria that underpin the hearings' legal determination of what constitutes the best interests of the child. Thus law and space are intertwined in ways that reveal how social actors map out material space in different, distinct and contested ways that reflect 'the field of power relations that links localities to a wider world' (Gupta and Ferguson 1997, 25).

Wilmsen, in Chapter 9, engages in constructing a social geography in order to map the processes by which law may have been fashioned to organize space in interior southern Africa during the eighth to the fifteenth centuries. Given the lack of written records for this period he turns to material artifacts to assess the trajectory of these social processes and the economic formations in which they functioned. He argues against the tendency today to regard things as inert and mute. Scaling these material objects up from the place they were found, he positions them within authority structures of a larger scale.

Drawing on the work of Locke and Marx he posits the proposition that human social relations are constructed by human agents through their labour and that human history and sociality are inextricably bound up with materials. He argues for recognition of the fact that material artifacts have the same ontological status as words. This is due to the fact that such artifacts are marked by the distinct intentions of their makers and their users and so can be viewed as potentially comprehensible as verbal documents. For they possess communicative as well as utilitarian functions. Thus the value that each party to a transaction places on an object is not an inherent property of that object but reflects a judgement made by persons that is mediated by transcendent temporal, cultural and social caveats. For objects become invested with meaning and are capable of accumulating histories. For this reason it should not be assumed that, for example, pottery vessels circulated in a purely functional capacity but rather that their materiality was invested with meaning through social interaction and accumulated histories linking persons and families across class distinctions in space and time.

In this way, Wilmsen designs a way of reconstructing patterns of law and power by means of archaeological finds of objects of authority in southern Africa. In that region, two principles of social organization compete, that is, those based on land and those based on lineage. Kinship and inheritance, according to Wilmsen, resolve this contradiction. He then goes on to ask how under these circumstances power can be maintained over long distances. This is only possible by means of controlling certain valuables and their transport. These items serve to create a power relationship between centre and periphery. Maintaining power involves three types of regulation: rules of who may possess certain things; rules of who may inherit certain things; and rules governing movement and transport. The spread of objects embodying power therefore provides us with clues for the localizations of authority. Thus, the exact dating of objects of power found in certain places, are indications of the ways in which these locations are connected to other locations and provide information about the localization of at least some core regulation that is required to establish and maintain power structures.

Maps, Law and Space

Maps of Law as Visualized Discourse

The spatial representations of law's claims to existence and validity, boundaries and spaces can be, and regularly are, plotted on maps of different size and scale. The ways this is done varies enormously depending on the purpose for which a map is made. It may range from the projection of whole legal systems to specific legal institutions and relationships. What is projected onto a map as well as what is left out signifies how that space is conceptualized, including its underlying political salience that may be implied from its concrete representations. Thus while maps are always abstractions, what underlies the form that such abstractions take is important. As Santos (1987) has shown, the mechanisms of scale, projection and symbolization inevitably lead to a misreading of the social reality in the actual social space mapped. Maps that emphasize waterways, vegetation, elevation or minerals but do not mention administrative or political boundaries, for example, often indicate that such administrative boundaries are unimportant when it comes to the management of these resources. Thus they depict the key features from which more specific concerns are being problematized. Maps are used to govern people. Worby (1994, 392) has analysed the use of tribal maps 'as instruments of colonial administration and domination'. As Scott (1998, 3) notes a 'state cadastral map created to designate taxable property holders does not merely describe a system of land tenure; it creates such a system through its ability to give its categories the force of law'.

Law defines space normatively in its own terms and negates other forms of spatio-temporality. It constitutes the places, spaces and boundaries with their legal consequences that should be there. While law can be used to construct images of reality, most legal constructions are not ways of description but rather of prescription, of imagining *the possible*, *the probable* and *the desired*.[30] Such normative maps invite, or require 'ground truthing', a systematic exploration of what actually goes on in the legally defined spaces and boundaries, in order to find out whether or not what has been normatively projected on space can be found on the ground.

The fact that maps of law are normative in that they depict what is regulated and ought to be in space (for example, territorial claims, sovereignty and lesser forms of legitimate political competence) and not necessarily what actually is in space makes them no less interesting. The representations of space on maps not only generate powerful ways of imagining and visualizing space but also provide important tools in contestations over it.[31] As Wood (1992, 43) notes, cartography is primarily a form of political discourse concerned with the acquisition and maintenance of power.[32] And mapped law is visualized as a discourse that expresses some characteristics and claims regarded as salient by the map makers. Such maps are usually made for purposes stated in the legal texts or which the makers of the legal maps had in mind, although later interpreters and users of the map may

30 See Geertz (1983); Santos (1987); and Benda-Beckmann and Benda-Beckmann (1991).

31 Blomley (1994, 74) describes how the common law was mapped by Coke around the end of the sixteenth century in England, to become 'the law of the land', and to eradicate other, competing, localized places of legal knowledge and practice. Law and land became locked together for all time (1994, 75).

32 See Worby (1994, 371) on the relation between the power to name and an imaginary knowledge of the relationship between ethnic identities and socio-geographic space. See also Anderson (1991).

give them a different significance (see Scott 1998; Gupta 2003; and Rosen-Zvi 2004). These legal constructions – this 'Space-in-Law', as Delany (2003, 69) calls it – can be usefully analysed or deconstructed as discourses of power and, in state legal orders, as expressing either a liberalistic or a totalitarian ideology. They thus represent a particular kind of empirical data for social scientists rather than analytical tools.

In Chapter 10, the particular question as to what extent law, in the sense of a complete legal system, can be mapped is an issue controversially addressed in the paper by Bavinck and Woodman. They formulate differing approaches to the issue of what the relationship is between law as mapped and social reality. They look towards a reality of law which is conceived in different ways: in processes of its enforcement à la Weber (Bavinck) or its (at least partial) observance (Woodman). In pursuing this relationship they are not concerned with drawing maps of specific legal fields, such as land law, fiscal law or of legal systems in the sense of a set of norms, or the claimed validity of legal systems. For they agree that these can all be mapped. Their disagreement centres on whether or not it is possible to map complete legal systems in the sense of a *particular body of observed norms*; law with a capital, as Woodman suggests calling this.

From Woodman's perspective (2003, 386) 'legal doctrine itself presents a conceptualization, and sometimes also depictions of law, but the view of legal doctrine cannot be conclusive. Indeed, it is factually inaccurate, for it is made not only with the objective of describing reality but also from a need to persuade the legality and authority of the law in question; it necessarily has a strong ideological element'. Thus Woodman adopts an empiricist point of view and maintains that it is not possible to map Law as observed norms. He argues that this is impossible for three reasons. First, Law, whether customary law or a state legal system, is often or even usually internally diverse. Second, Law is not a tightly coherent set of norms but rather a collection of disparate norms that defy internal uniformity. In addition what constitutes observance is ever shifting and untidy, making it impossible to draw boundaries so that 'the neat packages which have supposedly been represented by spaces on a map now disintegrate'. Third, there is the problem of the external boundaries of Law. Woodman argues that the notion of a map of a plural legal world, however untidy the internal structure of a Law may be, at least presupposes that it is clear where that Law ends and another begins. In reality, this is far from clear for the complexity of legal pluralism gives rise to contestation that renders it impossible to draw boundaries around distinct 'Laws'.

Bavinck (2004 and in Chapter 10) takes a pragmatic approach that starts from the assumption that any map is an abstraction from social reality. Any map thus contains generalizations and so he argues that it is possible to draw a map of Law. In this context he perceives of legal systems and their constituent elements, such as authorities as ideal types along the lines prescribed by Weber, and not as one-to-one representations of reality. What is important is to identify key features, actors and processes in order to be able to make comparisons between one setting and the next without getting bogged down 'in a plenitude of localized facts'. Rather than speculating about the existence of coherent rule systems he urges inquiring into authorities interested in developing and enforcing law. This is because authorities play such a crucial role in enforcing law and law observance that they can be used to map law. For what unites these authorities (be they politicians, judges or managers) 'is the use of power and the wielding of public authority' that not only enable them to implement, but also, to make law. He takes the view that it is possible 'to imagine law as a spider plus a web', and maintains that just as it makes more sense 'when one aims at achieving insight into the dynamics of insect life, to count spiders, rather than spider webs', it is more useful to 'take authorities as an index of living law than normative bodies'. The advantage of this approach is that having mapped, in an ideal typical way, the reach of the various legal systems it is possible to take account of the areas of overlap, and thus to become aware of where more than one legal system has influence that promotes 'forum shopping' and where authorities 'battle for their hold over matters and subjects'.

Use of Maps Made by Contributors to the Volume: Implications for Legal Anthropology

Legal anthropologists focusing on space not only study maps made by other actors and used in their negotiations and claims for resources. They also frequently draw up maps as analytical tools. Such maps can be a very useful visualization of the spatial distribution of legally relevant processes, including those envisaged by Bavinck, which otherwise could only with greatest difficulties be achieved. These maps can be overlaid on existing normative maps or on normative maps also made by anthropologists, to make the differences visible. In fact, many interesting aspects of plural legal orders, both their normative claims and a number of law-related social processes, can be mapped in all degrees of scale and detail, depending on the purpose for which the map is made. Such maps also allow one to relate spatial distribution of legal processes to other variables. Impressive examples are the legal maps that Markus Weilenmann (1996) produced of the use made of different courts and kinds of law applied in Burundi courts. He related the spatial differences in court use to climatic and soil fertility aspects and features of the political system. Similar maps could be made, for example, of the spatial distribution of number and kinds of marriages concluded; number of testaments made; per capita litigation rates; type of law applied: and the frequency of land transactions.

In this volume a number of authors also use maps to show contested spaces in plural legal constellations, where different rights, of different actors, based in different legal systems are projected on the same territory. Thus, the von Benda-Beckmanns visualize with the use of maps the specific ways in which competing legal categories and related legal claims are made in relation to the same land. For in West Sumatra, land can be classified competitively as village commons (*ulayat nagari*) or as state land, whereas the maps of a village on the island of Ambon show the competition between different forms of adat law with their spatial implications. Bakker, in Chapter 5, uses a map to visualize the claims two rivaling descendants of the sultan make to land that they claim to have been in the possession of their predecessor while Wiber utilizes maps to symbolize conflicting approaches to resource management. For those maps that derive from the dictates of global experts and that employ a two-dimensional perspective, have very different scalar and temporal frames when compared with those employed by the local users who operate on the basis of three-dimensional ocean spaces.

Thus maps are used as a means of description and analysis. However, like all maps, such legal anthropological cartographies of law are not politically innocent, and in that sense maps of legal pluralism have an 'insurrectionist' character (Pue 1990; and Blomley 1994, xii, 60). On the one hand, legal anthropologists' maps including more validity claims on the map than just the one of state law show the relative nature of all claims to exclusive validity of different legal orders. Maps of competing legal orders in actual space will show that any dominant law denying the (co)existence of other laws may lose their exclusivity, both at the level of normative constructions and of their involvement in social interaction. Maps depicting the normative claims to validity need not always reflect the hegemonic vision of powerful map makers. Alternative maps may be made, depicting other legal systems, such as ethnic people's (customary, traditional, folk) or religious law, with their own spatial validity claims. Comparing such a map with one that exclusively maps state law reveals the extent of the latter's distortion. On the other hand, maps of actual law involvement in social practices show the normativity and expose the ideological character of *all* normative claims of 'existence' in social and geographical space.

Law, Space and Place

The contributors to this volume demonstrate the importance of studying social and legal institutions, relations and practices as located and distributed in space. Space is a grounded, physical setting in which law affects the life of people. At the same time space also presents a more intangible universe. The volume thus acknowledges the diverse ways in which social relationships are created and regulated and the differing effects this entails. In exploring the interrelations between social, legal and physical spaces the authors highlight the ways in which law represents an arena in which the politics of space is enacted and negotiated. The volume shows that spatial constructions, as embodied in legal categories and regulation, are resources that create frameworks for the exercise of power and control over people and resources. Actors on varying scales ranging from international or transnational agencies, to state organizations, down to local actors utilize legal constructions of space in their struggle for power.

The variations in scale draw attention to the multifaceted nature of law that constitutes legal pluralism and that underlines the extent to which legal spaces are embedded in broader social and political claims. Multiple legal constructions of place not only open up a range of arenas for the exercise of political authority but also provide differing approaches to the localization of rights and obligations. They allow for the creation of social relationships and institutions that are characterized by different degrees of abstraction, different temporalities and moral connotations that reflect the different scales on which legal orders are projected and operate. In this process contradictory ways of constructing place can coexist peacefully or develop forms of hybridity. They may also, however, lead to serious conflicts as different legally defined spaces and spatially grounded rights and obligations become engaged in fights for control over people and resources.

References

Abramson, A. and Theodossopoulos, D. (2000) *Land, Law, and Environment: Mythical Land, Legal Boundaries*. London and Sterling, VA: Pluto Press.

Anderson, B. (1991) *Imagined Communities*, Revised Edition. London, New York: Verso.

Appadurai, A. (1990) 'Disjuncture and Difference in the Global Cultural Economy' in M. Featherstone (ed.) *Global Culture: Nationalism, Globalization and Modernity*. London: Sage, pp. 295–310.

Appadurai, A. (2003) 'Sovereignty without Territoriality: Notes for a Post-national Geography' in S.M. Low and D. Lawrence-Zuniga (eds) *The Anthropology of Space and Place: Locating Culture*. Oxford, UK: Blackwell, pp. 337–49.

Bavinck, M. (2004) 'How to Start Mapping Law – a Rejoinder to Woodman'. Paper given at the XIVth International Conference of the Commission on Folk Law and Legal Pluralism, Fredericton, New Brunswick, 26–29 August 2004.

Benda-Beckmann, F. von (1992) 'Uncommon Questions about Property Rights', *Recht der Werkelijkheid*, 1992(1): 8–14.

Benda-Beckmann, F. von (1999) 'Multiple Legal Constructions of Socio-economic Spaces: Resource Management and Conflict in the Central Moluccas' in M. Rösler and T. Wendl (eds) *Frontiers and Borderlands: Anthropological Perspectives*. Frankfurt am Main, Berlin, Bern, New York, Wien: Lang, pp. 131–58.

Benda-Beckmann, F. von (2001) 'On the Reproduction of Law: Micro and Macro in the Time-Space Geography of Law' in W. Fikentscher (ed.) *Begegnung und Konflikt – Eine kulturanthropologische Bestandsaufnahme.* München: C.H. Beck Verlag, pp. 119–31.

Benda-Beckmann, F. von and Benda-Beckmann, K. von (1978) 'Residence in a Minangkabau *Nagari*', *Indonesia Circle*, 15: 6–17.

Benda-Beckmann, F. von and Benda-Beckmann, K. von (1991) 'Law in Society: from Blindman's-bluff to Multilocal Law' in K. von Benda-Beckmann, F. von Benda-Beckmann and H.L.J. Spiertz (eds) *Living Law in the Low Countries. Special Issue of Recht der Werkelijkheid 1991/1*. Amsterdam: Vuga, pp. 119–39.

Benda-Beckmann, F. von and Benda-Beckmann, K. von (1994) 'Property, Politics and Conflict: Ambon and Minangkabau Compared'. *Law and Society Review*, 28: 589–607.
Benda-Beckmann, F. von and Benda-Beckmann, K. von (1998) 'Where Structures Merge: State and Off-state Involvement in Rural Social Security on Ambon, Indonesia' in S. Pannell and F. von Benda-Beckmann (eds) *Old World Places, New World Problems: Exploring Resource Management Issues in Eastern Indonesia*. Canberra: The Australian National University, Centre for Resource and Environmental Studies, pp. 143–80.
Benda-Beckmann, F. von and Benda-Beckmann, K. von (2003) 'Water, Human Rights and Legal Pluralism'. *Water Nepal, Special Issue*, 9/10: 63–76.
Benda-Beckmann, F. von and Benda-Beckmann, K. von (2006) 'How Communal is Communal and whose Communal is it? Lessons from Minangkabau' in F. von Benda-Beckmann, K. von Benda-Beckmann and M.G. Wiber (eds) *Changing Properties of Property*. Oxford: Berghahn, pp. 194–217.
Benda-Beckmann, F. von and Benda-Beckmann, K. von (2007) 'Ambivalent Identities: Decentralization and Minangkabau Political Communities' in G. van Klinken and H. Schulte Nordholt (eds) *Renegotiating Boundaries. Local Politics in Post-Suharto Indonesia, Verhandlingen van het KITLV 238*. Leiden: KITLV Press, pp. 417–42.
Benda-Beckmann, F. von and Taale, T. (1996) 'Land, Trees and Houses: Changing (Un)certainties in Property Relationships on Ambon' in D. Mearns and C. Healy (eds) *Remaking Maluku: Social Transformation in Eastern Indonesia*, Special Monograph no. 1, 1996, Darwin: Centre for Southeast Asian Studies, NT University, pp. 39–63.
Benda-Beckmann, F. von, Benda-Beckmann, K. von and Griffiths, A. (eds) (2005) *Mobile People, Mobile Law: Expanding Legal Relations in a Contracting World*. Aldershot: Ashgate.
Benda-Beckmann, F. von, Benda-Beckmann, K. von and Wiber, M.G. (eds) (2006) *Changing Properties of Property*. Oxford: Berghahn.
Bierschenk, T. and Olivier de Sardaen, J.-P. (1997) 'Local Powers and a Distant State in Rural Central African Republic'. *Journal of Modern African Studies*, 35: 441–68.
Blomley, N.K. (1994) *Law, Space, and the Geographies of Power*. New York: Guilford.
Blomley, N.K. (2006) 'From "what?" to "so what?": Law and Geography in Retrospect' in J. Holder and C. Harrison (eds) *Law and Geography*. Oxford: Oxford University Press, pp. 17–34.
Blomley, N.K., Delaney, D. and Ford, R.T. (eds) (2001) *The Legal Geographies Reader*. Oxford: Blackwell Publishing.
Blundo, G. (1996) 'Gérer les Conflicts Fonciers au Sénégal: le Role de l'Administration Locale dans le Sud-Est Bassin Arachidier' in P. Mathieu, P.-J. Laurent and J.-C. Willame (eds) *Démocratie, Enjeux Fonciers et Pratiques Locales en Afrique*. Paris: L'Harmattan, pp. 101–21.

Bohannan, P. (1967) 'Africa's Land' in G. Dalton (ed.) *Tribal and Peasant Economies*. Austin: University of Texas Press, pp. 51–60.

Breman, J. (1987) Het Dorp in Azië als Koloniale Schijngestalte. Amsterdam: CASA.

Brooijmans, W. (1997) 'The Plains of Tortuguero: Tropical Paradise or Paradise Lost?' in F. von Benda-Beckmann, K. von Benda-Beckmann and A. Hoekema (eds) *Natural Resources, Environment and Legal Pluralism, Special Issue of Law and Anthropology 9*, pp. 258–301.

Butler, J. (2007) *Who Sings the Nation-state? Language, Politics, Belonging*. London: Seagull Books.

Chanock, M. (1985) *Law, Custom and Social Order: The Colonial Experience in Malawi and Zambia*. Cambridge: Cambridge University Press.

Clammer, J. (1973) 'Colonialism and the Perception of Tradition in Fiji' in T. Asad (ed.) *Anthropology and the Colonial Encounter*. Atlantic Highlands, NJ: Humanities Press, pp. 199–220.

Delaney, D. (2003) 'Beyond the Word: Law as a Thing of this World' in J. Holder and C. Harrison (eds) *Law and Geography*. Oxford: Oxford University Press, pp. 67–84.

Dijk, H. van (1996) 'Land Tenure, Territoriality and Ecological Instability: A Sahelian Case Study' in J. Spiertz and M.G. Wiber (eds) *The Role of Law in Natural Resource Management*. The Hague: Vuga, pp. 17–45.

Economides, K., Blacksell, M. and Watkins, C. (1986) 'The Spatial Analysis of Legal Systems: Towards a Geography of Law?' *Journal of Law and Society*, 13: 161–81.

Engel, U. and Mehler, A. (2005) '"Under Construction": Governance in Africa's New Violent Social Spaces' in U. Engel and G.R. Olsen (eds) *The African Exception*. Aldershot, Burlington VT: Ashgate, pp. 87–102.

Featherstone, M. and Lash, S. (1995) 'Globalization, Modernity and the Spatialization of Social Theory' in M. Featherstone, S. Lash and R. Robertson (eds) *Global Modernities*. London: Sage, pp. 1–24.

Fisiy, C.F. (1997) 'State Dislocation of Customary Management Systems: Land Colonization on the Slopes of Mount Oku, North-West Province of Cameroon' *International Yearbook of Law and Anthropology,* Vol. 9 (special issue), pp. 124–45.

Fitzpatrick, P. (1992) *The Mythology of Modern Law. Sociology of Law and Crime*. London: Routledge.

Forman, G. (2006) 'Law and the Historical Geography of the Galilee: Israel's Litigatory Advantages during the Special Operation of Land Settlement'. *Journal of Historical Geography*, 32: 796–817.

Galanter, M. (1981) 'Justice in Many Rooms; Courts, Private Ordering and Indigenous Law'. *Journal of Legal Pluralism*, 19: 1–47.

Geertz, C. (1983) *Local Knowledge: Further Essays in Interpretative Anthropology*. New York: Basic Books.

Geisler, C. and Bedford, B. (1996) *Who Owns the Ecosystem*? Madison: Land Tenure Center, Paper 157.
Giddens, A. (1979) *Central Problems in Social Theory: Action, Structure and Contradiction in Social Analysis*. London: Macmillan Press.
Giddens, A. (1984) 'Agency, Institution, and Time-Space Analysis' in K. Knorr-Cetina and A.V. Cicourel (eds) *Advances in Social Theory and Methodology. Toward an Integration of Micro- and Macro-Sociologies*. Boston, London, Henley: Routledge and Kegan Paul, pp. 161–74.
Giddens, A. (1985) 'Time, Space and Regionalisation' in D. Gregory and J. Urry (eds) *Social Relations and Spatial Structures*. Basingstoke: Macmillan, pp. 265–95.
Gluckman, M. (1965) *The Ideas of Barotse Jurisprudence*. New Haven: Yale University Press.
Gluckman, M. (1971) *Politics, Law and Ritual in Tribal Society*. New York: Basil Blackwell.
Gooding, S.S. (1994) 'Place, Race and Names: Layered Identities in *United States v. Oregon*, Confederated Tribes of the Colville Reservation, Plaintiff-Intervenor' in E. Mertz (ed.) *Community and Identity in Sociolegal Struggles, Special Issue of Law and Society Review*, 28(5): pp.1181–229.
Greenhouse, C.J. (1998) 'Legal Pluralism and Cultural Difference: What is the difference? A Response to Professor Woodman'. *Journal of Legal Pluralism*, 42: 61–72.
Gupta, A. (2003) 'The Song of the Non-aligned World: Transnational Identities and the Reinscription of Space in Late Capitalism' in S.M. Low and D. Lawrence-Zuniga (eds) *The Anthropology of Space and Place: Locating Culture*. Oxford and Berlin: Blackwell Publishing and Carlton, pp. 321–36.
Gupta, A. and Ferguson, J. (eds) (1997) *Culture, Power, Place: Explorations in Critical Anthropology*. Durham and London: Duke University Press.
Hagberg, S. and Tengan, A.B. (eds) (2000) *Bonds and Boundaries in Northern Ghana and Southern Burkina Faso*. Uppsala: Acta Universitatis Upsaliensis.
Harvey, D. (1996) *Justice, Nature and the Geography of Difference*. Oxford: Blackwell Publishers.
Hatcher, L.J. (2006) 'Green Metaphors: Language, Land, and Law in Takings Debates' in J. Holder and C. Harrison (eds) *Law and Geography*. Oxford: Oxford University Press, pp. 445–64.
Holder, J. and Harrison, C. (eds) (2006) *Law and Geography*. Oxford: Oxford University Press.
Ingold, T. (1986) *The Appropriation of Nature: Essays on Human Ecology and Social Relations*. Manchester: Manchester University Press.
Kedar, A. (2006) 'On the Legal Geography of Ethnocratic Settler States: Notes towards a Research Agenda' in J. Holder and C. Harrison (eds) *Law and Geography*. Oxford: Oxford University Press, pp. 401–41.

Kelly, T. (forthcoming) 'Laws of Suspicion: Legal Status, Space, and the Impossibility of Separation in the Israeli Occupied West Bank' in F. von Benda-Beckmann, K. von Benda-Beckmann and J. Eckert (eds) *Rules of Law and Laws of Ruling*. Aldershot and Burlington: Ashgate.

Kemp, J. (1988) 'The Seductive Mirage: The Search for the Village Community in Southeast Asia'. *Comparative Asian Studies*, no. 3. Dordrecht: Foris Publications.

Kidder, R.L. (1978) 'Western Law in India. External Law and Local Response' in H.M. Johnson (ed.) *Social System and Legal Process*. San Francisco: Jossey-Bass, pp. 155–80.

Lash, S. and Urry, J. (1994) *Economies of Signs and Space*. London: Sage.

Lefebvre, H. (1991) *The Production of Space*. Oxford: Blackwell.

Long, N. and Roberts, B. (1984) *Miners, Peasants and Entrepreneurs: Regional Development in the Central Highlands of Peru*. Cambridge: Cambridge University Press.

Löw, M., Steets, S. and Stoetzer, S. (2007) *Einführung in die Stadt- und Raumsoziologie*. Opladen and Farmington Hills: Uni-Taschenbücher GmbH Stuttgart.

Low, S.M. and Lawrence-Zuniga, D. (eds) (2003) *The Anthropology of Space and Place: Locating Culture*. Oxford and Berlin: Blackwell Publishing and Carlton.

Malkki, L.H. (1997) 'National Geographic. The Rooting of Peoples and the Territorialization of National Identity among Scholars and Refugees' in A. Gupta and J. Ferguson (eds) *Culture, Power, Place. Explorations in Critical Anthropology*. Durham and London: Duke University Press, pp. 52–74.

Manderson, D. (2005) 'Interstices: New Work on Legal Spaces'. *Law Text Culture*, 9: 1–10.

Marcus, G. (1992) 'Past, Present and Emergent Identities: Requirements for Ethnographies of Late Twentieth-Century Modernity Worldwide' in S. Lash and J. Friedman (eds) *Modernity and Identity*. Oxford, Cambridge: Blackwell, pp. 309–30.

Merry, S.E. (1997) 'Legal Pluralism and Transnational Culture: the Ka Ho'okolokolonui Kanaka Maoli Tribunal' in R.A. Wilson (ed.) *Human Rights, Culture and Context*. London: Pluto Press, pp. 28–48.

Merry, S.E. (2005) 'Human Rights and Global Legal Pluralism: Reciprocity and Disjuncture' in F. von Benda-Beckmann, K. von Benda-Beckmann, and A. Griffiths (eds) *Mobile People, Mobile Law. Expanding Legal Relations in a Contracting World*. Aldershot: Ashgate, pp. 215–32.

Merry, S.E. (2006) 'Transnational Human Rights and Local Activism: Mapping the Middle'. *American Anthropologist*, 108: 38–51.

Mertz, E. (1994) 'A New Social Constructionism for Sociolegal Studies' in E. Mertz (ed.) *Community and Identity in Sociolegal Struggles, Special Issue of Law and Society Review*, 28(5): 1243–65.

Moore, S.F. (1973) 'Law and Social Change: the Semi-autonomous Social Field as an Appropriate Subject of Study'. *Law and Society Review*, 7: 719–46.
Orlove, B.S. (1991) 'Mapping Reeds and Reading Maps: The Politics of Representation in Lake Titicaca'. *American Ethnologist*, 18 (1): 3–38.
Perry, R.W. and Maurer, B. (eds) (2003) *Globalization under Construction: Governmentality, Law and Identity*. Minneapolis: University of Minnesota Press.
Peters, J.D. (1997) 'Seeing Bifocally: Media, Place, Culture' in A. Gupta and J. Ferguson (eds) *Culture, Power, Place: Explorations in Critical Anthropology*. Durham and London: Duke University Press, pp. 75–92.
Pue, W.W. (1990) 'Wrestling with Law: (Geographical) Specificity vs. (Legal) Abstraction'. *Urban Geography*, 11: 566–85.
Robertson, R. (1990) 'Mapping the Global Condition: Globalization as the Central Concept' in M. Featherstone (ed.) *Global Culture: Nationalism, Globalization and Modernity*. London: Sage, pp. 15–30.
Rosen-Zvi, I. (2004) *Taking Space Seriously: Law, Space, and Society in Contemporary Israel*. Burlington, VT: Ashgate.
Rösler, M. and Wendl, T. (eds) (1999) *Frontiers and Borderlands: Anthropological Perspectives*. Frankfurt am Main, Berlin, Bern, New York, Wien: Lang.
Saltman, M. (ed.) (2002) *Land and Territoriality*. Oxford and New York: Berg.
Santos, B. de Sousa (1985) 'On Modes of Production of Law and Social Power'. *International Journal of the Sociology of Law*, 13: 299–336.
Santos, B. de Sousa (1987) 'Law. A Map of Misreading: Toward a Post-modern Conception of Law'. *Journal of Law and Society*, 14: 279–302.
Schulte Nordholt, H. and Klinken, G. van (eds) (2007) *Renegotiating Boundaries. Local Politics in Post-Suharto Indonesia*. Verhandelingen van het KITLV 238. Leiden: KITLV Press.
Scott, J.C. (1998) *Seeing like a State*. New Haven, London: Yale University Press.
Spiertz, J. (1989) 'De Mythe van de Subak: Irrigatie op Bali in Rectsanthropologisch Perspectief'. *Recht der Werkelijkheid*, I: 6–33.
Stanford Law Review (1996) Special Issue on Symposium Surveying Law and Borders, Vol. 48(5).
Street, P. (2006) 'Spaces of Diversity in Diverse Spaces' in J. Holder and C. Harrison (eds) *Law and Geography*. Oxford: Oxford University Press, pp. 323–42.
Taylor, W. (ed.) (2006) *The Geography of Law: Landscape, Identity and Regulation*. Oxford, Portland: Hart Publishing.
Tickamyer, A.R. (2000) 'Space Matters! Spatial Inequality in Future Sociology'. *Contemporary Sociology*, 29: 805–13.
Tsing, A.L. (2005) *Fricton. An Ethnography of Global Connection*. Princeton and Oxford: Princeton University Press.

Weilenmann, M. (1996) *Burundi: Konflikt und Rechtskonflikt – Eine rechtsethnologische Studie zur Konfliktregelung der Gerichte*. Unpublished PhD Dissertation, Wageningen Agricultural University.

Werlen, B. (1988) *Society, Action and Space: an Alternative Human Geography*. London and New York: Routledge.

Wilmsen, E.N. (1989a) *Land Filled with Flies: A Political Economy of the Kalahari*. Chicago and London: University of Chicago Press.

Wilmsen, E.N. (ed.) (1989b) *We are Here: Politics of Aboriginal Land Tenure*. Berkeley and Los Angeles: University of California Press.

Winichakul, T. (1988) *Siam Mapped: a History of the Geo-body of Siam*. PhD Dissertation; University of Sidney.

Wood, D. (1992) *The Power of Maps*. London: Routledge.

Woodman, G.R. (2003) 'Why there Can be no Map of Law' in R. Pradhan (ed.) *Legal Pluralism and Unofficial Law in Social, Economic and Political Development*. Papers of the XIIIth International Congress, 7–10 April 2002, Chiang Mai, Thailand, Vol. III. Chiang Mai, Thailand: ICNEC, pp. 383–92.

Worby, E. (1994) 'Maps, Names, and Ethnic Games: The Epistemology and Iconography of Colonial Power in Northwestern Zimbabwe'. *Journal of Southern African Studies*, 20(3): 371–92.

Chapter 2

Peasant Community and Territorial Strategies in the Andean Highlands of Peru

Monique Nuijten and Davíd Lorenzo Rodríguez

Managing People by Means of Territorial Strategies

In this chapter we analyse the relation between territorial control and the formation of highland communities in the central Peruvian Andes, a remote and difficult to access area populated by indigenous populations. We discuss how the colonial regime and after that the independent Republic resorted to territorial strategies in their attempts to gain control over the population in the highlands. By territorial strategies we understand the regulation of access and use of land with the aim of forcing the population to act in certain ways. As we will show, the territorial techniques that were used by varying authorities differed from the issuing of a variety of laws, the demarcating of areas for specific use, to direct military intervention. In the case of one village in the region, Usibamba, we show how since the end of the nineteenth century state territorial strategies have shaped the formation of the local agrarian community. We relate the enacting of national laws and the nationwide political climate to internal divisions and events in Usibamba.

According to Sack (1986, 1) territoriality 'is best understood as a spatial strategy to affect, influence, or control resources and people, by controlling area'. In a similar way Vandergeest and Peluso (1995) point out that territoriality – in terms of the control over the variety in spatial ordering – implies control over land and land-related resources (forests, minerals, water, soils) in combination with control over the people that make use of these resources. So, territorialization includes the prescribing of specific activities within spatial boundaries. For example, the mandatory registration of land titles based on surveys, defining particular areas as natural forests, and marking out rights with respect to logging, grazing and mining, are all territorializing strategies, just like indicating specific areas as Indian property to be held under communal land tenure. The assignment of special use to particular spaces tends to be accompanied by legislation and regulation governing this special function.

The restriction of activities and the accompanying rules governing the use of space always go hand in hand with categorization of people. For example, the use that according to the law can be made of specially designated spaces is different for indigenous people, citizens, migrants, foreigners and so on. This means that territorialization also implies the definition of categories of people with different entitlements and practices of inclusion and exclusion of territorial subjects. Hence, territoriality is a strategy to establish different degrees of access and can be used to contain or restrain as well as to exclude (Sack 1986, 20).

Following these lines of thought, not all space is territory. Space becomes territorialized when access to it becomes confined and starts to be regulated. This also implies that 'as a strategy, territoriality can be turned on and off' (Sack 1986, 1). It means that several territorializing tendencies may work simultaneously.

Although the state certainly is the main agent in the field of territorialization, the state is certainly not the only actor in the field. For instance, agrarian communities have their own internal techniques of territorialization: rules about land use; localized registration of plots; definition of people with differing rights; resulting in particular forms of exclusion and inclusion. In addition, among communities and also villages fierce struggles may evolve around control over land and people. As Wilson (2004, 530) points out, territorializing is 'a process without closure, where claims to political/social space are constantly being brought into play (and constantly being questioned)'.

Vandergeest and Peluso (1995) point out that much discrepancy and contradiction exists between the 'lived space' that people experience in their daily life and the 'abstract space' that is created and imposed by the state. In other words, territorial land use planning tends to ignore and contradict people's lived interactions with the land. In mapping, cadastral surveying and legislation the state works with homogeneous units and administrative categories, which do not coincide with local languages and measures for space. Land registration and mapping by the state naturally involve more than a representation of reality, as boundaries are drawn, territories created and claims made which are enforced by courts of law (Craib 2004).

The aims with territorialization can be multiple but in the case of the state the main aims are taxing, surveillance (getting information about people) and – as we will see in the Peruvian highlands – forcing people to provide labour for the haciendas and not rebelling against exclusion and abject poverty. State rule in the form of property rights has important implications for the construction of space and power relations (Rabinow 2003, 355). Naturally, different state rationales may underlie territorial orderings. Orlove (1993) shows that, among other things, the coexistence of administrative and hegemonic rationales in territorial classification in Peru. The administrative rationale refers to the fact that a government must have some notion of the territory and population under its domain to be able to allocate resources, to implement plans and to ensure the enforcement of laws. 'The administrative impulse is a highly general one, common to all states which seek to impose some central authority over a diverse national territory' (Orlove 1993, 314). The hegemonic rationale refers to the making of classifications and regulations that privilege elite groups and the ruling classes at the expense of subordinate groups in society. In this way territorialization is central to how people's political identities as citizens are defined (Vandergeest and Peluso 1995, 385).

An interesting characteristic of territorial strategies is that they can be used to displace attention from the relationship between ruler and subject to territory. In other words, 'territory appears as the agent doing the controlling' (Sack 1986, 33). By designating certain areas for specific activities and populations, and issuing laws and regulations substantiating the management and enforcement of these rules, attention is displaced from the regional strongmen who are behind these policies to the 'neutral' laws and the area in question. In this way, territoriality helps make relationships *impersonal* (ibid.) and may function as a disguise of socio-political interests.

Despite the deliberate aims the state might have with its territorial strategies, these do not automatically result in the effective control of space and people. In many areas people follow localized practices that ignore or even resist the state's goals of territorial control. National laws often fail to achieve their effects on the ground (Benda-Beckmann, F. von 1993). This may in some occasions have the radical consequence of state coercion and military intervention against 'unruly' rural residents.

Territorial Control: The 'Land for Labour Deal'

Despite the terrible demographic catastrophe produced by the Spanish conquest, an indigenous population survived in the Andes. The legal and administrative systems of the colonial period distinguished among Indians, Spaniards, Africans and mixed caste-types (Orlove 1993, 322). The most important jurisdictional distinction was between the 'Republic of Spaniards' and the 'Republic of Indians', each with its own legal code, modes of authority, taxation and privileges (Poole 2004, 39). 'The Spaniards sought to change the spatial organization in order to control the population and facilitate the extraction of tributes' (Stepputat 2005, 65). Within this system, 'the Indians were a subject people, with a specific administrative status and a series of obligations to the state. Not only did the Indians form the majority of the population, but the colonial Peruvian economy would have been almost unimaginable without the fiscal contributions of the Indian head tax or without the Indian labour service' (Orlove 1993, 322). This was a colonial pact that guaranteed the access to land for the community of tribute-paying Indians. Spaniards, *Mestizos* and non-tribute-paying Indians were excluded from these reductions (Stepputat 2005, 65). Hence access to land was only granted in exchange for labour and tax. The *encomienda* was a grant over Indian labour provided to loyal Spaniards. This resulted in the emergence of large and semi-feudal landholdings or haciendas. In this system the indigenous nobles as well as the Spanish *encomenderos* administered justice, collected taxes and otherwise regulated relations between the crown and its colonial subjects (Poole 2004, 40).

Peru became officially independent in 1821. The nineteenth-century liberal land reforms tended to dissolve the colonial pact of the land tax nexus (Stepputat 2005). The law of 1828 declared Indians to be owners of the communal land they possessed but the same law barred illiterate Indians from property rights (Stepputat 2005, 68). Here we see several territorial mechanisms at work. First, access to territory is linked to ethnic categories. Second, by defining additional conditions these same ethnic categories are almost immediately excluded. By presenting these laws in terms of the 'neutral' administration of land, these processes of exclusion are impersonalized and obscured (Sack 1986). Formulating these new land laws in terms of territory, property rights and the condition of literacy sounds less crude than directly saying that Indians are excluded from property rights.

The nineteenth-century liberal reforms abolished the distinctive juridical status of the Indian Republic and banned the collective property rights that constituted the basis of its existence. However, until 1855 indigenous communities remained the basis for collecting the taxes that helped to finance the newly independent state. In this way, the semi-autonomous juridical, productive and political spheres of the indigenous communities remained the fiscal basis of the Peruvian state (Poole 2004, 41).

In 1855 the 'contribution', or 'tribute' levelled only upon the Indians, was abolished (Stepputat 2005, 69). Indians were no longer obliged to deliver labour to the haciendas. Yet, hacendados in the highlands relied on this colonial administrative invention to run their haciendas. Spalding (1974) argues that after the colonial political machinery disappeared hacendados deliberately created land scarcity for the Indians in order to force them to work for them. Only by offering Indian labourers access to land in exchange for their labour, was it possible to persuade them to work for the haciendas. Thus, in order to bind the indigenous labourers to the hacienda, the hacendados gave their shepherds (*huachilleros*) and their agricultural labourers (*colonos*) permission to use hacienda resources to herd their own animals and create their own vegetable garden. That the haciendas did not need the land for their own production became clear by the fact that they took the land without stocking it. According to Spalding this explains much of the expansion of the highland haciendas after independence. In this way the Indian population in the Peruvian Andes lost much of their remaining land to the hacendados who extended their landholdings by invading communal lands (Castillo 1992, 39). By these invasions the Indian peoples were forced to move towards the highest and poorest regions in the mountains. In their turn, on several occasions highland *comunidades* invaded haciendas (Martínez-Alier 1973, 20–74). Hence, indigenous communities were inserted into a larger economy and system of domination while they developed forms of resistance and opposition to that hegemony (Smith 1989, 29–84).

Summarizing, we see interesting forms of territoriality at work: Haciendas expanded their claims to land not because they needed it but in order to create a scarcity for Indians and hence oblige them to work for them in exchange for access to land. Smith (1989, 82) argues that 'it is undeniable that the effect of hacienda claims was to make community lands scarce, leading peasants into relationships with the hacienda'. Yet, according to Smith, the detrimental element for the Indian community was not creating land scarcity for pastoralists per se but rather undercutting a resource on which the politics of the community depended. The local community institutions were based on the organization and regular redistribution of access to communal land. *Comuneros* (community members) received land according to their efforts for the community. Hence, also within the communities territorialization was the central mechanism according to which land and people were managed and on which positions of power were based. Through this newly created scarcity the community authorities saw their position weakened as they had much less territory to manage (Smith 1989, 82). In short, the territorial strategy of creating land scarcity affected the position of communal authorities, whose control was largely based on the internal distribution of land in the communities.

In addition to the haciendas, the villages in the central highlands were subordinated to the valley towns. The highland villages were annexes (*anexo*) of the cities in the Mantaro Valley (*cabeceras, comunidades madres*), which meant that they had to carry out *faenas*, such as the construction of churches and bridges, and the cleaning of roads for the valley villages. The non-compliance with these obligations was severely sanctioned. Hence, urban centres, *comunidades indígenas* and haciendas formed a socio-political structure that was integrated through various mechanisms of control and domination. In this constellation territorial mechanisms were combined with administrative regulations. This vertical domination of valley over mountain areas obviously had racial and colonial dimensions as the valley people were mostly *mestizo* population descending from the Spanish colonizer, whereas the highlands were populated with indigenous communities. This structure of power and authority continued in the region till the second half of the nineteenth century when highland communities started struggles for independence and recognition as autonomous communities.

The Rise of a Peasant Ideology and the Search for Territorial Autonomy

By 1870 the region witnessed many conflicts between *cabeceras* and *anexos* over access to resources – pasturelands, commercial routes, taxes and labour rents (Mallon 1995a, 180). The Law of Municipalities of 1860 influenced this development through decentralizing the control over taxes and labour drafts. This policy increased the attractiveness of independent status, since *anexos* could, by declaring independence from a *cabecera*, directly control local rents, political posts and communal work parties. Villages that remained *anexos* – especially while growing economically or demographically – found that they contributed more than their share, in resources and labour power, to the *cabecera* of their district (Mallon 1995a, 180). It was not uncommon for the villages of a district to finance the development of the *cabecera* and get very little in return.

Much conflict in the late nineteenth and early twentieth centuries centred on the issues of district creation and district politics. As village populations grew, communities struggled to obtain independent district status, and thereby control their own revenue and labour drafts. The old district councils, for their part, attempted to block these bids and cement their dominance over *anexo* populations (Mallon 1983, 291).

In addition to competition over revenues and labour through struggles over the hierarchical classification of areas and populations, this period also witnessed other instances of territorialization. The difficult access to the highlands makes this region of Peru very suitable for resistance movements and warfare. This was a central dimension in the Pacific War between Peru and Chile at the end of the nineteenth century (1879–1884). Some authors argue that the Chilean invasion of the central highlands made them develop an elementary sense of nationalism which was grounded, above all else, in their love for the land and in a fierce sense of territorialism (Mallon 1995a, 170). This involvement of peasant fighters also had an impact on the power structure in the region. The regional elite became worried about the peasant mobilization. Although the peasants were fighting against the Chileans, the presence of well armed, mobilized peasant groups in the mountains was scary for the hacendados. Mallon (1995a) sees the fight against the Chileans as an explanation for the development of nationalist feelings among the peasants and the emergence of a strong popular movement against the hacendados. It is in this light that she views the ensuing land invasions.

Until 1920 the Indian villages in the Andean highlands had no official status. In other words, between 1824 and 1920 they existed 'in silence' as they were present in practice but lacked official recognition by the Peruvian State (Castillo 1992, 39). Here we see how the official governmental inscription of territoriality, or the lack of it, can be an effective strategy to establish degrees of access (Sack 1986). As Indian highland villages were not officially recognized as administrative category, they could not claim access to land and property rights, nor initiate legal proceedings as legal entity.

Consequently, fierce struggles over land developed in the entire Andean region (Sánchez 1981; and García-Sayan 1982). As Glave (1992) points out for the southern Andean region of Puno, the protests against abusive services and for access to land became more frequent and more ideological. In the documents of those times the indigenous communities spoke about the terrible crimes committed against them by this 'miserable race'. A strong peasant ideology developed. This occurred in a generalized context of growing violence and clashes (ibid., 59).

Finally, the Constitution of 1919 included the recognition and protection of the 'indigenous community' as a landowning corporation and in 1921 the Office for Indigenous Affairs was established. The official recognition of the first five indigenous communities in Peru took place in 1926 and today there are 5,680 *comunidades campesinas* (peasant communities) with 2 million members (Censo Nacional Agropecuario de 1994) (Castillo 2003). Increasing numbers of peasant villages began to apply for official recognition as Indian communities in the 1930s. According to some authors, 'the state actively encouraged official recognition, since it provided an avenue for more direct government control over village affairs' (Mallon 1983, 270). Hence, some authors contend that the recognition of communities constituted a state attempt to contain an unruly rural population (Stepputat 2005, 78). In their turn, 'the peasants were quick to use the new bureaucracy to resurrect age-old boundary conflicts with surrounding haciendas' (Mallon 1983, 271). The legal recognition of Indian communities could also challenge the legitimacy of land claims by hacendados, the Catholic Church or commercially-oriented farmers (ibid.). Even though the various state agencies usually decided in favour of the elite, there were instances in which government representatives were willing to uphold the side of the peasantry (Mallon 1983, 275). More changed in the 1930s, with the new national legislation and the strengthening of the Dirección de Asuntos Indígenas (Directorate of Indigenous Affairs).

Velasco's Agrarian Reform: Peasant Communities under State Tutelage

Peasant unrest in the Andean highlands continued and in 1968 the Revolutionary Government of the Armed Forces of President Velasco Alvarado decided to implement a large-scale land reform on the basis of a new agrarian legislation and new statute of *comunidades*. 'By eliminating large landholdings and abusive local powers, Velasco promised to rationalize production and attain equity in the distribution of land' (Poole 2004, 51). The new statute aimed to modernize the highland *comunidades* by recognizing the inalienability and imprescriptibility of their lands and stimulating their transformation into cooperative enterprises (Alberti and Sánchez 1974, 181). The official name of 'indigenous' was changed into 'peasant' and instead of *comunidad indígena* from 1968 onwards the official term is *comunidad campesina*. Under Velasco's land reform haciendas were expropriated and turned into cooperatives (in the lowlands) or associative enterprises (in the Andean highlands), the so-called SAIS (Sociedades Agrícolas de Interés Social) (Agrarian Association of Social Interest). In the central highlands huge cattle haciendas (sometimes owned by foreign corporations and highly capitalized) specializing in sheep production for wool export were expropriated.

Although the Agrarian Reform worked against the regional power holders (*gamonales*) it did not really work in favour of the peasants. Many hacendados de-capitalized their productive enterprises before they were expropriated. For that reason the cooperatives and SAIS had a difficult start. In the highlands most enterprises were too small and poor to allow for the payment of the functionaries that were going to be responsible for the exploitation (Martínez-Alier 1973, 36). As the members of the communities were displeased with the new developments more peasant unions were formed in this period.

Criticizers of the Velasco land reform argued that hacienda lands should have been handed over to the *comunidades*. They stated that 'in privileging the associative enterprises as a substitute for the traditional hacienda, Velasco's agrarian reform failed to resolve these historic demands for the lands stolen by hacendados' (Renique 1994, 226). Beneficiaries felt utterly betrayed by the fact that instead of receiving the land in the form of a restitution of what rightfully belonged to them, they were forced to become members of a landholding association run by external officials. In their view, this was far removed from the return of land that in the past had illegitimately been taken away from their forefathers. In addition, although the owners of the estates were removed, everything else remained the same (Sánchez 1989, 87–8). In fact, 'the associative enterprises reproduced the oppressive traits of the traditional haciendas' (Renique 1994, 241).

The military government of Velasco, however, was very proud of the SAIS, which they considered to be an invention that would result in the incorporation of the Andean Indian population into Peruvian society. Regional bosses (*gamonales*) would no longer be able to exploit indigenous communities who would from now onwards directly fall under responsibility of the state. It was propagated that by keeping the productive installations of the haciendas, the SAIS could produce a lot and help *comuneros* to capitalize themselves. In the Andean highlands the SAIS were expected to provide extension services and high quality sheep and other animals to the peasant communities. In this way the state would modernize the Peruvian agrarian production system by converting backward Indians (superstitious and lazy, almost by definition) into modern peasants (effective and dynamic entrepreneurs, commercially-oriented farmers). This corporatist state project employed territorial strategies to turn highland indigenous peasants into modern farmers and incorporate them into mainstream Peruvian society. For the indigenous villages this 'state care' meant that their access to territory was controlled by a highly institutionalized, top-down and state-led association.

Others have pointed out the less noble objective that 'by taking the "associative" option, the government sought the preserve the administration and assets of the expropriated estates while at the same time defusing and controlling peasant demands for land' (Renique 1994, 227). Through this territorial strategy in which land was collected and handed over to a cooperative instead of to the individual communities, the state was said to keep control over the *comunidades*. They did not give them the land directly but through a structure that they imposed and regulated from above. Whatever the aims were of the Velasco regime with the land reform and the associative enterprises, over time these reforms had results that differed very much from the official goals. Even if the Velasco regime wanted to 'free' the indigenous population from exploitation and support them in the development of large capitalist enterprises, the contradiction of this 'mobilization from above' was that the communities did not adopt the grateful, docile, pliant attitude that was expected from them.

In the next section we will look into the formation of one community in the central highlands, Usibamba. It is discussed how this community evolved in relation to centuries of external territorializing strategies. We will also analyse the development of processes within the community in relation to the opportunities and limitations created by external processes of state legislation and administrative rule.

Usibamba: The Founding of an Independent Community and the Rise of a Local Elite

Usibamba is a community of approximately 2,500 inhabitants[1] at an altitude between 3,600 and 4,100 metres, in the San José de Quero district, department of Junín. In past centuries Usibamba was an *anexo* of one of the biggest valley centres, Mito, and the Usibambinos worked as shepherds herding the cattle of the *Mitenos* (Castillo 1964; and Alberti and Sánchez 1974). As an annex of Mito, the Usibambinos also had to perform many other tasks for the head community (*comunidad madre*). For example, the church bells of Mito were fabricated in Usibamba. As part of the wider movement for recognition and independence of indigenous communities and backed by several laws issued at the end of the nineteenth century, the villagers of Usibamba started their struggle for independence from Mito. A group of families initiated legal proceedings against the Lozano family of Mito demanding the property rights to the land that they had been working for many years. In 1896 they won the law suit and were granted the property rights to this land on the basis of '*amparo de posesión*', meaning that they had been in continuous possession of the land.

It is interesting to look at the territorial breaking up of the Mito district and the accompanying political disintegration. The indigenous *comunidades* who managed to escape the dominant control by the *mestizos* of Mito took factual possession over the land and the decreasing economic situation forced several landowners of Mito to sell part of their lands. Because of new national legislation, the *mestizos* of Mito could no longer use the labour force of the *comunidades* for the maintenance and construction of public infrastructure. These conditions were accompanied by a strong decrease in the population of Mito. Mito was finally reduced to a valley village with no more than 25 square kilometres of extension, after having been one of the most extensive districts of the province of Jauja (Alberti and Sanchez 1974, 57–8).

When the mechanisms of domination that linked the annexes to the dominant group were breaking down, the dominant group lost its power bases and could no longer maintain its position. The indigenous people in the villages made use of this situation by seizing a greater role in local governments and stimulating movements that fought for the independence of annexes from the district. In this way the indigenous groups achieved more access to and control over land (Alberti and Sanchez 1974, 59).

As the debilitated landowners were increasingly prepared to sell their land, in 1907 the same families in Usibamba that had won the law suit against the Lozano family bought an additional tract of land from this family. The families who acquired this land maintained a strong control over village matters in Usibamba in

1 In 1993 Usibamba had 2,197 inhabitants according to the Resultados Definitivos de los Censos Nacionales: IX de Población y IV de Vivienda of 11 July 1993. The estimated population for 2003 is 2,345 according to the INEI projections of 30 June 2003.

the decades to come. Although the land was acquired in the name of the comunidad Usibamba these families claimed privileged access because of their efforts.

The phenomenon of leaders, who fought for the independence of their village and afterwards controlled the newly recognized community, was quite common throughout the region. As Roberts and Samaniego (1978, 249) point out: 'After attaining independence for their villages, these leaders appropriated large tracks of communal land for personal use, which they justified on the grounds that they had done most of the work in achieving independence. There is no evidence that the poorer families of the locality either derived much benefit from political independence or were particularly involved in the struggle for it.' On several other occasions, Usibamba acquires additional terrains through purchase and through legal claims on hacienda lands.

The national legislation plays a role in the struggle for autonomy of the mountain hamlets. As was mentioned above, the Peruvian Constitution of 1920 recognized 'indigenous communities' as a landowning corporation. The definition and registration of an indigenous community provided the means by which a village could attempt to protect and demarcate its potential land and labour resources that before were claimed by the valley villages and haciendas (Roberts and Samaniego 1978, 246). On 9 May 1939 Usibamba is officially recognized as an indigenous community by the Directorate of Indigenous Affairs in Lima.[2] At that time the population consists of 492 persons. Every year on 9 May Usibamba celebrates the anniversary of the *comunidad.*

From the very start, land distribution in Usibamba was highly unequal and controlled by a few families. Although land was officially held under communal tenure property relations in land soon developed into de facto private property. Poor people, especially, sold their land out of necessity. People in the village still speak about the tremendous poverty in those times when they even had to sell their land in order to pay for their own funeral. In other words, the poor families had to sell land out of misery. The general assembly of the *comunidad* allowed these land sales even though it went against community regulations. Obviously, those who could take most advantage of this situation were the wealthy *comuneros* who could buy up the land and let their herds of cattle graze on the large extensions of communal land. They took most of the lands and the best lands.

The poorer families in Usibamba opposed the domination in village matters of these 'founding families' and their monopolization of the land and started to explore legal ways to change the situation. Multiple letters from the first decades of the twentieth century, found in the archive of the Ministry of Agriculture, reveal severe internal conflicts in Usibamba and the demand of local people for external intervention by the state. In these letters to the ministry Usibambinos

2 Expediente relativo al Reconocimiento e Inscripción Oficial de la Comunidad de Indígenas de Usibamba, del Distrito de Aco, de la Provincia de Jauja, del Departamento de Junín. Dirección de Asuntos Indígenas. Sección Administrativa. Ministerio de Salud Pública, Trabajo y Previsión Social, 1939.

complain a lot about the inequality in the *comunidad*. They talk about the fact that the 'founding families' have taken the largest and best parts of the land, while the majority of people in the village do not possess any land. In these letters they talk about 'communal anarchy'. They refer to the fact that according to the law communal land tenure should be egalitarian and not monopolized nor turned into a de facto private property.

In 1930 this group finally manages to have the general assembly of the *comunidad* approve of the redistribution of plots in Usibamba in order to change the highly unequal land allocation. The 'founding families' who are going to be dispossessed of large parts of their land started a law suit. The inspector told the Usibambinos that they were not allowed to change the land distribution in the community without authorization of the General Directorate of the Ministry. The court of justice in Jauja decided in favour of the 'founding families' and declared that the internal redistribution of land in the *comunidad* had to be cancelled. Other studies reveal that struggles such as in Usibamba about the growing inequality in land tenure were common in the area. Laureano del Castillo (1992, 45) writes about a nearby *comunidad* (Misquipata) where they also tried to organize an internal redistribution. In this village a *comunero* argued that he had a private property title to the land and that it could not be taken away from him. He had bought the plot, but he was told that land sales within a communal regime were not valid.

Hence, here we see how poorer *comuneros* in Usibamba draw on national state legislation and search for state intervention in the form of inspectors, judges and even – as we will see later – the police and the military in order to break the domination by a few families. These families are often the ones who started the struggle for independence and afterwards monopolized the acquired land which they tried to turn into private property. Although in some cases the courts supported the *comuneros* favouring a more equal distribution, in many other cases the powerful local families were supported.

The Use of State Law for the Re-establishment of Local Territorial Rule

After their failed attempt in the 1930s, in the 1950s some *comuneros* in Usibamba again tried to break the dominant position of the 'founding families' and finally in 1959 and 1960, under the presidency of Belaunde, Usibamba carried out the first restructuring of the *comunidad*. Documents in the regional archive of the Ministry in Huancayo describe fierce conflicts and disorder in Usibamba in those years because of disagreements about the internal distribution of land. Despite many pressures and threats by the influential local families, the general assembly of the *comunidad* approves the decision of a total restructuring, implying a new parcelling out of plots and a redistribution of these plots among all *comuneros*. It was decided to first carry out an inventory and measurement of all arable land.

For this parcelling out and reallocation of plots rules were stipulated by the *comunidad* beforehand. Although this restructuring was a serious blow to the position of the rich families, they were still very much favoured in the new distribution. For the distribution different categories of *comuneros* were defined with different rights and only the 47 descendents of the 'founding families' would receive irrigated land, all other *comuneros* only received a rain-fed plot.

Support was asked from the Ministry and an engineer from Lima arrived to do the measuring of plots and carry out the restructuring. The costs were divided between the community and the ministry. In this redistribution of land in 1958, 804 hectares were redistributed and handed out to 305 *comuneros*. They received between 0.5 and 3 hectares each.[3] After the reallocation the *comuneros* directly moved to the plots that were assigned to them to build shelters and in this way mark their right to the plot.

The 'founding families' again tried to cancel the decision taken by the general assembly and accused the *comuneros* of invading their territory and constructing houses on their land. Again they went to court and asked for military support from Lima to remove the agitators from 'their' land. On the other hand the 'invading *comuneros*', accused the plaintiffs of the fact that they were abusive authorities in Usibamba, some monopolizing more than 20 hectares of land. In their letter they made reference to the norms guiding the use of communal land that said that a yearly equal redistribution had to be respected (*las normas en el uso de tierra comunal que dicen que se tiene que respetar una distribucion equitative anual*) in order to avoid disequalities and abuse. They also mentioned the fact that in the redistribution the rights of the three main local bosses were respected.

By now the political and legal climate had changed and this time the 'founding families' lost the court case. Some landholders left the village, when they realized that their protest was to no avail and that they were about to lose their plots.

The ministry sent an engineer to support the parcelling out and redistribution of plots in Usibamba. In his report the engineer described the work as quite complex and time-consuming. After the demarcation of plots, each plot was in turn divided into subplots. The reason behind this fragmentation is that *comuneros* prefer to have a variety of plots in different ecological zones. Family relations (wanting to have land close to different relatives) or the proximity of their houses are other reasons for having scattered plots. The adjudication of all these plots and subplots was registered in the 'book of adjudications' of the *comunidad*.

So, we see that in Usibamba, similarly to rural communities in other parts of the world, control over land means a position of domination in the village. People who possess most land and control the distribution of it are the ones who also dominate village administration in many other areas of life. So, also in the village itself control over space implies control over people. In the case of Usibamba,

3 Expediente Nº 25308. Ministerio de Trabajo y Asuntos Indígenas. Dirección General de Asuntos Indígenas. Departamento de Topografía y Catastro. Expediente relativo a la Parcelación de tierras de la Comunidad de Usibamba, (Distrito San José de Quero, Provincia Concepción, Departamento Junín). Iniciado el 8 de Abril de 1958 y concluido el 14 Abril de 1962. Recibido el 2 Septiembre 1969.

the families in a subordinate position drew on national legislation and state intervention in order to fight the domination of the 'founding families' who had monopolized the land and had turned it into de facto private property. The fact that these families still had much control over the villagers is illustrated by the fact that they were highly favoured in the new distribution of land.

Agrarian Reform and the Second Re-establishment of Local Rule in Usibamba

As was mentioned above, during the regime of Velasco Alvarado (1968–1975) a large land reform was carried out in which lands of haciendas were expropriated and organized into cooperatives or associative enterprises (SAIS). During this land reform Usibamba became one of the 16 member *comunidades* of the SAIS Túpac Amaru. In addition to the establishment of these cooperative associations, the Velasco government intended to address the problem of internal fragmentation of land within the *comunidades*. As we saw in Usibamba, *comuneros* generally possess many tiny parcels in different ecological zones. According to the Peruvian government this impeded the development of modern, progressive agricultural enterprises. The solution to this problem was seen in the complete surveying and redistribution of land in each *comunidad*.

Usibamba was chosen by the government to be the first example of this transformation. There were several reasons to choose Usibamba for this pilot project and for converting Usibamba into a 'model community' (*comunidad modelo*). Most importantly, the selection of Usibamba was based on the fact that several young *comuneros* of Usibamba had again initiated legal proceedings against local families who monopolized the land of the *comunidad*. For the government it was easier to introduce a radical redistribution of land in a community where there was already a movement going on in that direction. In order to facilitate the process, the government asked the German Mission – active in development projects in the region – to focus their activities on Usibamba and in this way support the restructuring and the development of collective projects. Among other things, the German Mission provided agricultural support to *comuneros* in Usibamba and introduced improved pastures. Much money was invested in Usibamba by the Germans. Hence, a variety of – partly territorial – techniques such as national legislation, government programmes and the steering of external funding were brought into action by the Peruvian state in an attempt to create an example of how to change patterns of land tenure and transform 'backward Indians' into 'modern farmers'.

Together with the support of the German Mission and engineers from the Ministry of Agriculture, the land distribution of the community of Usibamba was again reorganized. All land sales that had taken place since the 1920s were annulled by the authorities of the *comunidad*. For the second time in the history of the *comunidad* land was taken away from all *comuneros* and redistributed on a more equalitarian basis. The older landowning *comuneros* in the village, especially, were opposed to this transition as they were the ones with the largest extensions of land. Because of fierce opposition by some local groups, the army was sent to Usibamba to secure the implementation of this programme. That is why people tend to say that: 'Usibamba was restructured at the point of a gun (a punta de pistola).' So, physical military force was an additional technique used for the steering of people and their construction of space.

One of the Jesuit priests who worked in the region of Usibamba in the 1980s explained the following:

> The comunidades and their democratic model, their faenas [collective work parties] … the reality is not always that nice. In most cases a considerable internal differentiation exists. This was the case of Usibamba. The government chose a comunidad to implement the model of the restructured peasant community. Some had a lot of land and others had nothing. How do you convince the people? What they told us when we arrived in the region [in the beginning of the eighties] is that for the restructuring army trucks arrived in Usibamba, they took the people out of their houses and said: Those who want restructuring step forward and those who don't want restructuring get in the truck. It is a comunidad that was restructured 'a punto de pistola' [at gunpoint]. It was imposed by the government but accepted by the community. The final decision was taken at the communal assembly. It was an imposition but it worked. It was the 'model community'.

Usibamba was also promised to receive a preferential treatment in comparison with the 15 other member communities of the SAIS TA if they accepted the redistribution. As a reward for their reorganization of land tenure, the government determined that Usibamba would receive the highest percentage of the annual profits of the SAIS TA, namely 10 per cent.[4] Here we see that an alliance is forged between a group of *comuneros* that fight against the local monopolization of land and the state that needs a 'showcase' for the agrarian reform.

In the end, Usibamba would remain the only *comunidad* in Peru were the state implemented a reallocation of land. The *comuneros* refer to this period as 'complete restructuring' (*re-estructuracion total*), meaning that all land was taken and divided into equal parts. They are proud of the fact that they were the 'model community'. However, they do not tend to talk about the pressure by the government and the army. Although they do relate about the difficulties and heavy internal conflicts before and during the restructuring, they do not give much weight to outside forces. They convey the image of their own strong fight for justice. The image of the only *comunidad* that has carried out a total restructuring would obviously lose much of its ideological glamour by adding that they had been forced to do so.

---

4 Proyecto de adjudicación del complejo Cerro de Pasco a favor de la Sociedad Agrícola de Interés Social (SAIS) Túpac Amaru, 1969. Estatuto de la SAIS 'Túpac Amaru' Ltda. N° 1. Registrado la Modificación de Estatutos en el asiento N° 11, del folio 146° del tomo 1° de Sociedades Civiles de Junín. Huancayo, 28 de Junio de 1985.

The SAIS Túpac Amaru (TA): Controlling Communities via Territorial Strategies

The SAIS Túpac Amaru (TA) was established in 1970 through expropriation of 19 properties, c.q. haciendas. In total the SAIS TA received 216,499 hectares of land and all the installations of the former haciendas.[5] Of the communities which eventually formed the SAIS Túpac Amaru no less than 13 had claims against the enterprise by virtue of 'immemorial possession' or colonial land titles (Hobsbawn 1974, 148). The existence of law suits between the community and the former owner of the land, the Cerro de Pasco Corporation, was an official criterion for selection as a member of the new associative enterprise. Of the 30 communities who applied for membership of the SAIS TA only 16 were chosen. It was argued that existing legal problems about borders and land invasions could be resolved easier if the community would become a co-owner of the new associative enterprise, the SAIS. Although it was formally explained as a form of doing justice to the indigenous communities with outstanding claims, it can also be analysed in the opposite way of a form of co-optation of angry and possibly violent communities.

The SAIS TA was mainly oriented towards animal husbandry (sheep and wool production) and employed a large number of people who lived on the premises of the SAIS. The member *comunidades* all have one representative in the general assembly of the SAIS. The idea was that the SAIS would provide technical support and revenues of the enterprise to the member *comunidades*. In practice, however, the *comunidades* received hardly any benefits from their participation in the SAIS and most of them want to abolish the enterprise and receive the land that corresponds to them.

One of the properties that were expropriated for the establishment of the SAIS TA was the hacienda Consac that at that time belonged to the North American Cerro de Pasco mining company. Usibamba had a long history of working relations and border problems with this hacienda. The relations the Usibambinos developed with the SAIS TA were very similar to those with the hacienda. The newly established SAIS established his head office at the former hacienda Pachacayo and the SAIS administrator for Consac took his residence at the former hacienda Consac. So, also in this way there was little difference with the situation in the past. It is telling that although the SAIS refers to the 'production unit' Consac, the *comuneros* of Usibamba continue speaking about the hacienda Consac.

While the Velasco regime drastically transformed property regimes in the Andes, the *comuneros* felt that they maintained the same feudal relationships to

5 The 16 member communities were: Usibamba; San Antonio de Tanta; Canchayllo; Llocllapampa; Santa Rosa de Sacco; Huari; Suitucancha; Urauchoc; Santiago de Huayhuay; San Juan Bautista de Pachahaca; Huacapo; Purísima Concepción de Paccha; Chalhuas; Huancaya; Chacapalpa; and San Juan de Ondores. Proyecto de adjudicación del complejo Cerro de Pasco a favor de la Sociedad Agrícola de Interés Social (SAIS) Túpac Amaru, 1969.

the hacienda as to the SAIS. In fact, the great frustration of Usibamba has always been that they did not receive the lands of the hacienda Consac.

The SAIS TA hired many shepherds for their large herds of sheep and cattle. These shepherds are called *huacchilleros*. The *huacchillero* is an important figure that stems from the times of the hacienda when he carried out herding activities for the hacienda in exchange of being allowed to keep his own animals – called *huaccho* – next to the extensive herds of the hacienda. After the land reform, the *huacchillero* becomes an important figure in the relation between the SAIS and its member communities. In addition to their salary, *huacchilleros* are given the old usufructuary rights over the pastures of the SAIS. An additional task of the *huacchis* is to keep *comuneros* from invading the lands of the SAIS. The point is that member communities are not allowed to use the extensive SAIS TA pastures for the herding of their animals. Because of a lack of pasture land and the feeling that the SAIS TA lands is actually theirs, the *comuneros* have always violated this rule on pain of punishment by the *huacchilleros.*

The free use of the paths that cross the extensive SAIS TA properties and which people have to use to go from one part to another, is officially respected by the SAIS TA authorities. Hence, *comuneros* are entitled to use the trails of the SAIS TA for moving their animals. But when they are walking there and nobody is surveilling them, they can easily stop for a moment and let the cattle graze on the pastures besides the path. If they are caught during this activity they will be fined. This is locally called: *cobras por pasadero*. For that reason the *comuneros* used to go at night or at other moments that they would not so easily be caught. Other things that villagers 'steal' from the SAIS TA besides pasture and cow dung are the poles and wire used for the fences.

Here again we see that even today the relationship with the SAIS TA is very similar to that of the old hacienda. In the time of the hacienda the *comuneros* also had to pay for the use of pasture in the form of construction of irrigation canals or cutting pasture for the hacienda. In the past if people were found with their cattle on the pastures of the SAIS TA, the animals were locked up for 24 hours without food and water. Then the villagers could come and collect their animals if they paid a fine. Stories abound about the bad treatment by the *huacchis* of the SAIS TA, their abuse of women and children. For that reason they are called the assaulters (*maltratadores*) of the SAIS TA. What people in Usibamba resent most is not that the *huacchis* made them work as a form of punishment but the humiliation they had to suffer in order to get their animals back, the fact that the *huacchis* made them beg and cry. Over the years, several *huacchis* were beaten up by *comuneros* because of their abusive behaviour. These stories about abusive *huacchis* also contribute to the constitution of a collective communal identity against the SAIS as an oppressive institution that illegitimately owns lands that in fact belongs to the *comunidad.*

The *comuneros* feel that they are the rightful owners of the land, but they see few of its benefits. A great part of the profits of the SAIS is spent on remuneration for the workers, technicians and administrators, leaving no revenues for the member communities. This leads to the contradictory situation that the sector that officially ought to benefit most – the member communities and their *comuneros* – is the one that receives fewest profits from the SAIS. That is precisely the way the *comuneros* see this relationship.

Several member communities of the SAIS TA have continued to invade and incorporate more and more SAIS lands. Land invasion for them equalled the recuperation of their own land. This has been accompanied by much violence and political actions in the public arena and negative publicity about Indian rebels. For example, in newspaper reports about the invasion of SAIS land by member communities, *comuneros* were often accused of being 'communist agitators' and 'ultra leftists'. In fact, 'the categories of Indian, Communist and rebel overlapped considerably' (Orlove 1994, 84). The accounts did not represent uprisings as violent acts committed by the population against abusive authorities, but rather as a kind of barbarian savage acts which Indians were prone to do (ibid., 83).

From the day the SAIS Túpac Amaru was established, the member communities have also tried legal ways to dismantle the association and divide the land among themselves. The *comunidades* sustain their fight for the dismantlement of the SAIS TA through their representatives at the general assembly. Every meeting of the SAIS TA, one or more communities present petitions for land to be handed over to them. The SAIS TA has been confronted with countless lawsuits filed against them by the communities demanding 'their' land. In their turn, the directives of the SAIS TA have tried to annul these pressures, even through killings if thought necessary. For instance, a well-known case is that of Moises Camacho, a *comunero* from Chalhuas, who was killed because of his vigorous intents to dismantle the SAIS during his term as representative of the community at the SAIS.

As the abolishment of the SAIS TA through legal ways has proven impossible to achieve, several member communities just invade and incorporate SAIS TA lands under their own communal regime. The problem with those invasions is that it creates division among the communities who claim rights to the SAIS property. For example, on several occasions Usibamba has turned against invasions by other communities as they fear losing land that they consider theirs. This is especially worrisome for Usibamba as it is the largest member *comunidad* of the SAIS TA with most entitlements. Another difficulty with invasions is that influential local families often use the figure of the *comunidad* to gain individual access to land of the SAIS. In their turn, the SAIS TA has used several territorial strategies to keep the communities 'at a distance'. For example, they have handed out several tracts of land to the different communities under usufructuary rights. The SAIS also uses the strategy of 'living frontiers', handing out land in such a way that communities have to cross the properties of other communities and fight among themselves rather than against the SAIS TA.

In the next section we will show how the violent struggles of the Maoist guerrilla movement, the Shining Path in the Andean region, changed territorial control and the relation between the SAIS TA and its member communities. Due to the violence the *comunidades* have acquired more control over territory and have started more openly using and invading SAIS land.

The Shining Path and Contestation of Territorial Claims

In the 1980s the region suffers a lot from the violence of the Maoist guerrilla movement, the Shining Path (*Sendero Luminoso*). Initiated by intellectuals in the city of Ayacucho, *Sendero Luminoso* moved from there to other Andean regions and the capital of Lima (Degregori 1996). *Sendero* propagated a revolutionary agenda directed against 'the enemies of the people'. All authorities were suspected but especially those of the state (Degregori 1996; and Fumerton 2001). The abolition of the SAIS as a state-run enterprise and the restitution of the land to the highland communities fitted well *Sendero*'s political agenda.

In general the population in the highlands was sympathetic to *Sendero*'s agenda of social order, including the fight against thievery and adultery. What peasants in Usibamba liked most, however, was *Sendero*'s agenda of bringing down the SAIS TA and dividing the property between the member communities. All SAIS in the Andes were violently attacked by *Sendero* and many of its directors killed. Consequently, some of the SAIS were closed down. At times attracted by *Sendero*'s propaganda or 'moved by the threat of force, dozens of peasants participated in the massive attacks on the associative enterprises and in the sacking of goods and livestock which took place after the armed attacks' (Renique 1994, 235). What caused disenchantment and horrified the community populations, however, were the brutal killings of authorities and the regime of violence that the *senderistas* introduced. Instead of a visionary project towards a more egalitarian future, the revolutionaries turned life into a nightmare of violence, threats and war (Starn 1995, 552). The rebels also angered the villagers with their demands for food and forced recruitment.

In Usibamba relatively few people were killed and no authorities were sacrificed by *Sendero*. For that reason other communities sometimes accuse Usibamba of having worked together with *Sendero*. This type of accusation is used in conflicts within and between communities. Also within *comunidades* there is much talk about families or persons who are said to have been involved with *Sendero*. However, division lines were not clear-cut and they certainly did not remain the same over time.

Being one of the largest associations, the SAIS Túpac Amaru received much support and protection by the national military and police. In this way the SAIS TA survived although they suffered many attacks in which 13 people were killed.

Usibamba, as well as other communities used this time of political unrest to officially request land from the SAIS TA. For example, in a letter written by the authorities in Usibamba to the director of the Ministry of Agriculture in 1987, they argue the following:

> As we are overpopulated in the little village where we live with only 3,810 hectares of land to support 2,840 inhabitants … this is a continuing problem which we try to resolve through your respected intervention, through … an extension of 12,000 hectares, which corresponds to us as member of … the SAIS Túpac Amaru.

When the Usibambinos talk about the 12,000 hectares that correspond to them, they refer to the 12,000 hectares of the hacienda Consac.

In 1988, during the presidency of Alan García Pérez (1985–1990) many letters and requests are written by peasant confederations to the president of the republic in which is declared that it is obvious that the member peasant communities are not benefiting from the SAIS TA. They talk about the exploitation of the rural population. Usibamba also requests the abolishment of the SAIS, meaning the distribution of land, animals and machines among the member communities and in this way – in their words – 'finalizing the process of Agrarian Reform'.

In 1988, the SAIS Túpac Amaru transfers some land to Usibamba. Even though the SAIS only transfers the usufructuary rights to the land and remains the official owner, the Usibambinos were pleased to receive the land 'in their own hands'. Yet, the Usibambinos continue their fight and in 1990 they again send a letter to the assembly of the SAIS demanding the dismantlement of the association, as it is not fulfilling the aims for which it was created for its member communities.

During the *Sendero* period communities who were involved in land claims, were labelled by the SAIS TA as pro-*Sendero* and therefore as potential 'terrorists'. The management of the SAIS TA accused the *comuneros* of Usibamba of being actively involved with *Sendero*. Although some villagers indeed actively participated in *Sendero*'s activities, most *comuneros* tried to keep a distance from the violent conflict. The period of worst violence in this region was between 1987 and 1989. Six *comuneros* of Usibamba disappeared during the years of violence.

In 1991 civil defence committees (*rondas campesinas*) were organized to protect the population and a national army base was established in the region. The heads of the *rondas* were trained by the military. Although officially the army came to protect the people against *Sendero*, in many instances the military themselves turned into a violent enemy of the *comuneros*. As a *comunero* put it: 'The *terruco* [*te hacia abuso*] betrayed you, the armed forces betrayed you and the police betrayed you.'

With the escalation of war in the late 1980s, numerous military checkpoints were installed in order to control the Andean territory and fight the Shining Path. In 1991 the army began the massive distribution to Andean peasants of more than 10,000 'shotguns' (Starn 1995, 553). In 1992 Peru's president Alberto Fujimori even arrived by helicopter to visit Usibamba's neighbouring village Chaquicocha to hand over arms to the *rondas*. In Usibamba they cherish the photos where they appear together with the Peruvian president. Finally, in 1992 the leader of the movement, Abimael Guzmán, was captured by the Peruvian army and life in the Andes became more peaceful. The self-defence committees functioned in this region until 1996.

Yet, relations between the SAIS and their member communities, already uneasy, had now been further disrupted. Territorial claims assumed new forms. As several *comuneros* from Usibamba said: 'It is only since *Sendero* that the SAIS started to respect us.' In former times, if the *huacchis* found *comuneros* herding on the lands of the SAIS TA, they took their animals for 24 hours and they had to pay a fine. After the Shining Path period the SAIS TA has become less severe to the intruders. Every morning, many women and children leave their homes in Usibamba for their trip with the animals to the pastures of the SAIS. They leave the village, cross the river and pass the fence of the SAIS. If the '*huacchis*' find them they throw them out of the hacienda. Sometimes they also annoy the villagers by taking their ropes, hats and other belongings. In contrast to the past, however, this illegal herding takes place quite openly during the day and people no longer try and hide what they are doing. Even if they see the *huacchi* coming towards them they continue herding the animals without giving them much importance. If the *huacchi* throws the people out of the SAIS the people just wait till the *huacchi* goes out of sight in order to pass the fence and enter the SAIS again.

Although it certainly is an improvement, the member communities keep on fighting for what really interests them: the transfer of their land. In order to appease the communities the SAIS TA recently agreed to hand over 30,000 hectares: 2,000 hectares to each of the communities. Yet, even this is very little considering the total extent of the company: more than 200,000 hectares. So, member communities, dissatisfied, have continued their invasions and law suits. In January 2004 one of the member communities, San Juan de Ondores, occupied 14,000 hectares of land of the SAIS TA and immediately fenced it. The executive committee of the SAIS started a law suit, which they lost and the police came to defend the people of Ondores. Yet, the directors of the SAIS continue their fight for the survival of the company. As the SAIS lawyer said in public: 'If terrorism did not end with the SAIS, neither will Ondores end with it.'

Since 2001 several meetings have been convened in the different member communities of the SAIS TA in remembrance of Moises Camacho – the *comunero* from Chalhuas who was killed by the SAIS because of his struggle for dismantlement of the association – with the slogan 'the land for the one who tills it' (*la tierra para el que la trabaja*). In these meetings the *comunidades* tried to close the ranks and not let themselves be divided by the SAIS.

Conclusion: Differential Effects of Territorial Strategies

Over the centuries and under different political regimes, the central administration in Peru has employed a variety of territorial strategies to levy taxes, draw on labour and subordinate the Indian population in the Andean highlands. The Indian labour was necessary for the herding of animals, agricultural activities and the construction of roads, churches and houses in the valley towns. The colonial regime created the Indian Republics and granted some territorial rights to Indian communities that complied with tax and labour requisites. This institution disappeared with the new Peruvian Republic. After independence and the removal of the colonial labour obligations another strategy had to be invented by regional power holders to draw on the Indian labour force. So, haciendas created an artificial land scarcity by claiming and invading more and more indigenous community lands. They did not make use of this territory but because of this new land shortage the Indian population was forced to work on the haciendas in exchange for access to land.

During all this time, however, the indigenous population fought against the invasion of their land and their subordinate position. Towards the end of the nineteenth century, when peasant invasions and revolts became increasingly strong, the state started to grant more rights to indigenous groups. This development was strengthened by the fact that the war against Chile had shown the force of the armed peasantry in the Andean highlands. New laws were enacted granting territorial rights to indigenous communities against hacienda interests. Although many court cases concluded in favour of the regional strongmen, more and more sentences also favoured indigenous communities. This development continued into the twentieth century. According to Vandergeest and Peluso (1995, 385), modern states have increasingly turned to territorial strategies to control what people can do within particular geographic regions within national boundaries.

Although the state gradually granted more rights to land and autonomy to the indigenous communities, the demands of these communities became increasingly fierce and violent. As they did not have much power to change the law or influence the functioning of the judicial apparatus, the territorial strategy employed by the communities was direct invasion and occupation of hacienda lands. This contributed to the image of the indigenous population as being violent, in addition to being 'stupid' and 'backwards'. 'Roving, highland peasants are notoriously independent figures throughout history, invariably escaping attempts to control them, and the chasms, slopes, and peaks in which [they] worked made this especially so' (Smith 1989, 53). Through a variety of technologies of power the Peruvian state attempts to 'manage' or 'pacify' these populations and in this way transform these 'unruly subjects' and the civilizationally 'other' into lawful subjects of the state (Das and Poole 2004, 9). As Poole points out, it is in those areas that are said to be both spatially and socially 'marginal' to the nation state, that 'we see the relationship between the spatializing images and tropes through which the state lays claim to both territory and particular forms of life' (Poole 2004, 36–7). For the state and in the public imagery 'the "margin" represents a zone of instability and danger' (ibid., 54).

In 1968 the Revolutionary Government of Velasco Alvarado finally implemented an extensive agrarian reform based on a new agrarian legislation and the new statute of *comunidades*. This statute aimed to modernize the *comunidades indígenas*, by recognizing the inalienability and imprescriptibility of their lands and stimulating their transformation into cooperatives or associative enterprises. Large landholdings, especially commercial cattle haciendas, in the Andean highlands were expropriated and turned into so-called SAIS of which indigenous communities – from now on called peasant communities – became members. The idea was that the member communities would share in the profits of these commercial enterprises and would receive extension, improved agricultural inputs and other forms of support. In practice, however, the communities saw very little profit from the SAIS as most money was spent on the labourers and administrators or just 'disappeared'. For that reason the *comunidades campesinas* felt increasingly unhappy with the SAIS, which they saw as companies led by external agents, occupying land that was theirs. So, while the agrarian reform was presented as an important transformation of the agrarian question in Peru and a way to finally incorporate indigenous *comuneros* as modern farmers in Peruvian society, in the end it led to great dissatisfaction and revolt among highland communities.

Other types of legislation introduced with the official aim to protect indigenous peoples – such as the legal recognition of indigenous communities in the beginning of the twentieth century – also had the contradictory effect of bringing them more under state control. Through administrative procedures aimed at the registration of communities and their territory, the state indirectly exercises control over people. For that reason, some authors concluded that 'the state actively encouraged official recognition, since it provided an avenue for more direct government control over village affairs' (Mallon 1983, 270). Other authors have also analysed Velasco's land reform programmes of the 1970s in Peru as an attempt to impose greater control over rural regions. However, we should not simplify political programmes or analyse state–civil society relations as strictly oppositional and state power not as only coercive (Nugent 1994). 'Thus, on the one hand, law is seen as a sign of a distant but overwhelming power. On the other hand, it is also seen as close at hand – something to which local desires can be addressed' (Das and Poole 2004, 22). For indigenous communities the effects of many laws aimed at their recognition and protection was double sided.

One should also take into account that even if territorial laws and programmes are issued with specific aims their ultimate effects might be very different. National laws and procedures do not necessarily have the expected effects, especially not in these physically and socially 'remote' regions. The limited effects of central regulation explain that the state often recurs to physical violence through military intervention to control these areas. As Das and Poole (2004, 6) convincingly show, key to 'the problem of margins is the relationship between violence and the ordering functions of the state'. On various occasions during the last two centuries, military intervention took place in the Andean highlands, often at the request of local groups. The most recent and very violent period of military intervention was during the rebellion of the Shining Path in the 1980s and 1990s.

As Sack (1986) points out, territoriality is socially constructed and involves multiple levels of reasons and meanings. Setting places aside and enforcing degrees of access means the inclusion of some activities and people together with the exclusion of others. For that reason, territoriality and power are intricately linked and influence each other. In the history of the region, 'land and political autonomy cannot be separated. The two questions interlocked and reverberated constantly in the ongoing struggles over power and meaning that formed communal and regional political cultures' (Mallon 1995b, 320). Territorial practices can be deliberately used to support or weaken positions of power. 'Whether the peasant views himself as part of an imposed territory or not, the crucial issue is that, from above, the central authorities do' (Sack 1986, 74). Territorial strategies tend to arise from centres of power with aims of control.

Territorial strategies are often used in combination with non-territorial strategies. However, in the case of the Andean highland communities, the Peruvian state has above all recurred to plain territorial strategies in their attempts to administer and control the population. Apart from the original aims with the creation of the SAIS, in the end this institution turned into a territorial mechanism through which Andean populations were refrained from direct access to 'their' territories. Over the years, the SAIS TA employed a variety of territorial strategies in their attempts to oppose legal requests for dismantlement and invasions by member communities; handing out usufructuary rights to certain parts of the land; creating division among communities by handing out land in such a way that border problems arose between them and fluctuating the punishments of *comuneros* who trespassed onto the SAIS pastures with their animals. Sometimes physical violence was used in the form of support of the army against invasion of SAIS land or the killing of *comuneros* who became too resolute in their initiatives for the dismantlement of the association. The period of the Shining Path, which also fought for the dismantlement of the SAIS, somewhat changed the relationship between the SAIS TA and its member communities. The SAIS has handed out more land and is less severe in punishing trespassing of the SAIS boundaries.

It is in this context of territorial struggles that the indigenous highland *comunidades* are formed and shaped over the centuries. Within the communities themselves similar territorial strategies are used to administer the village and control people. In Usibamba several times groups of *comuneros* have searched for support from the state in the form of engineers to survey the land, the military and legal proceedings to fight internal struggles and oppose practices of monopolization and privatization of land tenure in the community. Hence, we contend that it is impossible to understand the history of the Andean *comunidad* in Peru without taking into account the interlinkage and contestation of territorial strategies employed by a variety of powers.

References

Alberti, G. and Sánchez, R. (1974) *Poder y Conflicto Social en el Valle del Mantaro (1900–1974)*. Lima, Peru Problema 10, Instituto de Estudios Peruanos (IEP).

Benda-Beckmann, F. von (1993) 'Scape-goat and Magic Charm: Law in Development Theory and Practice' in M. Hobart (ed.) *An Anthropological Critique of Development: The Growth of Ignorance*. London and New York: Routledge, pp. 116–34.

Castillo, H. (1964) *Mito: The Orphans of its Illustrious Children*. Ithaca, NY: Cornell University.

Castillo, L. del (1992) 'Tienen Futuro las Comunidades Campesinas?' *Debate Agrario*, 14: 39–53.

Castillo, L. del (2003) 'Propiedad Rural, Titulación de Tierras y Propiedad Comunal' *Debate Agrario*. Centro Peruano de Estudios Sociales (CEPES) 26: 61–79.

Craib, R.B. (2004) *Cartographic Mexico: A History of State Fixations and Fugitive Landscapes*. Durham: Duke University Press.

Das, V. and Poole, D. (2004) 'State and its Margins: Comparative Ethnographies' in V. Das and D. Poole (eds) *Anthropology in the Margins of the State*. School of American Research Advanced Seminar Series. Oxford: James Currey, pp. 3–34.

Degregori, C.I. (ed.) (1996) *Las Rondas Campesinas y la Derrota de Sendero Luminoso*. Lima: Instituto de Estudios Peruanos.

Fumerton, M. (2001) 'Rondas Campesinas in the Peruvian Civil War: Peasant Self-defence Organisations in Ayacucho'. *Bulletin of Latin American Research*, 20(4): 470–97.

García-Sayan, Diego (1982) *Las tomas de tierras en el Perú*. Lima: DESCO.

Glave, L.M. (1992) 'Personero o Cabecilla'. *Debate Agrario*, 14: 55–73.

Hobsbawm, E.J. (1974) 'Peasant Land Occupations'. *Past and Present*, 62: 120–52.

INEI (1993) *Resultados Definitivos de los Censos Nacionales: IX de Población y IV de Vivienda Realizado el 11 de Julio de 1993*.

Mallon, F.E. (1983) *The Defense of Community in Peru's Central Highlands: Peasant Struggle and Capitalist Transition, 1860–1940*. Princeton: Princeton University Press.

Mallon, F.E. (1995a) 'Comas and the War of the Pacific' in O. Starn, C. Degregori and R. Kirk (eds) *The Peru Reader; History, Culture, Politics*. Durham: Duke University Press, pp. 168–86.

Mallon, F.E. (1995b) *Peasant and Nation: The Making of Postcolonial Mexico and Peru*. California: University of California Press.

Martínez-Alier, J. (1973) *Los Huacchilleros del Perú. Dos Estudios de Formaciones Sociales Agrarias*. Paris: Ruedo Ibérico.

Nugent, D. (1994) 'Building the State, Making the Nation: The Bases and Limits of State Centralization in "Modern" Peru'. *American Anthropologist*, 96(2): 333–69.

Orlove, B.S. (1993) 'Putting Race in its Place: Order in Colonial and Postcolonial Peruvian Geography'. *Social Research*, 60(2): 301–36.

Orlove, B.S. (1994) 'The Dead Policemen Speak: Power, Fear and Narrative in the 1931 Molloccahua Killings (Cuzco)' in V. Das and D. Poole (eds) *Anthropology in the Margins of the State*. School of American Research Advanced Seminar Series, Oxford: James Currey, pp. 63–96.

Poole, D. (2004) 'Between Threat and Guarantee: Justice and Community in the Margins of the Peruvian State' in V. Das and D. Poole (eds) *Anthropology in the Margins of the State*. School of American Research Advanced Seminar Series, Oxford: James Currey, pp. 35–65.

Rabinow, P. (2003) 'Ordonnance, Discipline, Regulation: Some Reflections on Urbanism' in S. Low and D. Lawrence-Zuniga (eds) *The Anthropology of Space and Place: Locating Culture*. Oxford: Blackwell, pp. 353–62.
Renique, J.L. (1994) 'Political Violence, the State, and the Peasant Struggle for Land (Puno)' in D. Poole (ed.) *Unruly Order: Violence, Power, and Cultural Identity in the High Provinces of Southern Peru*. Boulder: Westview Press, pp. 223–46.
Roberts, B. and Samaniego, C. (1978) 'The Evolution of Pastoral Villages and the Significance of Agrarian Reform in the Highlands of Central Peru' in N. Long and B. Roberts (eds) *Peasant Cooperation and Capitalist Expansion in Peru*. Austin: University of Texas Press, pp. 241–63.
Sack, R.D. (1986) *Human Territoriality: Its Theory and History*. Cambridge: Cambridge University Press.
Sánchez, R. (1981) *Toma de tierras y conciencia política campesina. Las lecciones de Andahuaylas*. Lima: Instituto de Estudios Peruanos (IEP).
Sánchez, R. (1989) 'Las SAIS de Junín y la alternativa comunal'. *Debate Agrario*, 7: 85–101.
Smith, G. (1989) *Livelihood and Resistance; Peasants and the Politics of Land in Peru*. Berkely: University of California Press.
Spalding, K. (1974) *De Indio a Campesino. Cambios en la Estructura Social del Perú Colonial*. Lima: Instituto de Estudios Peruanos.
Starn, O. (1995) 'To Revolt against the Revolution: War and Resistance in Peru's Andes'. *Cultural Anthropology*, 10(4): 547–80.
Stepputat, F. (2005) 'Violence, Sovereignty, and Citizenship in Postcolonial Peru' in T.B. Hansen and F. Stepputat (eds) *Sovereign Bodies: Citizens, Migrants, and States in the Postcolonial World*. Princeton and Oxford: Princeton University Press, pp. 61–81.
Vandergeest, P. and Peluso, N.L. (1995) 'Territorialization and State Power in Thailand'. *Theory and Society*, 24(3): 385–426.
Wilson, F. (2004) 'Towards a Political Economy of Roads: Experiences from Peru'. *Development and Change*, 35(3): 525–46.

Official Documents

Expediente relativo al Reconocimiento e Inscripción Oficial de la Comunidad de Indígenas de Usibamba, del Distrito de Aco, de la Provincia de Jauja, del Departamento de Junín. Dirección de Asuntos Indígenas. Sección Administrativa. Ministerio de Salud Pública, Trabajo y Previsión Social, 1939.
Proyecto de adjudicación del complejo Cerro de Pasco a favor de la Sociedad Agrícola de Interés Social (SAIS) Túpac Amaru, 1969.
Estatuto de la SAIS "Túpac Amaru" Ltda. N° 1. Registrado la Modificación de Estatutos en el asiento N° 11, del folio 146° del tomo 1° de Sociedades Civiles de Junín. Huancayo, 28 de Junio de 1985.

Chapter 3

Migrants, Settlers and Refugees: Law and the Contestation of 'Citizenship' in Bhutan

Richard W. Whitecross

Travelling from the plains of West Bengal towards Bhutan, Bhutan rises sharply a thousand meters above the plain. A tall, crumbling concrete wall separates the Bhutanese town of Phuentsholing from its neighbour, Jaigon, in West Bengal. Recently, this wall has been moved at various points in the town minimally increasing the size of Phuentsholing. The 'Gateway to Bhutan' arches across the main road between Phuentsholing and Jaigon, with Bhutanese and Indian officials on either side. Symbolically marking entry to the Dragon Kingdom, the Gateway seeks to emphasize the ability of the Bhutanese state to control access to and, equally important, exit from its territorial space. The notion of a frontier, a border policed on one side by Indian and on the other by Bhutanese personnel is quickly revealed to be little more than a bureaucratic and legal conceit. Living in the peripheral border zone, dayworkers pass through official and unofficial routes to work in Bhutan. Internal checkpoints along the only road linking Thimphu, the capital, with India attempt to regulate movement within the country but fail to prevent Bhutanese employers bringing in unauthorized labour from West Bengal and Bangladesh.

The porous nature of Bhutan's borders is the cause of deep concern for the Bhutanese government. In the 1990s, separatists' guerrilla forces from Assam established bases in the dense jungles of southern Bhutan and were forcibly removed during a military campaign in 2003. Similarly, the arrival and settlement of Nepalese migrant workers in the southern districts during the twentieth century led to increasingly vocal concerns in the National Assembly that the identity and character of Bhutan was under serious threat. Referred to as Lhotshampa, 'the people of the southern border', by the late 1980s these Nepalese migrants and their descendents represented between one quarter and one third of the total population of Bhutan, mainly settled in the more fertile southern valleys close to India.[1] Tensions between the Bhutanese authorities and the Lhotshampa community increased in the late 1980s and led to violent clashes. As a result of the conflict and reported government pressure to leave, a significant number of Lhotshampa left Bhutan and were settled in refugee camps in southeast Nepal.

---

1 There are no reliable or accurate population figures for Bhutan during this period that provide information of the different ethnic groups in Bhutan.

In my chapter, I approach the theme of law and space through the changing criteria of citizenship in Bhutan and their impact on the Lhotshampa. I examine the legal development of citizenship laws and locate the legislation within the broader framework of a country emerging from a feudal monarchy to a 'nation state'. I illustrate how the changes impacted at the local level on rights to own land, on those Lhotshampa who remained in Bhutan after the escalation of conflict in 1990–1991 and on the 90,000 to 100,000 Lhotshampa who fled what they considered to be their homeland for the 'non-places' or 'spaces of non-existence' of the refugee camps (Auge 1992; and Coutin 2000). My approach to space, therefore, is abstract in the sense that I focus on how law is being used to 'imagine' Bhutan as a homogenous nation within its borders. Further, these laws create barriers and obstacles for Lhotshampa in seeking official recognition of land claims, as well as transforming public spaces into highly difficult spaces to negotiate in daily life, creating a sense of powerlessness and vulnerability for Lhotshampa going about routine, everyday actions.

As a result of the changes to the legal grounds for citizenship a series of categories or, more precisely, gradations of citizenship and legal rights have been created that place a significant number of Lhotshampa Bhutanese in a liminal legal space – caught between neither being Nepalese nor able to establish their legal rights to be granted full Bhutanese citizenship. Through its ability to prescribe the criteria for citizenship, the Bhutanese state controls landownership through the categories of person who are either included or excluded from claiming and receiving full citizenship. In effect, law in Bhutan is a key arena in which the politics of space and rights, in particular cultural rights and the right to own land, have been, and continue to be, contested. The citizenship laws have been used in a variety of ways to create a range of frameworks for the exercise of power and control, notably by government officials and the police, that although presented in the apparently neutral language of the law have specifically impacted on the Lhotshampa. As Kedar (2006, 412) notes 'while law plays an important role increasing and organizing spaces of inequalities, it simultaneously conceals and legitimizes these inequalities beneath a neutral and professional discourse'.

Arrival in Bhutan: Migrants and Settlement

Borders, frontiers and their control are highly problematic, indeed, sensitive issues in Bhutan. The northern border with the Tibetan Autonomous Region remains undefined despite ongoing discussions with the Chinese over its demarcation. To the south, Bhutan historically extended beyond its current borders to include sections of Darjeeling and the plains immediately to the south of its mountains that form the northern edge of West Bengal. Following the Treaty of Sinchula in 1865 between the British and the Bhutanese, Nepalese migrants were moved into the newly acquired Duars. The Duars, or plains, had been ceded by Bhutan following a brief war in 1864. In the late nineteenth century, Nepalese from the eastern hill tribes (notably from the Rai, Tamang and Gurung), encouraged by the British colonial authorities, began to settle in Sikkim, Darjeeling and further west in Assam. However, according to British colonial reports, few Nepalese settled in Bhutan for fear of antagonizing the Bhutanese.

The first wave of migration into Bhutan, by Nepalese, began in the late nineteenth century when permission was given for them to enter the southern border region of Bhutan. After this initial wave, a second wave of migrants entered and settled permanently during the 1950s and 1960s. There is a lack of reliable data, however it does appear that by the 1970s the Nepalese community, referred to as Lhotshampa, made up between 20–40 per cent of the population. The Lhotshampa developed a society based on Nepalese culture and social structure – though it should be noted that it did not carry with it all aspects of the Nepalese Hindu caste system (Hutt 2003).

The Nepalese migrants cleared and planted the fertile valleys that had previously been uncultivated, creating small farms and villages across the southwest of Bhutan. The subsequent waves of migration in the mid-twentieth century occurred as major social, economic and political reforms were being introduced. More importantly, these waves of migration coincided with the development of a conscious move towards creating a national identity that transcended local ethnic and linguistic identities and loyalties. In the 1960s, labour was required for the economic expansion set out in a series of five-year plans funded by the Indian government. Accordingly, inward migration was encouraged and, as discussed below, full citizenship was available provided qualifying periods of residency could be established. Central to this process of nation building was the new legislative institution, the National Assembly and the creation of the first national code of law.

Reform and Modernization: Law and Nation Building

From a historical perspective Bhutan belongs to a category of countries – such as Nepal and Thailand – that were not colonized (Collister 1987). Remaining outside foreign control, Bhutan avoided the impact of colonial regimes on its internal social and political structure. Bhutan was, indeed remains, conscious of its precarious existence. As with Nepal and Thailand, Bhutan had a feudal monarchy and faced a range of internal and external pressures in the course of the twentieth century to modernize. Starting in the 1950s Bhutan sought to effect legal reforms to protect its independence and to tackle political pressures both from within, notably the formation in 1952 of the Bhutan State Congress by members of the Lhotshampa community, and externally with the Chinese occupation to the north.

Central to the process of modernization was the preparation and enactment of the Supreme Law in 1959. The Supreme Law was the most significant piece of legislation passed by the National Assembly following its creation in 1953. The Supreme Law set out the first comprehensive and recognizably modern code of laws. Equally significant, the Supreme Law set out a new vision of the emerging Bhutanese nation state replacing the earlier view of Bhutan as a religious estate established by the Buddhist hierarch, Ngawang Namgyal in the early seventeenth century. The political and social developments instigated by the third King, Jigme Dorji Wangchuck (reigned 1952–1972), were supported by a series of reforms that can be seen as necessary preconditions for a sovereign nation state: namely the creation of a centralized civil service and the introduction of a system of unified modern laws and the creation of new legal institutions, notably the High Court of Justice in 1968.

Legislating Citizenship: Creating Legal Categories

The Bhutanese legislation governing citizenship underwent major revisions in the 1970s and 1980s. In this section, I outline the introduction of Bhutanese citizenship legislation in the 1950s, its changes during the 1970s and 1980s as the result of political concerns over the size of the Lhotshampa population. Finally, I set out the relevant article from the first written constitution published by the Bhutanese government in 2005 and enacted in 2008. Specifically, I highlight that as a result of wider, at times inchoate, fears over immigration and the perceived threat to Bhutan's political and cultural survival there was a radical shift in the legal grounds for full citizenship.

Yet, a sense of unease and mistrust emerged in the late twentieth century among the governing elite over the presence of a sizeable Lhotshampa minority located mainly in the south of Bhutan. Schicklgruber (1997, 14) notes that 'to understand such fears one need only look at the neighbouring Sikkim. Nepali immigrants there reached such proportions that the original inhabitants came to constitute a minority'. The emergence of political awareness and activism among the Lhotshampa during the late 1940s and early 1950s, mirroring political developments in Nepal – notably the overthrow of Rana rule in 1951 and a brief move towards democracy in Nepal presented the first potential political challenge to the Bhutanese monarchy beyond the traditional and small elite. The emergence of the Bhutan Congress Party formed by Lhotshampa contrasted with the lack of political awareness among the other ethnic minorities in Bhutan. Political change in Nepal together with other political developments in Tibet and India formed the broader background to the reforms of the third king. Among these was the first Act dealing with citizenship in Bhutan, the Nationality Act 1958.

Nationality Act 1958

The Nationality Act 1958 was the first formal piece of legislation regulating citizenship and marked a major political shift. In part, the Nationality Act appears to be a response by the third king to demands by the Nepali activists who formed the Bhutan State Congress Party in the early 1950s. The Bhutanese government presented the 1958 Act as a 'grant of citizenship' to the Lhotshampa and there is documentary evidence to suggest that the Nationality Act was intended to 'offer full rights to practically all existing Nepalese in the State' (Rustomji 1978, 182). However, the 1958 Act was, in my opinion, not simply passed to address the question of the rights of Lhotshampa who had settled in the southern regions. In addition, as part of his social reforms undertaken in the early years of his reign, the third king abolished the various categories of serfs which existed and instituted a process of land reallocation, including the capping of land holdings at a maximum of 25 acres.[2] These former serfs together with the descendants of migrant Nepalese had to be accommodated within the new state and this was accomplished by the Nationality Act.

The Nationality Act 1958 reflected both the desire and need to regulate the wider Bhutanese population and reflected the gradual emergence of a new conceptual framework of Bhutan as a nation state. Equally, the 1958 Act represents the first legislative attempt to regulate citizenship. Before 1958 citizenship as a legal concept was absent. Bhutan as a polity was united under the monarchy but lacking a strong national identity. Therefore, while on one level the Nationality Act 1958 introduced the legal category of 'citizen', it sought to create and promote a 'national' identity as Bhutanese, rather than as Ngalong, Sharchop, Lhotshampa or any of the other minority ethnic groups within Bhutan.[3] Under the Nationality Act 1958, Bhutanese nationality was to be granted to any person who had resided in Bhutan for ten years and owned agricultural land. Those applying for Bhutanese nationality had to have reached the age of majority and were required to swear an oath of loyalty to the king once their application was accepted by the Home Ministry. Those who did not own land, but satisfied the residency requirement and had worked for the government for at least five years also qualified. It therefore appears that any new migrants settling in Bhutan could claim Bhutanese nationality after ten years. However, it does appear that under the provisions of the Nationality Act 1958 that landless and sharecroppers were ineligible. The 1958 Act therefore seeks to create the concept of citizenship as a legal category in relation to the territorial space of Bhutan, while at the same time requiring proof of residency within its borders to be granted citizenship. Unlike the legislative changes described below, the 1958 Act did not create gradations of belonging – an individual would either be a full citizen or not.

2 The serfs (*drap* and *'zab*) probably did not account for more than 10 per cent of the population at the time of their manumission in 1959 (Wangchuk 2000, 61).

3 Ngalong, Sharchop and Lhotshampa are the three largest minority groups. There are, however, another 16 linguistic groups ranging from a few hundred to several thousand each located in separate valleys. See Pommaret (1997); and Driem (1998).

Citizenship Act 1977

Nineteen years later and the general political situation was significantly different. The fourth king came to the throne on the early death of his father in 1972. The style of government remained based on direct royal rule with the National Assembly sanctioning royal policies. From this date onwards, the debates of the National Assembly revealled a conservative shift in government policies.[4] China had suppressed Tibet after the March Uprising in 1959 and set about destroying its cultural heritage during the Cultural Revolution of the 1960s. To the west, the semi-independent kingdom of Sikkim was annexed in 1975 by the Indian Republic following a major political crisis as ethnic Nepalese in Sikkim pressed for merger with India (Crossette 1995). These events unsettled the Bhutanese authorities who became increasingly concerned at the high numbers of Lhotshampa settled in the south – the most productive agricultural area in the country. As a result of these increasingly vocal concerns, the grounds for citizenship were reconsidered and a new Citizenship Act passed by the National Assembly in 1977.

The Citizenship Act 1977 redefined the legal grounds for eligibility to Bhutanese nationality. Sections Ka 1 and 2 amended the required period of residence from ten years to twenty, and from five years to fifteen for those in government service. Unlike the 1958 Act, the new Citizenship Act introduced the requirement of being able to read and write the national language, Dzongkha and to know about Bhutan's history and customs. This final condition set out in Ka 3 needs to be placed in context. Dzongkha was only made the official language of Bhutan during the 1960s and the majority of Lhotshampa located in southern Bhutan used Nepali, rather than Dzongkha. These apparently small changes to the formal legal criteria for eligibility reflect a conscious move by the Bhutanese authorities to restrict and limit legal claims to citizenship. The changes in effect limited the ability of significant numbers of Lhotshampa to be able to demonstrate their eligibility based on residence. As a result their rights were restricted, for example, only Bhutanese citizens can either own land or register a land title.

Prior to any grant of citizenship, the Home Ministry investigated the application before it was granted. On the award of citizenship, the individual was required to take an oath of allegiance to the king, to uphold the laws and observe the customs and traditions of the country. The customs and traditions are those of the Buddhist majority, rather than those of the Lhotshampa. The Citizenship Act 1977 for the first time set out a requirement that the applicant for citizenship was not to commit any act against the *Tsa Wa Sum* – a phrase referring to the 'King, Nation and People'. This trinity of the 'King, Nation and People' became increasingly used to underscore the importance of loyalty to the state and the desire of the government

---

4 There are earlier indications in the archival reports of the National Assembly which indicate an emerging emphasis on dress and national identity, for example, in 1964, Bhutanese national dress was discussed and made a requirement for Bhutanese women, army personnel and all guides entering public buildings.

to promote a national, rather than regional or linguistic, identity. Implicit within the concept of the *Tsa Wa Sum* is the importance of loyalty to the emerging concept of the Bhutanese state that was still intimately linked with the person of the monarch. With the amendments to the eligibility for citizenship set out in the 1977 Act, we can see the intertwining of legal processes and requirements with an increasingly exclusionary vision of what it meant to be 'Bhutanese'.

Citizenship Act 1985

Concerns continued to mount regarding the potential threat to Bhutan's cultural heritage and political survival. Calls for a Greater Nepal issued by the Gorkha National Liberation Front in north Bengal and the recognition that the Lhotshampa were generally better educated, therefore more politically aware than their northern counterparts, disturbed the Bhutanese government. These fears were fuelled by the belief that there had been a steady influx of (illegal) migrants from Nepal throughout the 1960s and 1970s. In 1985, a new Citizenship Act was endorsed by the National Assembly. Once again the grounds of eligibility were altered. The 1985 Act remains the applicable legislation for claims of nationality.

Under the 1985 Act, both parents (unlike the 1958 Act) must be Bhutanese for citizenship to be acquired by birth. Otherwise, an individual can be naturalized provided that they were 21 years of age, or 15 if either parent is Bhutanese. Government employees are still required to show 15 years of residency and all others 20 years. All such periods of residency had to have been registered prior to 31 December 1958 and appear in the records of the Department of Immigration and Census. Further conditions apply included being mentally sound; able to speak; read and write Dzongkha proficiently (though no indication is given as to what would pass as proficiency in Dzongkha); to possess a good knowledge of the customs; traditions and history of Bhutan; have no criminal record; and to not have acted or spoken against the *Tsa Wa Sum*. The Ministry of Home Affairs remains responsible for investigating all applications and the decision of the ministry is final with no right of appeal provided for in the Act.

There is an additional aspect which I want to draw attention to – namely the role of marriage. Prior to the 1977 Citizenship Act, nationality or citizenship could be acquired through either parent. A non-national parent could take an oath of loyalty and become a naturalized citizen. However, under the 1977 Act, Bhutanese women could no longer pass on citizenship to their children. Therefore, any child born of a Bhutanese mother and a foreigner was required to apply for naturalization and generally were awarded 'special residence permits' which allowed them access to health care and education. It is perhaps worth noting at this point that in 1978 the National Assembly adopted a policy which provided payment of 5,000 ngultrim as an incentive for marriage between Lhotshampa and northern Bhutanese. However, there was a low take-up rate and the policy was abandoned in 1991.

Census 1988

Three years after the passing of the 1985 Citizenship Act, the Bhutanese government began a fresh census in the southern districts where the resident majority were Lhotshampa. Hutt notes that the census was carried out, according to official documents, to 'identify foreigners and issue citizenship identity cards to all bona fide Bhutanese nationals' (2003, 152). Each member of every household had to present her/himself to the census team and provide either a tax receipt dated 1958 or a certificate of origin in the event that they had moved village since 1958. The recently issued Citizenship Identity cards were no longer accepted as proof of Bhutanese nationality. Each person had to complete a separate form and their names were added to one of seven lists based on the following categories:

F.1 – Genuine Bhutanese citizens
F.2 – Returned emigrants
F.3 – Dropout cases (that is people not around at the time of the census)
F.4 – Children of Bhutanese father and non-national mother
F.5 – Non-national father married to Bhutanese mother and their children
F.6 – Adopted children
F.7 – Non-nationals

Lee (1998) argues that the 1988 Census was undertaken on the assumption that the 1985 Citizenship Act repealed both the 1958 Nationality Act and the 1977 Citizenship Act. This is despite there being nothing to suggest this in the 1985 Act itself. As a result, tensions between the officials and civilians increased, especially since it was not made clear what would happen to those categorized as F.7 – Non-nationals. Hutt describes how the census teams returned time and time again to the villages and it was claimed that the census had revealed 100,000 illegal immigrants. From the accounts of refugees it does appear that the 1985 Act was being misinterpreted. This misinterpretation by Bhutanese officials was compounded by the absence of legal redress, either by way of legal challenge to the interpretation of the Act or to the actions of the officials. Furthermore, the reliance on documentation appears procedurally straightforward, yet certificates of origin became increasingly difficult to obtain and their accuracy was questioned by census officials. Tax receipts from 1958 or earlier were hard to find or the names on the receipt no longer matched those in possession of them or the land to which they referred.

The 1988 Census marked a major escalation in the tensions between the Lhotshampa and the Bhutanese government. Government reports argued that Bhutan had attracted thousands of illegal migrants due to its prosperity and the generosity of the government in providing health care and schools. The presence of so many 'illegal' migrants was presented in debates in the National Assembly as a major threat to Bhutan's unique identity and cultural survival. These themes were to be repeated annually during the National Assembly sessions. As a result of these debates, there appears to have been a shift in attitudes towards the Lhotshampa by their fellow Bhutanese. One Bhutanese informant noted that she had gradually found herself 'pulling away from my Lhotshampa friends' during this period. She could not explain why beyond a growing sense of uncertainty about their status as Bhutanese or perhaps as Nepalese. On reflection, she feels that her ability to trust Lhotshampa was eroded and admitted that she remains distrustful towards Lhotshampa.

Citizenship and the Constitution

Based on a royal edict (*kasho*) of the fourth king issued in November 2001, a committee of 37 members began the process of drafting a constitution which has undergone several periods of revision before it was finally made public. The Constitution was published on 26 March 2005 and came into effect in 2008. Citizenship is defined as follows:

> **Article 5**
>
> **Citizenship**
>
> 1. A person, both of whose parents are citizens of Bhutan shall be a citizen of Bhutan.
>
> 2. A person domiciled in Bhutan on or before Thirty First of December Nineteen Hundred and Fifty Eight, and subject to the laws, and whose name is registered in the official record of the Government of Bhutan, shall be a citizen of Bhutan by registration.
>
> 3. A person who applies for citizenship by naturalization shall:
>
> (a) Have resided in Bhutan for at least fifteen years;
> (b) Not have any record of imprisonment for criminal offences within the country or outside;
> (c) Be able to speak and write Dzongkha;
> (d) Have good knowledge of culture, customs, tradition and history of Bhutan;
> (e) Have no record of having spoken or acted against the King, the Country and the People of Bhutan;
> (f) Have renounced the citizenship, if any, of the foreign State; and
> (g) Take a solemn Oath of Allegiance to the Tsa-Wa-Sum as may be prescribed.
>
> 4. The grant of citizenship by naturalization shall take effect by a Royal Kasho of His Majesty.
>
> 5. A person who voluntarily acquires the citizenship of a foreign State shall not be entitled to be a citizen of Bhutan and, if any citizen of Bhutan acquires the citizenship of a foreign State, he shall be liable to have his citizenship terminated.
>
> 6. Subject to the provisions of this Article, law shall regulate all other matters relating to citizenship.

Article 5 retains the 15-year residency requirement, as well as the emphasis on an ability to write Dzongkha (despite its complex orthography), and the reference to the customs and traditions of the country. In effect, it reiterates the 1985 provisions.

The ability to demonstrate residence in a particular locale is the lynchpin for claims to full citizenship as a 'genuine Bhutanese'. The legislation moves from being abstract and neutral to having a concrete effect for the person applying for citizenship. Legal documents and official proof of residence are central to the process not only of establishing ownership of property, but to the right to be a citizen and able to access the full range of resources offered by the state. Furthermore, the criteria emphasize the importance of not being connected with another nation state – dual citizenship is not permitted. Dual citizenship is not favoured by many states, but in Bhutan there is no provision for an individual to chose which citizenship to surrender – by holding another citizenship that person automatically loses his or her Bhutanese citizenship. A question mark over the loyalty to the nation appears to be raised in those circumstances that must exclude that person from being a full citizen and be reduced to one of the seven remaining categories discussed above. This in turn is intertwined with the other requirements, for example, to not have a criminal record, to know the language and customs that illustrate the complex intertwining of law and the wider political and social frameworks.

In 2004 the Department of Immigration and Census started to issue new identity cards, officially called 'Citizenship Cards'. Identity cards are very important documents – permitting an individual to vote, to travel and, accordingly, play an important part in controlling the population. The new identity cards were described as 'exclusively meant for "genuine" Bhutanese' (Kuensel 2004, 20). More specifically, those Bhutanese who hold resident permits, marriage certificate cards (these are typically non-Bhutanese – or those treated by the state as not being Bhutanese – married to Bhutanese) and time bound certificates are specifically excluded from receiving the new citizenship card. Furthermore, it was announced that as the census data for the census undertaken in 2004 is checked and any individual is found to have dual citizenship, they will lose their Bhutanese citizenship. Therefore, we see that the Bhutanese state is creating and enforcing important differences of status, excluding and including within the national community through different levels of legal documentation reflecting official categories, with important legal effects.

The increasing restrictions on access to full citizenship, for example, the exclusion of children where one parent is a non-Bhutanese, hint at an underlying logic to the legal formalities outlined above. There is an explicit need set out in the legislation drafted by the government and sanctioned by the National Assembly to demonstrate a proper commitment to, and identification with the Bhutanese state. Underlying this is a concern about the invisible bonds by which the Bhutanese, both individually and collectively, establish and maintain this commitment. Children of mixed marriages are implicitly not seen by the Bhutanese state as being fully part of the imagined community (Anderson 1983). Where do they fit in the 'One Nation, One People' vision?

Official Spaces and Public Places: Dress and Decorum

In 1989 a royal decree was promulgated in which *driglam namzha* formed part of the official theme of the sixth Five-Year Plan (1987–1992). *Driglam namzha* refers to a code of formal behaviour and etiquette governing matters from appropriate dress, to greeting officials, gift giving and a range of ceremonial occasions. Originally derived from monastic codes of conduct and applied only to officials, both monastic and lay, of the Zhabdrung's government, it came to represent in the National Assembly debates a distinctive feature of 'being' Bhutanese. It is the core of the legal requirement to 'have a good knowledge of culture, customs, traditions' (Article 5, Constitution 2005).

Under the theme 'One Nation, One People', it set out as one of the nine policy objectives the 'preservation and promotion of national identity'. This policy went beyond simply maintaining traditions, stating that 'every effort must be made to foster the unfailing faith, love and respect for the country's traditional values and institutions' (NAB 1988, Res.18). Karma Ura, *driglam namzha* is a 'system of rules of physical conduct and external forms, applied on an individual basis to forge a sense of nationhood' (Ura 1997, 247). Yet, as mentioned above, *driglam namzha* is not merely about physical conduct and deportment. The code of conduct and etiquette govern not only dress and manners, but architectural styles and official etiquette. Above all, it regulates public behaviour and conduct.

Official signs outside government buildings, schools and monasteries advise the public that they must be appropriately dressed before entering and this is the key feature of *driglam namzha* – it seeks to tightly regulate public appearance and behaviour. The presence and role of these official signs reminds us that the presence and reach of law and regulation have greatly extended into ever increasing areas of everyday life in Bhutan, as it has done elsewhere. Wikan cites an elderly Bhutanese nun as declaring that 'China occupied Tibet, India occupied Sikkim, and we are occupied by our own government' (1996, 282). Similar small notices and announcements can be found throughout Bhutan and in all the administrative buildings and state-supported monasteries, a reminder both of the official policy of *driglam namzha*, and demonstrating that law and regulation effectively are 'cultural code[s] of conduct' (Passavant 2001, 727).

The fines imposed for breaching *driglam namzha* highlight the emphasis on public conduct while creating a distinction between public and private spaces. In private, especially in the urban areas, men, especially young men, often dress in Western-style clothes. Speaking with a young driver from eastern Bhutan, he spoke of his dislike of *driglam namzha*, or at least of the requirement to wear traditional dress. 'I like wearing my tracksuit or my jeans. But I know I will get stop by the police … then I just say that I am on my way to play football. They cannot fine me since they can't prove I am not.' (F/N 6 June 2001). While my informant's questioning of *driglam namzha* is not uncommon among young Bhutanese, its role as a symbol of unity and cohesion is now widely accepted. However, the royal decree in 1989 had major implications for the Lhotshampa.

At the time the royal decree was being issued in January 1989, the 1988 Census was still ongoing. Many Lhotshampas were encountering officials who requested a range of documents to establish their residency. Relations between the government and the Lhotshampa were already strained as a result of the 1985 amendments to the conditions for citizenship. The police and local officials were responsible for the enforcement of *driglam namzha*, which included the levying of a 100 Nu fine (about $3), half of which could be kept by the police as an incentive. An already tense situation quickly escalated as increasing numbers of Lhotshampa faced fines for not wearing the national costume. Often referred to by critics as 'Bhutanisation' (Strawn 1994), the emphasis on what was seen as 'northern' Bhutanese customs and practices, became a feature of the dispute over citizenship which reached a new intensity in 1990–1991 (ibid.). The Bhutanese government has since admitted that the application of the royal decree was, especially in the southern districts which have the highest Lhotshampa populations, 'implemented by overzealous functionaries … in a provocative manner' (Thinley 1994, 60).

For Lhotshampa, the need to wear the traditional costume associated with the northern Bhutanese is more than a tedious burden. To wear the traditional costume is to publicly demonstrate loyalty to the country and deny its own cultural heritage. By wearing traditional dress, as one Lhotshampa informed me, 'you try to avert the suspicion that you are, by being Lhotshampa, a threat to Bhutan. You show that you belong here. But, I don't like to wear *baku*'.[5] This suspicion towards the Lhotshampa communities remains a major source of anxiety for Lhotshampa and the ongoing promotion of *driglam namzha*, for example, in the weekly column on *driglam namzha* in the Dzongkha language version of Kuensel underscores the need for conformity, in public at least, with its complex rules.

Tsa Wa Sum: Citizen or Anti-national

The preservation and promotion of the values and the changing criteria for citizenship, discussed in the previous sections, coalesce around the emergence of the official trinity of *Tsa Wa Sum*. There is no reference to *Tsa Wa Sum* in the 1958 Nationality Act, issued a year before the Supreme Law. However, as described above, loyalty to the *Tsa Wa Sum* is expressly mentioned in Ka 4(iv) of the Citizenship Act 1977 and in the 1985 Citizenship Act.[6] The promotion of this concept of *Tsa Wa Sum* can, I believe, be directly linked to the emergence of a particular definition of what it means to be Bhutanese and the shaping of an increasingly vocalized ethno-nationalism. However, it is with the debates of the 65th Session of the National Assembly in 1989, just as the tensions with the

5 Baku–Nepali term for the male national dress of Bhutan (Dzongkha: *gho*).

6 The *Tsa Wa Sum* may be further extended to include the idea of the division between executive, legislative and judiciary as set out in the constitution.

Lhotshampa were approaching their violent climax, that the term reappears in the debate over 'anti-nationals'.

Following the clashes between the Bhutanese authorities and Lhotshampa in 1990–1991, either forced out by the Bhutanese or encouraged to leave by political activists, a significant number of Lhotshampa left their homes in southern Bhutan. The government viewed these people as 'anti-nationals'. Concerns over 'anti-nationals' and their lack of 'loyalty for the country' and intent 'to *harm* the *Tsa Wa Sum*' (NAB 1992, 92, my emphasis) in the National Assembly and reported in the media raised question marks over the remaining, not insubstantial, Lhotshampa community. There appears to have been a gradual, but definite shift in perceptions towards the Lhotshampa. Listening to Bhutanese talking over the last few years, there is a sense that the rhetoric of mistrust and association of anti-national activities with this community has had an impact. Sitting one evening with a family of northern Bhutanese, a middle-aged business man that I know well sneered as he declared 'Lhotshampa are not Bhutanese … they steal our land and don't belong here'. This outburst, as we discussed proposals by the family to buy land in one of the southern districts, surprised me. I knew that the business man had been raised and educated by a Lhotshampa woman, a widow with several other children. She and her family had fled Bhutan in the early 1990s and he had, as he admitted later, visited her and her family in Kathmandu. Listening to him, I began to realize that the government representation of the threat posed to Bhutanese identity and national integrity was unquestioned, rather it had being internalized. In part, the demonization of the 'anti-national' has been used to focus fears and uncertainties caused by the changes in Bhutanese society away from more tangible problems that face the government. Equally, the spectre of the 'anti-national' has ruptured relations between the remaining Lhotshampa and the majority northern Bhutanese population. Demands voiced by National Assembly members during the late 1980s and through the 1990s that the Lhotshampa reaffirm their loyalty underscores this rift.

The Lhotshampa interviewed discussed how they were, and still are, held under suspicion by the Bhutanese authorities because of their familial relationship with so-called 'anti-nationals'. One Lhotshampa who was studying at university in India when the violence broke out in his village in 1990/1991, informed me that it took him eight years to clear his name because several of his relatives had been listed as 'anti-nationals'. Commenting on the trial and sentencing of 111 Bhutanese in September 2004 for collaborating with the various guerrilla forces expelled in 2003, another informant highlighted that half of the names of those sentenced were Lhotshampa, especially from the two southern districts of Sarpang and Gelephu. 'We are always the first suspects.'

Other Lhotshampa commented on the frequency with which they are stopped by police and immigration officials and asked for their papers. One woman living in Thimphu and working as a domestic servant, described immigration officials visiting her home and demanding to see her papers. When they saw her papers which gave her place of residence in one of the southern districts, they began to question her about her family, how long they had lived in Bhutan and whether or not she had relatives living in the refugee camps in Nepal. As a result of her experience and her fear of the authorities, she is planning to leave Bhutan. These comments highlight another indirect effect of the suspicions towards the Lhotshampa, namely the impact on their mobility around Bhutan. Moving around the country can be problematic and attracts unwanted official attention. There is a further twist; jealous neighbours may choose to draw official attention to Lhotshampa increasing the sense of mistrust on all sides.

These suspicions have tangible implications for Lhotshampa living in Bhutan. Although nine Lhotshampa candidates were successful in the first elections between competing political parties in March 2008, there remain daily obstacles in everyday life for many Lhotshampa. The law and the rights it either confers or denies illustrates an underlying cultural logic and set of unspoken (at least in official discourse) assumptions underpinning the legal arguments and regulations concerning citizenship. I argue that apparently neutral regulations or inclusionary laws and principles (for example, equality before the law) create alternative spaces for 'an implementation based on exclusionary principles and practices' (Stoller 1995, 212–13). Implicit within the citizenship acts are concerns over land and access to land. The clearing of the dense forests in the southern districts revealed more productive and fertile settlements than elsewhere in Bhutan. Although these concerns may have been inchoate, it is worth noting the sharp increase in land purchases in the south by northern Bhutanese. By permitting northern Bhutanese to settle in the south, the government may be able to dilute the remaining Lhotshampa communities.

Life in the Refugee Camps: Living In-between

Although their relatives remaining in Bhutan may face various challenges, the Lhotshampa refugees have remained in their camps since 1991. Transformed in the minds of many Bhutanese into 'anti-nationals' due to the violent and criminal acts of a few members of their refugee community, the Lhotshampa refugees have been suspended in 'permanently temporary' camps. The Nepalese authorities have no desire to integrate them into Nepalese society, while the camps serve as physical markers of their separateness from their host country. During fieldwork in Nepal in 1999 and 2000, I encountered, by chance, some young Lhotshampa refugees who described their sense of being suspended in a no-man's-land; neither Nepalese nor Bhutanese – unwanted by both states. One young woman, Radha, described that she felt 'time has stopped for us. We are not settled, yet we aren't moving'. When asked what she meant by 'not settled', she replied, 'We cannot settle where we do not want to be, or belong.' The flight of these young people's parents from Bhutan began with the law, its apparent neutrality and its operational affect. Their parents, grandparents, aunts and uncles lost their property, their homes and live, according to Radha, 'nowhere'. The experience of these refugees mirrors what

Coutin describes as 'spaces of non-existence'. Fleeing Bhutan, either as the result of pressure from more militant members of the Lhotshampa community or as the result of violence and pressure by the Bhutanese authorities, the refugees and their families are socially isolated while being physically, politically and legally removed (see Coutin 2000).

In 1994, the governments of Bhutan and Nepal established a joint verification process. Under the terms of this agreement, two teams of Bhutanese and Nepalese officials would examine each of the refugees' claims to Bhutanese citizenship. Those who were deemed to be genuine would be permitted to return and resettle in Bhutan. Following the verification process at Khudunbari camp 70.55 per cent were categorized as having voluntarily emigrated from Bhutan and only 2.4 per cent as genuine refugees. The joint verification process was disrupted in December 2003 when frustrated residents of Jhapa camp violently attacked the Bhutanese verification team. Space and time for these refugees, as suggested by Radha above, appear to have been suspended until recent moves by various governments, notably the United States, Canada and Norway, to accept up to 60,000 Lhotshampa refugees broke the impasse.

There is one final aspect that is worth commenting on. The refugees physically removed from Bhutan, confined in theory, if not in practice, to their camps may not be recognized as possessing any legitimate claim to Bhutanese citizenship, yet they do appear to have some form of legal existence in Bhutan. Newspaper reports often present details of criminals or 'anti-nationals' including the name of their refugee camp. This suggests, although physically and politically excluded from Bhutan, the Bhutanese authorities maintain or at least appear to maintain detailed records of those who have settled in the camps.

Conclusion

In my chapter, I have attempted to reflect on the intimacy of law in defining and redefining citizenship in Bhutan as experienced by a minority, ethnic community. At the same time, I illustrate how in seeking to examine the spatialization of law, specifically the laws around citizenship, we need to pay attention to the complex interrelationship of different legal spaces ranging from the abstract, apparently neutral language of the law text to the practical effects of the laws at the local, everyday level. Gupta and Ferguson (1997) illustrated how physical and legal presence are conflated by the citizen who is assumed to be located within particular national boundaries. However, for the Lhotshampa, this conflation of physical and legal presence is problematical with the emergence of a disjuncture between physical presence (residence) and legal authorization (citizenship).

In Bhutan, the citizenship laws illustrate how legal rules and their application have direct, localized effect on individuals' rights and obligations. Yet the legal rules themselves are intimately linked to political, social and economic concerns and in this case, to the emergence of an official ideology of 'One Nation, One

People'. By examining the citizenship legislation across the late twentieth century, I have detailed how the laws and its associated practices 'render undocumented immigrants' and their descendents 'legally absent' (Coutin 2000, 28). The immigrants in this case may or may not be first generation, yet what we have seen is that the Bhutanese have sought to limit the number who could claim to be second or third generation migrants. The need for documentation to establish residence from before 1950 presents a key obstacle for many Lhotshampa whose families settled in Bhutan during the early waves of migration. Without this documentation their presence could not be used to meet the residency requirements. As a result, whole families of several generations are unable to seek legal recognition as 'full citizens' of Bhutan.

Akhil Gupta, citing Brackette Williams, describes nationalism 'as a distinctively modern cultural form' that attempts to create 'a new kind of spatial and mythopoetic metanarrative, one that simultaneously homogenizes the varying narratives of community while, paradoxically, accentuating their difference' (Gupta 2003, 329). The Bhutanese authorities in seeking to present Bhutan as a homogenous nation state have drawn on particular aspects of Bhutanese culture, for example, the 1989 decree reintroducing *driglam namzha*. By stressing conformity to an ideal, the Bhutanese authorities and its officials have accentuated differences, increasing official and popular concerns over the presence of those who could not be easily assimilated. By the same token, the relationship between the Lhotshampa and everyday spaces, including their own homes and farmsteads are reconstituted and transformed.

Griffiths and Kandel (Chapter 8) note in their conclusion that 'space in and of itself is never inherently safe or dangerous'. I agree but would add that if we view the law and its political significance, everyday spaces for minority groups can assume a subtly sinister dimension that creates and reinforces existing forms of hegemony. The challenges for those Lhotshampa who remain in Bhutan are complex and subtle. Indirect discrimination, for example, not being granted passports to travel or promoted at work, is reported yet is difficult to establish. The uncertainty of their legal status – either as full citizens or more typically under one of the other gradations set out in the legislation has conflated them in the minds of other Bhutanese with illegal migrants at the more benign level to 'anti-nationals/traitors' at the other extreme.

The development and the use of the citizenship laws in Bhutan serve to highlight how law is a powerful tool that exercises control over people and resources. In Bhutan, the legal rules on citizenship cannot be separated from access to land and other resources. Being unable to establish the right to full Bhutanese citizenship, as illustrated in my chapter, blocks the right to own land. It drives an invisible, yet significant, wedge between those who can own land and those denied this right. Kedar notes that law can be used 'to shape a landscape of … inequitable distribution of public resources and political disenfranchisement' (2006, 412–13). I have sought to illustrate how the citizenship laws created a legal space in which political, social and legal control of the minority Lhotshampa was made possible.

This increasingly led to the state exerting its control over land cleared and worked by Lhotshampa and the confiscation of the lands and homes of those who fled the country. Finally, for those Lhotshampa continuing to reside in Bhutan everyday life carries with it a range of compromises each to be negotiated in a variety of everyday spaces, while their relatives who left Bhutan remain in 'permanently temporary' camps or more recently rely on being allowed to resettle in a third country. Yet for all these effects there is a sense of law's fragility and the state's inability to effectively control and assert its authority.

References

Anderson, B. (1983) *Imagined Communities: Reflections on the Origins and Spread of Nationalism*. London and New York: Verso.

Auge, M. (1992) *Non-Lieux: Introductions á une Anthropologie de la Surmodernitie*. Paris: Sueil.

Collister, P. (1987) *Bhutan and the British*. London: Serindia.

Coutin, S.B. (2000) *Legalising Moves: Salvadoran Immigrants' Struggle for US Residency*. Ann Arbor: University of Michigan Press.

Crossette, B. (1995) *So Close to Heaven: The Vanishing Buddhist Kingdoms of the Himalayas*. New York: Alfred A Knopf.

Driem, G. van (1998) *Dzongkha*. Leiden: Brill Publications.

Gupta, A. (2003) 'The Song of the Non-aligned World: Trans-national Identities and the Re-inscription of Space in Late Capitalism' in S.M. Low and D. Lawrence-Zuniga (eds) *The Anthropology of Space and Place: Locating Culture*. Oxford: Blackwell Publishing, pp. 321–36.

Gupta, A. and Ferguson, J. (1997) 'Discipline and Practice: "The Field" as Site, Method and Location in Anthropology' in A. Gupta and J. Ferguson (eds) *Anthropological Locations: Boundaries and Grounds of a Field Science*. Berkeley: University of California Press, pp. 1–46.

Hutt, M. (2003) *Unbecoming Citizens: Culture, Nationhood, and the Flight of Refugees from Bhutan*. Oxford: Oxford University Press.

Kedar, A. (2006) 'On the Legal Geography of Ethnocratic Settler States: Notes towards a Research Agenda' in J. Holder and C. Harrison (eds) *Law and Geography*. Oxford: Oxford University Press, pp. 401–41.

Kuensel, (2004) 'New Citizenship ID Cards', 28 August, xix(34) 1, 20.

Lee, T.L. (1998) 'Refugees from Bhutan: Nationality, Statelessness and the Right to Return'. *International Journal of Refugee Law* 10(1/2): 118–55.

National Assembly of Bhutan (1988) *Report of the National Assembly*. Thimphu: Royal Government of Bhutan.

National Assembly of Bhutan (1992) *Report of the National Assembly*. Thimphu: Royal Government of Bhutan.

Passavant, P.A. (2001) 'Enchantment, Aesthetics, and the Superficial Power of Modern Law' *Law and Society Review*, 35(1): 709–29.

Pommaret, F. (1997) 'Ethnic Mosaic: Peoples of Bhutan' in F. Pommaret and C. Schicklgruber (eds) *Bhutan: Mountain Fortress of the Gods*. London: Serindia, pp. 43–59.

Rustomji, N. (1978) *The Dragon Kingdom in Crisis*. Delhi: Oxford University Press.

Schicklgruber, C. (1997) 'Introduction' in F. Pommaret and C. Schicklgruber (eds) *Bhutan: Mountain Fortress of the Gods*. London: Serindia, pp. 13–27.

Stoller, A.S. (1995) *Race and the Education of Desire*. Durham, NC: Duke University Press.

Strawn, B. (1994) 'The Dissidents' in M. Hutt (ed.) *Bhutan: Perspectives on Conflict and Dissent*. Gartmore: Kiscadale Asia Research Series no. 4, pp. 97–128.

Thinley, J. (1994) 'Bhutan: A Kingdom Besieged' in M. Hutt (ed.) *Bhutan: Perspectives on Conflict and Dissent*. Gartmore: Kiscadale Asia Research Series no. 4, pp. 43–76.

Ura, K. (1997) 'Tradition and Development' in F. Pommaret and C. Schicklgruber (eds) *Bhutan: Mountain Fortress of the Gods*. London: Serindia, pp. 239–51.

Wangchuk, T. (2000) 'Changes in Land Use in Bhutan: Ecology, History, Culture and Power'. *Journal of Bhutan Studies*, 2(1): 54–85.

Wikan, U. (1996) 'The Nun's Story: Reflections on an Age-old, Post-modern Dilemma'. *American Anthropologist*, 98(2): 279–89.

Chapter 4

The Spatial and Temporal Role of Law in Natural Resource Management: The Impact of State Regulation of Fishing Spaces

Melanie G. Wiber

> Place is any locality that has significance for a person or a group of persons.
>
> (Yi-Fu Tuan 1978)

> Communities and the territories within which they operate represent a very different subject and space than is evident in current fisheries science and management.
>
> (Kevin St. Martin 2001)

Introduction

Administrative law in the arena of natural resource management, taken together with various management regimes, has progressively 'deskilled' the members of communities that directly rely on those natural resources. This happens in two ways. First, regulations rely on a combination of spatial and temporal management that either excludes locals from access to resource stocks or significantly limits times or areas open for access and withdrawal. This has the effect of constraining the creation and maintenance of local knowledge. Second, management regimes increasingly rely on the spatial/temporal expertise emanating from highly technical 'epistemic communities', thereby discounting practice-based knowledge. The end result is that irreplaceable longitudinal knowledge is disappearing along with the resource stocks. Relying on case material from the Canadian Bay of Fundy, this chapter examines how the expanding realm of regulation of the sea has interacted with local knowledge systems. The aim is not to naïvely advocate local users as naturally more in tune with the environment but rather to draw attention to the ways in which space and time concepts within the law are framing knowledge generation and degeneration. Given the destruction of commercial fish stocks in the North Atlantic, we clearly need to develop alternative management regimes. I argue here for a more nuanced analysis of the potential relationship between law, space, time and knowledge as an important first step in developing such regimes. This approach cannot be limited to examining how 'place' is conceptualized locally and how this relates to valuable ecological knowledge based on place-based livelihoods and quotidian practice. It must also ask critical questions about how the local and the global are intertwined in the spatial and temporal work of the law.

The Research Context

In early 2005, the national media arrived in one of the fishing communities working with us in participatory research on resource management,[1] and the community subsequently appeared on the national evening news. But in this coverage, their political struggle to retain some local say in fisheries management was represented as a nostalgic longing for a historic connection with place. While the narrator spoke about how this village was the oldest continuous fishing village in Canada, the camera played on the pink fuzzy slippers of the woman hosting a kitchen meeting to discuss the town economic crises, and on the handmade cardigans of the mayor and his deputy. While the narrator represented the community as a place of *historic* interest (camera panning to small, colourful houses perched above the sea), he also explicitly placed it in a *present day* situation of joblessness and poverty (camera panning to abandoned cars, derelict fishing plants and empty storefronts). The narration managed to suggest that a sense of history, of attachment to community and of pride of place were all very well but that all of these should yield to economic rationality. The total package while appearing sympathetic, recast a political struggle over access to and benefit from public resources, to one of clinging to traditional and outmoded lifestyles and attachments to place.

This media coverage illustrates the difficulty of discussing issues of place without falling under the influence of longstanding and deeply intertwined Western notions of space and time, particularly of the different values that come to bear in ascribing significance to place and of the explicit or implicit links between these and notions of time. Under the influence of globalism, of hype or of actual transformations, the local has become problematic (Agrawal and Gibson 1999; and Tsing 2000) with time and space ratcheted ever more tightly to scalar notions of social difference and distance (Harvey 1989; and Massey 1994). Particularly when local people question values, ideas or legal regimes that 'come from away', place gets conceptualized as the opposite to all things global: static to progressive;

1 This multidisciplinary research focused on multiple sites in the Canadian Maritime provinces with the object of building local research capacity in support of community-based management of the inshore fisheries (see Wiber et al. 2004). I am grateful to the Social Sciences and Humanities Research Council of Canada for providing the Research Development Initiative funding for the research. An early version of this paper was developed with a student intern, Shirley von Sychowski, who worked with one fishery organization in New Brunswick. I also acknowledge the contributions of John Kearney, Tony Charles, Fikret Berkes and members of the fishing organizations involved in the project.

cyclical to linear; insular to cosmopolitan; and particular to universal. The political ramifications of this for local places cannot be overstated.

These polar constructs about space and time enter into political discourse and frustrate local attempts to direct change. Carter et al. (1993, ix) note, for example, that nation states employ universalistic arguments to restrict place-based difference to the private sphere, 'beyond the scope of politics and negotiated consensus'. Thus, Canadian fisher families who lose access to the sea under new management regimes are advised to 'follow the jobs elsewhere' and their loss of livelihood is thereby represented as a matter of individual choice rather than one of public concern. Ong and Collier (2005, 13) note that such 'distinctive forms of calculative rationality associated with the market environment' are one of the favoured 'impersonal principles' that figure in global rhetoric. They are useful in rejecting any 'heterogeneous conception of the public sphere' (Carter et al. 1993, x) that might constrain the deployment of capital in local places. It is such distinctive forms of rationality that Escobar (2001, 142) rejects in trying to privilege place in support of sustainable environment, of social justice and of political legitimacy. Homogenous constructs of the nation, meanwhile, are ironically constructed on a foundation of countryside and of folk, constructs harmonized and made bland in the urban (and globally connected) centres of political and economic control (Pigg 1992, 492; and Wiber 2004, 59–61). While this has led some academics to dichotomize rural and urban spaces (Buttimer 1980; and Wilson 1980), Hirsch (1995, 13) warns against any easy dichotomy between those who 'live' their landscape and others who 'entertain an objectified concept of it'.

For the workshop that formed the basis of this volume, we were asked: 'In which kinds of social processes do we perceive "the existence of law"?' In the research on which this chapter is based, we were interested in both living in a landscape *and* constructing objectified concepts of that landscape; both are social processes that make visible the existence of space and time in the work of the law.[2] Livelihoods are one way of living in a landscape and of objectifying that landscape through their connection with resource dependency. State law, as another means of objectifying place, constrains or enables livelihoods and employs concepts of space and time to justify and depoliticize those objectifications. In marine spaces,

2 In this chapter, I refer primarily to state law and somewhat less so to international legal conventions that affect spatial and temporal access to ocean-based resources. However, in discussing the effects of these larger normative orders on local places, I do not mean to represent local normative orders as a less important source of data in legal studies. Fishermen have in the past and continue in the present day, to think about local access to resources using local notions of fairness, equity and justice. Often these local notions are used to resist those normative orders originating in bureaucratic authority and often they continue to serve as important guides to local behaviour, thus creating a situation often characterized as legal pluralism. For examples of the development of local rules of access, see Acheson (2000; 2003). For the interaction of such local rules with state and international law under conditions of legal pluralism, see Graham and Idechong (1998); and Benda-Beckmann, F. von (2001).

for example, the political struggle over resource control is often played out through boundary marking to better delimit/control areas and their permitted uses. In this chapter, I consider how the state and international law employed in that boundary marking also thereby constrains or enables knowledge about places and about the environmental impacts of that boundary marking.

Consider, for example, the authoritative claims made on the maps produced by the Canadian Department of Fisheries and Oceans (DFO) in support of their regulatory regimes. The marine environment is particularly marked by 'volumetric complexity' (Sutherland 2005), a result of the overlap in use of marine spaces in three dimensions, including: the water surface; water column; submerged lands and subsoil. Nevertheless, formal state maps come in many different types of two-dimensional representations, that fix in place and time a variety of permitted activities and objects, including communication cables; offshore oil installations; toxic dumps; ship wrecks and hazards; traffic lanes; harbours; fishing zones; and many others. These maps, primarily because of their authoritative two-dimensionality, employ very different scalar and temporal frames than those employed by the local users of three-dimensional ocean spaces. The regulatory maps downplay the resulting complexities and smooth over the overlapping claims. A comparison of the two spatial and temporal frameworks demonstrates that an important consequence of the legal struggle to codify marine spaces is that this process is actively and without reflection, *constraining or enabling both livelihoods and knowledge generation*. Both livelihoods and their attendant knowledge generation, then, are social processes in which law is implicated.

In examining place dependent livelihoods and the creation, maintenance and suppression of place-based knowledge, this chapter does not break new ground.[3] But the body of research on situations of legal pluralism and that of critical theory together generate new questions about the consequences of transforming local livelihoods, by asking both how international and state law supercedes local rights of access, and about the environmental consequences of that. When state or supra-state organizations implement management regimes that are solely focused on economic values of efficiency and maximum utility for capital accumulation, both the environment and local people who rely on it are irrevocably harmed.[4] And one

3 These issues have been well explored in research into traditional ecological knowledge (TEK), or the conflict between aboriginal peoples and state administrators in resource management (see Berkes 1999).

4 A recent assessment of regional fisheries management organizations (RFMOs) reported that these international actors have failed in several ways, including: 'to prevent over-exploitation of straddling and highly migratory fish stocks, to rebuild overexploited stocks and to prevent degradation of the marine ecosystems in which fishing occurs. Not only have broader, international expectations not been met but RFMOs have also largely failed to meet the objectives of their own governing conventions, generally characterized as conservation and sustainable utilization of target stocks under their mandate' (Willock and Lack 2006, iii). For a critique of globalization in fisheries management, see Cole (2002).

of the most vulnerable arenas of social action under such conditions is the local knowledge system.

Brulle (2000, 75), following Habermas, argues that a vital part of any process of environmental degradation is 'the systematic blocking of communicative action'. He sees one remedy as the individual acquisition of key technical knowledge so that individuals (as ecological citizens) can participate 'meaningfully in discussions of collectively binding actions' (ibid., 63). Agrawal (2005), on the other hand, argues that this is to proceed 'as if subjects emerged and existed independent of a historical, political, and social ground'. Is only technical knowledge relevant in building ecological citizens and does only a single unitary civil society exist in which to debate potential (re)actions? The legal pluralism literature illustrates that the role of multiple and poorly collated levels of law are increasingly a feature of globalization, transforming places, concepts of time and schemes for natural resource management (Wiber 2005). Further, the contributions of a socio-legal focus can be enriched in borrowing from embodiment theory, governmentality of space and critical geography on place in order to pay 'close attention to practice' (Agrawal 2005). Taken in this framework, the question of place-based knowledge becomes very complex.

Polarizing Concepts: Global and Local

Globalization, both in anthropology and in law, has been a buzz word for a focused attention on large-scale transfers of capital, relocation of jobs and workplaces across international boundaries; mobility of labour; affects on national sovereignty; emergence of international business law regimes; and on the various 'scapes' created by such developments.[5] Escobar (2001, 141) argues that while this research has alerted us to the many people who are 'placeless', that is less geographically-bounded in their notions of culture and self-identity, the central importance of place to many *other* people has been demoted in social theory, leaving people and ideas about their identity construction strangely disconnected from landscape and from geographical place.[6] Any expression of an emotional and physical (livelihood) dependency on a particular geographic space becomes, at least in social theory, relegated to a nostalgic longing for the past, or at best, the political maneuvering required by contested identity constructs. This is an unfortunate and unintended effect of questioning the theoretical invisibility of place, an invisibility that may have been overstated from the outset.

Gupta and Ferguson (1992), for example, argue that globalization theory addressed an imbalance in classical anthropology where culture was viewed

5 See Appandurai (1990; 1991); and Schuerkens (2003). For an edited volume bringing many of the arguments together in one place, see Held and McGrew (2002).

6 A critique also voiced by Creed and Ching (1997); Lovell (1998); and and Hyatt (2001).

as hyper-localized and place as relatively static. It was assumed that under the classical approach, place occupied a central organizing principle but at the same time disappeared from analytical view. But in fact, place has been critically conceptualized by many disciplines over the past century, including sociology, anthropology[7] and critical geography. Durkheim introduced the notion of social space in the 1890s (cited in Wilson 1980, 135); sociologists took that in a subjective direction (subjective meanings of space) while geographers largely took it in the objective or concrete direction (land use, habitat, geopolitical landscapes). In anthropology more recently, common perceptions of place have been linked to identity construction and common actions in space linked to 'body-ballet' (Seamon 1980) and later to embodiment studies (Shilling 2001). Meanwhile, Foucault's interest in governmentality led to interesting new directions in the theorizing of spatial governmentality (Rose 1996; see also Merry 2001). Perhaps, as Gupta and Ferguson (1992) argue, the assumed isomorphism between place and culture resulted in a failure to see or adequately deal with 'the topography of power', or to understand how distinctive identities resulted from the 'intersection of specific involvement in the hierarchically organized spaces' within that topography (ibid., 8), but even here they may have overstated their case. Historically contingent political struggles in the cultural construction of place have concerned a number of disciplines, many of which addressed the relationship between power and landscape.[8] While the focus on globalization was designed to address the topography of power, Escobar has tackled the same problem through *place*-based critical theory. This convergence of approaches only serves to illustrate the extent to which place and global are intertwined.

My argument here is that an unfortunate side effect of emphasizing the cultural construction of place has been to make all places seem less authentic; as multiple conflicting constructions attach to any one place, none has any apparent superiority over another. Further, with the attention focused on political struggles to invent salient constructs of place, the impact of alternative constructions on ecological sustainability (or on livelihoods) or on social justice has received less critical attention. While many social geographers and political theorists would be surprised by this critique given that they pursue a better understanding of power in the construction of place, the combined influence of their work has been to make place more 'constructed' than lived in. This has the perverse effect of *depoliticizing* the construction of place.

Much spatial analysis follows Pred (1984), but neglects a dimension to which he paid particular attention. Relying on structuration theory, Pred argued for a 'time-space specific' focus, one that incorporated the 'interplay between long-term commitment and everyday practice' (ibid., 286).[9] He advocated paying attention

7 See the reader edited by Low and Lawrence-Zuniga (2003).

8 See Hirsch and O'Hanlon (1995); Swyngedouw (1997); Stokowski (2002); Williams (2002); Heasley (2003); and Robbins (2003).

9 See also Benda-Beckmann, F. von (2001).

to the 'formation of individual biographies', arguing that 'the life path-daily path dialectic is central to the local and wider reproduction of group, class, and gender differences' (ibid.). In doing so, Pred remained concretely focused on the human interaction with the environment and the processes by which the two were mutually constructed over time. Interestingly, Pred saw regulation as a vital component of this process and particularly focused on the resulting control not only over what people do, but what they subsequently know and what they are able to perceive, think, say and pass on as knowledge about a place.

Tsing (2000) has commented on this connection between space and time in recent globalism discourse. In this discourse, the past is viewed as associated with geographically-tied people operating under local law developed through practice-based learning that focuses on maintaining the past. On the other hand, the state is associated with a wider geography administered under rational scientific policy focused on growth and the future. Transcending the state can either be positively valued as an exciting new global landscape of the future (Gupta 1992; and Appandurai 2003) or negatively assessed as the end of sovereignty (Strange 2003). International legal policy, while remaining largely state-centric in its focus, seems increasingly polarized between reinforcing local power through decentralization and enhancing global governance through international institutions.[10] Between international levels of organization and community-based management, there seems little common ground. But these constructs, as Tsing notes, tend to polarize the debate, unnecessarily dividing the local from the global as if these were two separate spaces.

Following Tsing (2005), I argue that when we break out of simple dichotomizations, we are better able to understand how place is a space within global processes, a place that reflects all of the larger processes and influences but which also has influence itself. I also argue that this approach best explores temporal and spatial aspects of law. Law is one of the most important and under-theorized components of the construction of place and in the relation of place to larger spaces; thus, attention to legal pluralism can better tease out the many dimensions that go into cultural understandings of processes that affect us all.

The Bay of Fundy: Livelihoods and Knowledge

Under the influence of burgeoning international law and national management regimes, the ocean is increasingly conceptualized as a constructed landscape of intersecting rights and responsibilities. But how has this development of a globalizing marine regulation interacted with longstanding human livelihoods that

10 Haas (2004, 7), for example, argues for 'decentralized, information-rich systems' for dealing with 'managing complex problems like global environmental issues'. Meanwhile, those same problems are approached through empowering localities in Kerans and Kearney (2006).

have been deeply intertwined with the sea? Given the wide experience with land-based 'eco-government' (see Goldman 2001), the answer will surprise few of us. Local fishermen have found themselves labelled with 'potent cultural markers' of marginalized class, lifestyle and status, and as having little to contribute to the development of economically or environmentally appropriate management regimes (Walley 2002).

Recent research, however, demonstrates the practical utility of local fisher's knowledge in understanding resource stocks, their relationship with local environments and the transformations of both over time (see Neis and Felt 2000). This is especially true of the small boat fisheries. In those coastal regions highly dependent on the fisheries, most shallow, inshore waters have a history of small boat fisheries whereby production practices have brought fishers, an ocean territory and various marine species into regular, close contact. In these inshore fishing technologies, the fishermen handle the fish that they land, giving them the opportunity to assess weight, general health, breeding status and reproductive cycles. As inshore fishermen typically rely on a large number of species for their annual cycle of catches, their boats are out on the waters at all times of the year, routinely travelling the same ocean territory and accessing information on a number of different stocks. In addition, fishermen make first-hand observation of tides, currents, wind, water temperature, seasonal weather systems and the impact of human uses of the ocean environment. Such livelihoods have over time created 'systems' of local knowledge that represent a resource widely shared among community members,[11] a knowledge system that is able to place fish in particular ocean spaces, to ask questions about changes in those patterns of distribution and to link these in turn to other ecological or environmental changes. These knowledge systems have not only allowed fishermen to successfully catch fish, but they have also allowed fishermen to regulate their approach to marine spaces over time.[12]

These conditions of production have pertained for many generations in the Scotia-Fundy region of the Canadian Maritimes (Davis and Wagner 2003, 480). The names humans have given to marine spaces in that region are one indication of the knowledge system at work.[13] Such names reflect fisher knowledge of the underwater topography, ocean currents, and marine ecology – knowledge that has only been enhanced by their enforced participation in gathering data for

11 See Poizat and Baran (1997); Neis et al. (1999a; 1999b); Pálsson (2000); Olsson and Folke (2001); and Davis and Wagner (2003).

12 See Acheson (1988); Dyer and McGoodwin (1994); Neis and Felt (2000); and Gezelius (2002).

13 According to a recent study of local knowledge about fish spawning grounds in the Bay of Fundy (Graham et al. 2002), haddock prefer to spawn on The Gravelly or on the Pollock Humps, areas of ocean bottom known to contain the hard, smooth rock, or sand and gravelly bottom that are good foraging ground. Cod are not so discriminating, spawning in The Shipping Lane (at the mouth of the Bay) and on The Rip where currents are fierce.

government marine science.[14] But more importantly, the local knowledge system charts the broad ecological changes that have happened in the Scotia-Fundy region over the last 50 years with the introduction of new technologies and changing patterns of use of the Bay (see Wiber and Kearney 2004).

But in the Bay of Fundy, knowledge has not led to power. Local mapping projects have been developed rather naïvely as one means to document and make available to the federal regulators, knowledge that might improve resource management policy for the Bay. These efforts have been largely unsuccessful in getting the Canadian federal regulators to rethink how they protect spawning habitats or rebuild commercial stocks. One reason for this, as I will explain further below, is another knowledge system that runs counter to local knowledge. Since the Second World War, longitudinal and place-based fisher knowledge has being devalued in favour of federal bureaucratic and university-based marine research, and in favour of urban-centred values and economic interests, including: oil and gas installations; tourism; whale watching; aquaculture and the industrial; and offshore fishing fleets. Resource management policy has leaned on scientific expertise, and in the process has transformed the rules of access to and use of the Bay of Fundy. This has gone hand in hand with significant transformation of the ocean bottom, change in flora and fauna, and decline of major commercial fish stocks. Law has played a significant role in transforming the way local people use local resources, in allowing new users to proliferate, and in repressing or in destroying alternative knowledge about the impact of all of the above. A few recent examples will illustrate the clash of rules about spatial use before I turn to how the situation in the Bay of Fundy links to legal pluralism and to space and time concepts within the law.

Contested Places, Contested Values

Like other places around the world, the Bay of Fundy has become a site for numerous contests over sustainable use and appropriate development as each new economic opportunity brings new players into conflict with established users (Wiber 2004). In recent years, these clashes have escalated, as the economy of the region has been directed away from resource extraction and towards industrialization. The fishers' organizations that our participatory project has worked with have had to confront so many new threats to their traditional fishing grounds that the available resources to deal with them have been overwhelmed. These threats include: two proposals for new liquid natural gas (LNG) terminals and harbour facilities on the New Brunswick and Maine coasts that would close down adjacent fishing grounds

14 Inshore fishermen must participate in the Department of Fisheries and Oceans stock assessment surveys as a condition of their license. They contribute time and personal resources to bureaucratic/scientific technical data gathering, but are allowed no part in assessing what that data means.

to make room for shipping lanes; loss of fisher wharf privileges in Saint John under new anti-terrorism regulations; harbour dredging practices that dump toxic sludge into areas of lobster habitat; numerous new aquaculture sites, including a proposal for a massive and experimental new site in the centre of the Bay on an area of scallop beds; a proposal for a large gravel quarry requiring expanded shipping lanes on the Nova Scotia side of the Bay; and the imminent collapse of the remaining fish stocks under pressure from mid-shore dragger fleets that push into areas supposedly off limits to that technology. While a number of these developments, such as the LNG terminals, are themselves on land, they all involve increasing shipping or infrastructure that contribute to 'volumetric complexity' (Sutherland 2005) in that they affect in varying degrees the water surface, the water column and/or the sea floor. They therefore displace fishers.

Most of these projects have been developed without meaningful consultation with local fishers, and the fishing industry, vital as it is to local economies, often finds that an effective voice in governance of local resources is difficult to obtain. Fishing industry requirements are often not well understood in the wider society, but when fishers complain about the impact of such developments, many people assume they can simply fish elsewhere (Recchia 2005, 2). But fishers cannot relocate to new grounds for several reasons, including: their licenses restrict them to particular marine areas; their knowledge-base is place sensitive, and all inshore fishing grounds are subject to the same pressures. Even DFO bureaucrats, who better understand these relocation constraints, dismiss fishers' concerns about the impact of such projects on the grounds that they are mere ploys to protect fishers' selfish interests. Government bureaucrats, on the other hand, excuse new economic actors who act in a self-interested way, on the grounds that they will contribute to economic growth. For example, when the DFO chaired a meeting to discuss compensation between the Saint John LNG site developers and local fishers, they began the meeting by informing all parties that the DFO had *a legal opinion* that in marine space, navigation takes priority over fishing,[15] so that there is no need for compensation for temporary or permanent exclusion as a result of development of the terminal. Not surprisingly, the site developers were subsequently reluctant to negotiate compensation, although they continued to meet with fishers to discuss limiting the size of the exclusion zone. Meanwhile, in negotiation with the city and the province, these same developers threatened to withdraw their proposal if regulatory requirements were not 'fast tracked' and tax concessions immediately forthcoming. The city councilors of Saint John, concerned with an economic downturn in that port and under threat of losing economic opportunities to neighbouring Maine where another LNG proposal was in process, met in closed session to grant these concessions. The resulting public outcry over 'tax

15 However, they were not willing to share this legal opinion with the fisher's organization.

concessions for the rich' generated media interest in the LNG proposal whereas the fishing industry environmental concerns had been unable to do so.[16]

Often research that substantiates fisher concerns is unable to stem the tide of industrial development. This has been of particular concern lately for lobstermen. Lobster viability is vital for most inshore fishers as lobster is the last remaining species that is both commercially valuable and in relative abundance. It has become the backbone of the inshore fishing household economy. Fishers all down the adjacent Canadian and American coast take lobsters originating in the Bay of Fundy. Saint John harbour dredge spoil and materials – sometimes toxic – are transported further down the coast and dumped at sea. A fisher-supported study was able to demonstrate how resulting particulate matter in the water column affected juvenile lobster, while adult lobster mortality occurred on the ocean floor at the dredge dumpsite. But so far, dumping regulations remain unchanged. Lobstermen also report problems with lobster taken adjacent to aquaculture sites, perhaps as a result of exposure to chemicals used regularly in the aquaculture feed or preventative medications. But aquaculture operators argue that their use of chemicals meets or exceeds provincial regulation and reject any potential link between aquaculture feed and lobster shell deformity.

Mid-shore draggers, who form a different sector of the fishery than the inshore sector, also affect other users of the ocean space in multiple ways, both as surface traffic, in the water column as their large gear is pulled behind their boat and on the bottom as their gear drags along the ocean floor. They are said to be pushing the boundaries of appropriate places for their technology. Some have been reported dragging close to shore and even into the mouths of rivers. Inshore fishermen view the dragger technology as very damaging to fish spawning habitat and fish refuge sites,[17] but the federal regulator seems concerned only to repress conflict between the two sectors using spatial regulation. Longstanding areas where lobster traps could be safely set on the bottom are now regularly used by dragger gear which catches up and destroys lobster traps, and under the influence of DFO adjudication processes, dragger fleet zones are said to be expanding at the expense of both lobster fishing and other fishing technology such as long liners and gillnets.

A more recent conflict in the Bay of Fundy involves the water column as well as the ocean bottom. This was triggered by the proposed introduction of fish traps, which unlike net technology, would sit on the bottom with a line and buoy riding

16 See the coverage by the Canadian Broadcasting Corporation at http://www.cbc.ca/nb/story /print/nb-lndmlas20050506.

17 Ecological groups, such as the Halifax-based Ecology Action Center, agree. There is mounting evidence around the world that such dragger or trawler technology is extremely damaging to ocean floor habitats (see the 19 May 2006 BBC report at http://news.bbc.co.uk/1/hi/sci/tech/4996268.stm). I discuss an unsuccessful lawsuit against the DFO for allowing draggers to operate on Georges Bank in what follows. For a discussion of the ecological and social impact of the dragger fleet in the Digby Neck area of the Bay of Fundy, see Wiber and Kearney (2004).

up through the water column. The advantage of the traps is that they would allow by-catch, or fish species that are not sought by fishermen, as well as undersized or spawning fish to be returned to the water unharmed.[18] The DFO has so far rejected the introduction of such technology in the Bay, or even to allow trap testing in the Bay waters, arguing that it would multiply the gear hanging in the water column and increase conflict with draggers. In these space use conflicts, the small boat, inshore sector is noticeably losing ground to other technologies, in effect, losing access to ocean spaces.

Contested Knowledge, Contested Rules

Such conflicts over spaces in the Bay of Fundy involve many players (environmental groups, inshore fishermen associations and industrial proponents) and bring poorly organized and funded inshore fishers groups up against better organized environmental lobbyists, as well as provincial and federal bureaucracies and large industrial interests. While all of these more powerful players argue that they recognize other legitimate users of the oceans, they largely reject arguments that such pre-existing claimants have any detailed knowledge of local marine environments. Only technical experts are thought to hold valuable knowledge, and they are consulted during environmental assessments mandated under the law. The knowledge on which such assessments are made, while privileged under the law, is often quite different than local, practice-based knowledge – as different as are the rules for use that each side endorses given their unique knowledge perspectives (see Pálsson 1995).

Most people who are acknowledged experts on the marine environment or on resource stock characteristics do not recognize the local knowledge systems of inshore fishers – a phenomenon that has been called 'The Two Cultures Theory of Fisheries Knowledge' (Wilson 2003). Marine biologists employed by the federal regulator, for example, view the knowledge of fishers as lacking scientific validity or reliability, largely because of fisher economic dependency on marine resources (Finlayson 1994). Biologists do not trust that fishers will constrain their incomes in order to protect and sustain commercial fish stocks. Arguments about the untrustworthy nature of fishers go further. Many biologists, who work closely with fishers on routine stock assessment, argue that fishers spoil the data whenever possible, making scientific stock management impossible.[19] Fish

18 By-catch can be a significant problem and where federal regulators have set a very low catch level for a particular species, can shut down a fishery as most groundfish gear is not discriminating enough to select for one or two species.

19 See the summary of the session on Fisheries Management from the retrospective of the 2003 Ocean Management Research Network National Conference (at www.omrn.ca). All of the presenters disparaged fishers' contribution to knowledge and the session summary published online states: 'Independent of the management regime in place, fish

harvesters thus serve as a handy scapegoat when scientific data collection fails to yield better management outcomes.

Many fishers will agree that they resent the time and effort put into survey data required as a condition of license and that some will 'make up' the data just to fulfill their legal obligations. But many fishers also drag their feet on scientific data collection because they reject the validity of the technical, scientific methods that they are forced to follow. They question scientific theoretical assumptions as in stock models that assume stability over time and scientific methods, such as the random sampling procedures that demand samples from areas where experience indicates particular species will not be found.[20] The means of reconciling divergent local and technical knowledge are also under dispute. Davis and Wagner, for example, studied fisher knowledge systems on the Northumberland Strait and argued that while local knowledge is different in kind and quality from scientific knowledge, the two could reinforce and complement each other through a process of *scientific validation of local knowledge* (2003, 476). Many fishers reject such an approach as giving too much power to science, and some worry that any collaborative effort would simply hand government more power to restrict fishing effort (Wiber and Lovell 2003, 93).

Law and the Construction of Knowledge Systems

While there are considerable equity, social justice, epistemological and science aspects of the problem, my concern in this chapter is with the long-term effects of changing resource use patterns on local knowledge about, and related conceptualizations of, ocean spaces. As the above examples illustrate, competing perspectives on the utility of place are clearly evident in ocean management where overlapping boundaries, debates about wise use and a lack of agreement about how environmental resources can be sustained create several legal challenges. How spatial scales are variously used to frame environmental knowledge and to mobilize particular social practices has been largely ignored to date, so that discourses of law shape 'place' even as they often misread and mismanage the landscape. Brulle (2000, 38) notes that the 'juridification' of the 'lifeworld' is part of the process that shuts down the ability of civil society to 'generate meaning'. But Agrawal (2005, 180) notes that in recent community forest management in India, 'intimate government' has encouraged local assessment of environmental practices and their consequences – and this in turn has generated shared meanings

harvesters will continue to misreport, creating data fouling that confounds reliable stock assessment.'

20 Wilson (1990) provides an example of a scientific approach that fishermen find seriously flawed. Wilson notes that in fisheries economics, fish are largely 'assumed to be either randomly or evenly distributed in the ocean' – an assumption that is 'mathematically convenient' but far from empirical reality.

that encourage the development of 'environmental subjects'. These observations suggest the many ways that law, as a contested field itself, can both constrain and enable knowledge generation.

A final example can illustrate how the law has deflected sustainability assessment in the Canadian fisheries. The Ecology Action Center in Halifax recently launched a court case to have the federal regulation of dragger fishing off the southwest coast of Nova Scotia evaluated for its environmental impact, making the argument that federal law required justification of any technology that damages fish habitat. They hoped for a landmark decision that would expose the illogic of making one government department responsible for both promoting the fishing industry and protecting fish stocks and habitat. To obtain this outcome, they needed to make a direct link between the DFO opening a particular place to draggers and the subsequent environmental damage to spawning grounds for a particular stock. However, while it is clear that draggers do a lot of damage, the court rejected the argument that the DFO minister should be held accountable for failing to uphold federal regulation.[21] Instead, the judge accepted the DFO argument that the department *acted within its powers* when it permitted dragging to occur on Georges Bank. She also ruled that the DFO could not be held responsible if fishers subsequently fished in a way that damaged the environment, saying that no direct link had been established between an order allowing the opening of Georges Bank to dragger fishing and any subsequent damage to fish habitat. Finally, she made no ruling on the question that the Ecology Action Center specifically wanted addressed: is the federal regulator facilitating the destruction of fish habitat in contravention of the Fisheries Act by allowing draggers to operate *in that place*?

The point I want to emphasize here is that any space in which dragging is allowed is by nature unworkable for many other types of fishing gear of which draggers 'run foul'. Conflicts between draggers and other gear sectors usually result in areas being restricted to gear sector, so that the non-draggers become excluded from ever increasing areas of the fishing grounds. This in turn limits the knowledge generated about those areas by other types of fishermen. In other words, by agreeing to exclusive dragging grounds (see McMullan et al. 1993), the new regulatory regimes de facto eliminate the possibility of gathering knowledge on a daily basis about the damage draggers (and thus the regulations) do. The local rules for fishing activities derive directly from local knowledge of marine resources, which is one reason why dragger technology has always been contentious within fishing communities. The challenge is to document how these local normative orders are negotiated, how areas are thereby closed or open to access, how local knowledge is refused recognition or undercut, and to situate all of this in relation to the political economies that make them possible. As Goldman (2001) has argued, global regulatory regimes that theoretically focus on the environment in fact actually target resource-based populations in order to

21 See decision of 19 August 2004 (at http://decisions.fct-cf.gc.ca/fct/2004/2004fc1087.shtml).

compel them to participate in the new neoliberal process of capitalist expansion. The science of judging what is needed in resource management, then, is critical to interventions and investments – much too critical to be challenged by local knowledge that may contradict such processes.

The law becomes very visible in supporting neoliberal interventions in particular places. It would be naïve to assume that members of a community automatically share a value system that drives the wise use of resources (see Bradshaw 2003). Yet when widespread agreement does exist within resource dependent communities, it can be easily undermined using state law. For example, the government creates the legal category of 'stakeholder' and then decides who qualifies as stakeholder for any particular regulated place. The very act of delineating and identifying a set of stakeholders in contrast to the larger community inherently includes and empowers some while excluding others. Further, the state often 'consults' with privileged stakeholders as if they were all equally knowledgeable about the relevant space, as well as equally endowed with social and political resources to enter into contests about that space. This bypasses the thorny issues of whose standards and values should apply in determining wise uses of space. Since the definition of a place and the uses to which that place can and should be put can be so contested, we need to recognize the ways in which multiple layers of law differently define and constrain uses of legal space, with unanticipated consequences for understanding place. As space is regulated differently, quotidian practices that shape and define place change, and this changes too the generation of knowledge over time – displacing some knowledge in favour of other knowledge – with some severe ecological consequences.

Concluding Thoughts on Place and Sustainability

Rights-based policies in fisheries management, as with quota rights in fish stocks, have been deployed around the world to displace fishermen who are no longer recognized as having legitimate claims – thus governments have responded to the claim that 'too many fishermen are chasing too few fish'. Fishermen have responded with attention to 'history' – keeping careful logs and fish landing records in order to demonstrate their reliance on fish stocks in particular places and to claim rights in those stocks for themselves. The result has often only accelerated the decline in fish stocks. In the past, for example, if fishing in one place or for one type of stock was unprofitable for some reason, fishers had the flexibility to move to alternative grounds or species in order to reduce the pressure on stocks suffering a decline. Now, with specific licenses and quota tied closely to a single area and to a single species, fishing in multiple places or for multiple species is discouraged, if for no other reason than that fishing rights now cost money to acquire. Only the capital and technology-rich corporate sector is likely to acquire and hold onto fishing rights. But they in turn need high catch rates as a return on their higher investments. Thus, a rights-based approach to management, some fishers argue, leads to over-exploitation and inflexibility. More importantly, the resulting loss of exposure to fishing (particularly in the more 'hands on' fishing sectors) has had a direct effect in valuable fishing knowledge that in turn might have helped to evaluate the ecological impacts.

It is alarming how frequently state and international law dodges the issue of wise stewardship when the impact of particular regulation is being examined. There are many layers of law applied to marine spaces, most of them rationalizing away place-based understanding of the ecosystem in favour of economic efficiency, and most of them taking a rather static approach to time and environmental change. Under these conditions, creating the legal space for local rules to operate and for quotidian practice to perpetuate environment knowledge *over time* becomes very difficult. Young men in eastern Canada no longer go out on the water with their fathers to fish, and the practice-based knowledge of fish stocks, of fish environments and of environmental change is being lost. It will be difficult to recover such local knowledge if future regulation is to have better long-term consequences for the environment. This is one unavoidable consequence of the operation of law in this place and at this time. In a very real sense, 'Local Knowledge has come knocking on Science's door', but Law has already emptied the till inside.

References

Acheson, J. (1988) *The Lobster Gangs of Maine*. Hanover, NH: University Press of New England.

Acheson, J. (2000) 'Distribution Fights, Coordination Games, and Lobster Management'. *Comparative Studies of Society and History*, 42(1): 209–38.

Acheson, J. (2003) *Capturing the Commons: Devising Institutions to Manage the Maine Lobster Industry*. Hanover, NH: University Press of New England.

Agrawal, A. (2005) 'Environmentality. Community, Intimate Government, and the Making of Environmental Subjects in Kumaon, India'. *Current Anthropology*, 46(2) April 2005: 161–90.

Agrawal, A. and Gibson, C.C. (1999) 'Enchantment and Disenchantment: The Role of Community in Natural Resource Management'. *World Development*, 27(4): 629–46.

Appandurai, A. (1990) 'Disjuncture and Difference in the Global Cultural Economy'. *Theory, Culture and Society* 7, pp. 295–310. Special issue edited by M. Featherstone on *Global Culture, Nationalism, Globalization and Modernity*. London: Sage Publications.

Appandurai, A. (1991) 'Global Ethnoscapes. Notes and Queries for a Transnational Anthropology' in R.G. Fox (ed.) *Recapturing Anthropology. Working in the Present*. Santa Fe: School of American Research, pp. 191–238.

Appandurai, A. (2003) 'Sovereignty without Territoriality: Notes for a Post-national Geography' in S.M. Low and D. Lawrence-Zuniga (eds) *The Anthropology of Space and Place. Locating Culture*. Oxford, UK: Blackwell, pp. 337–49.

Benda-Beckmann, F. von (2001) 'On the Reproduction of Law: Micro and Macro in the Time-space Geography of Law' in W. Fikentscher (ed.) *Begegnung und Konflikt – eine kulturanthropologische Bestandsaufnahme*. München: Verlag der Bayerischen Akademie der Wissenschaften, pp. 119–31.
Berkes, F. (1999) *Sacred Ecology. Traditional Ecological Knowledge and Resource Management*. Philadelphia: Taylor and Francis.
Bradshaw, B. (2003) 'Questioning the Credibility and Capacity of Community-based Resource Management'. *The Canadian Geographer*, 47(2): 137–50.
Brulle, R.J. (2000) *Agency, Democracy, and Nature. The U.S. Environmental Movement from a Critical Theory Perspective*. Cambridge: MIT Press.
Buttimer, A. (1980) 'Home, Reach, and the Sense of Place' in A. Buttimer and D. Seamon (eds) *The Human Experience of Space and Place*. New York: St. Martin's Press, pp. 166–87.
Carter, E., Donald, J. and Squires, J. (1993) 'Introduction' in E. Carter, J. Donald and J. Squires (eds) *Space and Place: The Theories of Identity and Location*. London: Lawrence and Wiskart Publishers, pp. vii–xv.
Cole, H. (2002) 'Contemporary Challenges: Globalisation, Global Interconnectedness and that "there are not Plenty more Fish in the Sea". Fisheries, Governance and Globalisation: is there a Relationship?' *Ocean and Coastal Management*, 46: 77–102.
Creed, G.W. and Ching, B. (1997) 'Recognizing Rusticity. Identity and the Power of Place' in B. Ching and G. Creed (eds) *Knowing your Place. Rural Identity and Cultural Hierarchy*. New York and London: Routledge, pp. 1–38.
Davis, A. and Wagner, J.R. (2003) 'Who Knows? On the Importance of Identifying "Experts" when Researching Local Ecological Knowledge'. *Human Ecology*, 31(3): 463–89.
Dyer, C.L. and McGoodwin, J.R. (eds) (1994) *Folk Management of the World's Fisheries*. Boulder: University of Colorado Press.
Escobar, A. (2001) 'Culture Sits in Places: Reflections on Globalism and Subaltern Strategies of Localization'. *Political Geography*, 20: 139–74.
Finlayson, A.C. (1994) *Fishing for Truth*. Institute of Social and Economic Research, Memorial University of Newfoundland, St. Johns. Social and Economic Studies no. 52.
Gezelius, S. (2002) 'Do Norms Count? State Regulation and Compliance in a Norwegian Fishing Community'. *Acta Sociologica*, 45: 305–14.
Goldman, M. (2001) 'Constructing an Environmental State: Eco-governmentality and other Transnational Practices of a "Green" World Bank'. *Social Problems*, 48(4): 499–523.
Graham, J., Engle, S. and Recchia, M. (2002) *Local Knowledge and Local Stocks. an Atlas of Groundfish Spawning in the Bay of Fundy*. Antigonish, Nova Scotia: The Center for Community-based Management.
Graham, T. and Idechong, N. (1998) 'Reconciling Customary and Constitutional Law: Managing Marine Resources in Palau, Micronesia'. *Ocean and Coastal Management*, 40:143–64.

Gupta, A. (1992) 'The Song of the Nonaligned World: Transnational Identities and the Reinscription of Space in Late Capitalism'. *Cultural Anthropology*, 7(1): 63–79.

Gupta, A. and Ferguson, J. (1992) 'Beyond "Culture": Space, Identity, and the Politics of Difference'. *Cultural Anthropology*, 7(1): 6–23.

Haas, P.M. (2004) 'Addressing the Global Governance Deficit'. *Global Environmental Politics*, 4(4): 1–15.

Harvey, D. (1989) *The Condition of Post-modernity*. Oxford: Basil Blackwell.

Heasley, L. (2003) 'Shifting Boundaries on a Wisconsin Landscape: Can GIS Help Historians Tell a Complicated Story?' *Human Ecology*, 31(2): 183–213.

Held, D. and McGrew, A.G. (2002) *The Global Transformations Reader: An Introduction to the Globalization Debate*. Cambridge: Polity Press.

Hirsch, E. (1995) 'Landscape: Between Place and Space' in E. Hirsch and M. O'Hanlon (eds) *The Anthropology of Landscape. Perspectives on Place and Space*. Oxford: Oxford University Press, pp 1–30.

Hirsch, E. and O'Hanlon, M. (eds) (1995) *The Anthropology of Landscape: Perspectives on Place and Space*. Oxford: Clarendon Press.

Hyatt, S.B. (2001) 'Review Essay: "Writing against Globalization"'. *Anthropological Quarterly*, 75(1): 205–12.

Kerans, P. and Kearney, J. (2006) *Turning the World Right-side up. Science, Community and Democracy*. Halifax: Fernwood Publishing.

Lovell, N. (1998) 'Introduction' in N. Lovell (ed.) *Locality and Belonging*. London and New York: Routledge, pp. 1–24.

Low, S.M. and Lawrence-Zuniga, D. (2003) *The Anthropology of Space and Place. Locating Culture*. Oxford, UK: Blackwell.

Massey, D. (1994) *Space, Place and Gender*. Minneapolis: University of Minnesota Press.

McMullan, J.L., Perrier, D. and Okihiro, N. (1993) 'Regulation, Illegality and Social Conflict in the Nova Scotia Lobster Fishery'. *Journal of Legal Pluralism*, 33: 121–46.

Merry, S.E. (2001) 'Spatial Governmentality and the New Urban Social Order: Controlling Gender Violence through Law'. *American Anthropologist*, 103(1): 16–29.

Neis, B. and Felt, L. (eds) (2000) *Finding our Sea Legs: Linking Fishery People and their Knowledge with Science and Management*. St. John's, Newfoundland: ISER Books.

Neis, B., Felt, L., Haedrich, R. and Schneider, D. (1999a) 'An Interdisciplinary Method for Collecting and Integrating Fishers' Ecological Knowledge into Resource Management' in D. Newell and R.E. Ommer (eds) *Fishing Places, Fishing People: Traditions and Issues in Canadian Small-scale Fisheries*. Toronto: University of Toronto Press, pp. 217–38.

Neis, B., Schneider, D., Felt, L., Haedrick, R., Fischer, J. and Hutchings, J. (1999b) 'Fisheries Assessment: What Can be Learned from Interviewing Resource Users?' *Journal of Fisheries and Aquatic Science*, 56: 1949–63.

Olsson, P. and Folke, C. (2001) 'Local Ecological Knowledge and Institutional Dynamics for Ecosystem Management: A Study of Lake Racken Watershed, Sweden'. *Ecosystems*, 4: 85–104.

Ong, A. and Collier, S.J. (2005) 'Global Assemblages, Anthropological Problems' in A. Ong and S. Collier (eds) *Global Assemblages*. Malden, MA and Oxford, UK: Blackwell, pp. 3–21.

Pálsson, G. (1995) 'Learning by Fishing: Practical Science and Science Practice' in S. Hanna and M. Munasinghe (eds) *Property Rights in a Social and Ecological Context: Case Studies and Design Applications*. Stockholm: Beijer Institute, pp. 58–97.

Pálsson, G. (2000) '"Finding one's Sea Legs": Learning, the Process of Enskilment, and Integrating Fishers and their Knowledge into Fisheries Science and Management' in B. Neis and L. Felt (eds) *Finding our Sea Legs*. St. John's, Newfoundland: ISER Books, pp. 24–38.

Pigg, S.L. (1992) 'Inventing Social Categories through Place: Social Representations and Development in Nepal'. *Comparative Studies in Society and History*, 34(3): 491–513.

Poizat, G. and Baran, E. (1997) 'Fishermen's Knowledge as Background Information in Tropical Fish Ecology: A Quantitative Comparison with Fish Sampling Results'. *Environmental Biology of Fishes*, 50: 435–49.

Pred, A. (1984) 'Place as Historically Contingent Process: Structuration and the Time-geography of Becoming Places'. *Annals of the Association of American Geographers*, 74(2): 279–97.

Recchia, M. (2005) 'LNG Terminal: Irving Oil Refuses to Compensate Mispec Fishermen'. *Fundy North Fishermen's Association Newsletter*, October.

Robbins, P. (2003) 'Beyond Ground Truth: GIS and the Environmental Knowledge of Herders, Professional Foresters, and other Traditional Communities'. *Human Ecology*, 31(2): 233–53.

Rose, N. (1996) 'The Death of the Social? Refiguring the Territory of Government'. *Economy and Society*, 25(3): 327–56.

Schuerkens, U. (2003) 'The Sociological and Anthropological Study of Globalization and Localization'. *Current Sociology*, 51(3/4): 209–22.

Seamon, D. (1980) 'Body-subject, Time-space Routines, and Place-ballets' in A. Buttimer and D. Seamon (eds) *The Human Experience of Space and Place*. New York: St. Martin's Press, pp. 148–65.

Shilling, C. (2001)'Embodiment, Experience and Theory. In Defense of the Sociological Tradition'. *The Sociological Review*, 49(3): 327–44.

St. Martin, K. (2001) 'Making Space for Community Resource Management in Fisheries'. *Annals of the Association of American Geographers*, 91(1): 122–42.

Stokowski, P. (2002) 'Languages of Place and Discourses of Power: Constructing New Senses of Place'. *Journal of Leisure Research*, 34(4): 368–82.

Strange, S. (2003) 'The Declining Authority of States' in D. Held and A. McGrew (eds) *The Global Transformations Reader*, 2nd edn. Cambridge: Policy Press, pp. 127–34.

Sutherland, M. (2005) 'Marine Boundaries and Good Governance of Marine Spaces', unpublished PhD dissertation, Geodesics and Geomatics. University of New Brunswick.

Swyngedouw, E. (1997) 'Neither Global nor Local. "Glocalization" and the Politics of Scale' in K.R. Cox (ed.) *Spaces of Globalization. Reasserting the Power of the Local*. New York, London: Guilford Press, pp. 137–66.

Tsing, A. (2000) 'The Global Situation'. *Cultural Anthropology*, 15(3): 327–60.

Tsing, A. (2005) *Friction. An Ethnography of Global Connection*. Princeton, NJ: Princeton University Press.

Walley, C.J. (2002) '"They Scorn Us because We are Uneducated": Knowledge and Power in a Tanzanian Marine Park'. *Ethnography*, 3(3): 265–98.

Wiber, M.G. (2004) 'Finding Common Ground in the Fisheries Field: Agency in the Ethnographic Encounter'. *Zeitschrift für Ethnologie*, 129: 49–70.

Wiber, M.G. (2005) 'Mobile Law and Globalism: Epistemic Communities versus Community-based Innovation in the Fisheries Sector' in F. and K. von Benda-Beckmann and A. Griffiths (eds) *Mobile People, Mobile Law: Expanding Legal Relations in a Contracting World*. Aldershot: Ashgate, pp. 131–51.

Wiber, M.G. and Kearney, J. (2004) 'Learning Communities and Legal Spaces: Community-based Fisheries Management in a Globalizing World'. Paper presented at the International Conference on Developing the Anthropology of Law in a Transnational World, Edinburgh, 17–19 June 2004.

Wiber, M.G. and Lovell, P. (2003) 'Property, Kinship and Cultural Capital: The Ethics of Modeling Kinship in Sustainable Resource Management'. *Anthropologica*, 46: 85–98.

Wiber, M.G., Charles, T., Berkes, F. and Kearney, K. (2004) 'Participatory Research Supporting Community-based Fishery Management'. *Marine Policy*, 28(6): 459–68.

Williams, D.R. (2002) 'Leisure Identities, Globalization, and the Politics of Place'. *Journal of Leisure Research*, 34(4): 351–67.

Willock, A. and Lack, M. (2006) *Follow the Leader. Learning from Experience and Best Practice in Regional Fisheries Management Organizations*. World Wildlife Fund International and TRAFFIC International.

Wilson, B.M. (1980) 'Social Space and Symbolic Interaction' in A. Buttimer and D. Seamon (eds) *The Human Experience of Space and Place*. New York: St. Martin's Press, pp. 135–47.

Wilson, D.C. (2003) 'Examining the Two Cultures Theory of Fisheries Knowledge: The Case of Bluefish Management'. *Society and Natural Resources*, 16: 491–508.

Wilson, J.A. (1990) 'Fishing for Knowledge'. *Land Economics*, 66(1): 12–29.

Yi-Fu Tuan (1978) 'Space, Time, Place: A Humanistic Frame' in T. Carlstein, D. Parkes and M. Thrift (eds) *Making Sense of Time*. London: Edward Arnold Publishers, pp 7–16.

Chapter 5
The Sultan's Map: Arguing One's Land in Pasir

Laurens Bakker

Return of a Sultan?

This chapter concerns a land dispute in Indonesia, in the district of Pasir, East Kalimantan, in which three parties present different versions of local history, social circumstances and cultural values to substantiate their views of the legal validity of the claim and the status of the land.[1] The parties are unequally matched from a formal legal perspective, but those not having formal authority on their side make up by bringing in the power of social support.

A descendant of Pasir's last sultan, whom we shall call Pak Keturunan, or Pak Tur, owns an old map.[2] Drawn in black ink on pink silk, in places eaten by moths and weighed down with official seals, it confirms a stretch of land as the sultan's private property. Basing himself on national inheritance law and sustaining his claim with references to customary and historical rights, Pak Tur claims the land as his private property. His claim is disputed by another sultan's descendant, Pak Tio, who maintains that Pak Tur's version is nonsense and a local NGO, the PBA, who champion the rights of the local indigenous population, the Orang Paser or Paserese, argue that the sultan never had anything to say about land in Pasir in the first place. The official authorities that have to deal with these claims lack expertise of Paserese customary law and only realized the threat of losing state land to a private party when the claim threatens to become a public conflict.

The case is being judged according to formal Indonesian law by relevant courts of law, but the courts' decisions are not undisputed. Parties refer to conflicting

---

1 This chapter is based on research by the author in Paser from 2004 to 2006 as part of the Indonesian–Dutch INDIRA project. The author would like to thank Fakultas Kehutanan of Universitas Mulawarman, Lembaga Ilmu Pengetahuan Indonesia, Tropenbos International Indonesia and the Van Vollenhoven Institute of Leiden University for their kind support of the research. Financial support was provided by the Royal Netherlands Academy of arts and Sciences (KNAW), the Treub Foundation, the Netherlands Foundation for the Advancement of Tropical Research (WOTRO) and the Adatrechtstichting. I am grateful to Donald Tick for material and critical input.

2 Pak Keturunan is not this person's real name. As this discussion does not require us to use his actual identity, the interests of privacy prevale.

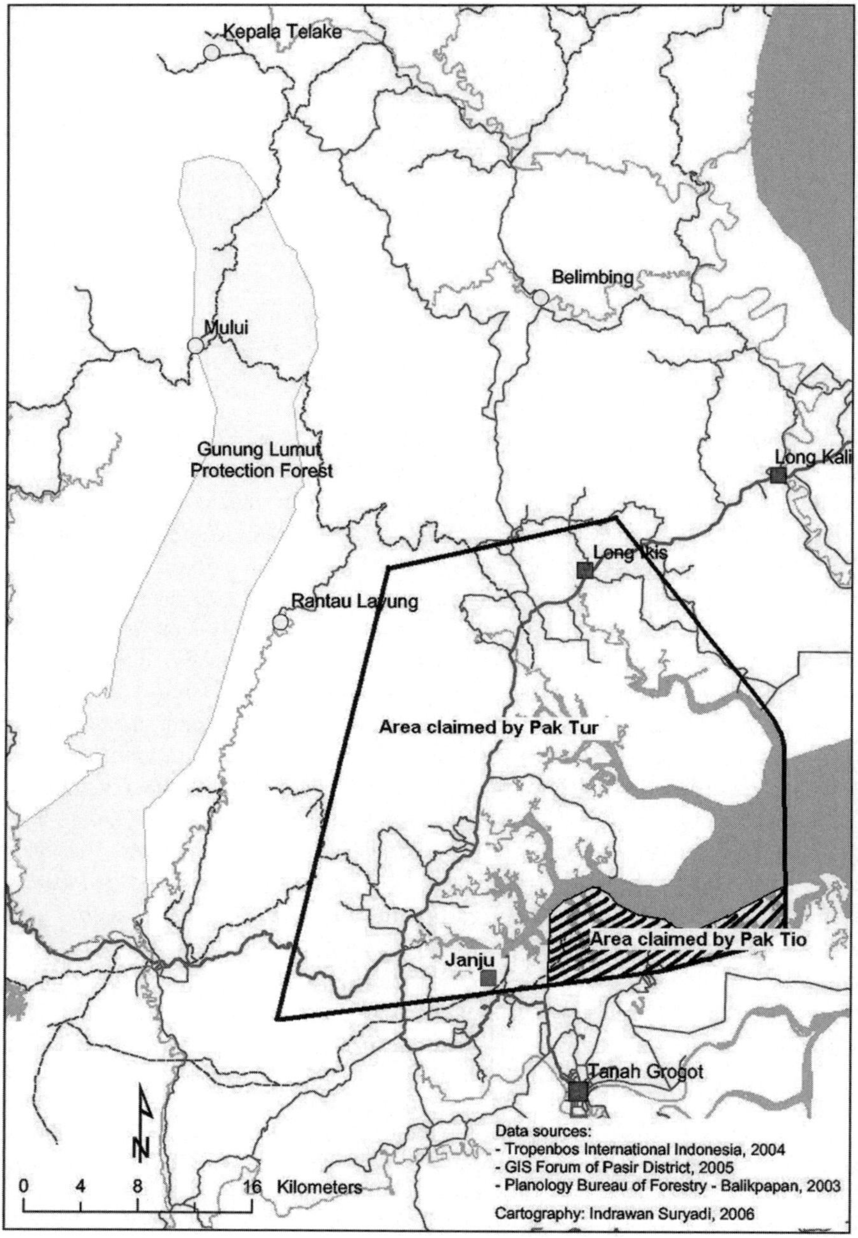

Map 5.1 Central Pasir and the location of the claims

Cartography: Indrawan Suryadi and Laurens Bakker.

versions of local history, customary rules and social norms as legitimate sources of authority to refute the courts' – and each others' – versions of how the claim ought to be solved. These arguments are distinctly local in range. Used alongside formal Indonesian law they, thus, contribute to a legal process that is distinctly Pasirese in character and evolution, and contains developments that would not be legal in the eyes of a non-local judge.

Today's Indonesia offers considerable opportunities for such developments. Following President Suharto's resignation in 1998 after an intense and widespread call for government reform and increased democracy, his successors decided to end the central government's totalitarian grip on the nation and decentralize considerable administrative powers to the regional authorities.[3] As a result local identity, culture, tradition and ethnicity, which used to be subordinated to the central government's drive for national unity, became a major issue in regional politics. Capitalizing upon feelings of neglect of local issues by the regional government, successful local power brokers managed to turn such aspects of identity into local power bases. As novel competition, these newly emerged influentials weakened the authority of prescribed or 'legitimate' access to power and introduced alternatives.

In this chapter, I analyse the spatiality of the legal process surrounding the question of recognition of Pak Tur's claim. I find that the various contesting normative systems (versions of local 'law' versus national Indonesian law and versus each other) gain their validity (or lack thereof) from the specific spatial setting in which they are applied. Parties' success depends on referring to the correct normative system and sentiments at each location. This cannot be done without a thorough knowledge of circumstances at the location and access to its authorities. The disruption of Indonesia's government structure has made this easier, but this disruption has also recasted local identity as a niche where power can become available to those looking for it. These factors made 'valid law' a spatially diverse and dynamic source of authority that can be managed and steered by those with sufficient knowledge of, and influence in, the local situation.

Positioning Authority

The validity of authority is limited. Spatial borders, defined mainly by social circumstances, pose boundaries to specific authorities' powers (Bromley 2003). Hence a map of authority would be subject to frequent revisions as borders and regimes alter and hybrid forms of law arise where borders fluctuate (Musson 2005, 1–2) or frontiers persevere. Pak Tur's map is no different. Drawn up at the end of the nineteenth century during the last decades of the Pasirese sultanate, it depicts a situation and quotes authorities that no longer exist. From a strictly legal

3 The hierarchy of government levels in Indonesia in descending order is: national (central), province, region, subregion, village.

perspective Pak Tur could argue that the authority of the sultanate passed on to the Dutch colonial authorities and from there to the Indonesian state, all guaranteeing land rights given out by their predecessors under certain conditions, but his line of reasoning would stand little chance of popular acceptance without additional support – or at least no opposition – from the major social powers.

Social and political constellations at the regional level of Indonesian society are dynamic alignments. Regional leaders are, as Watson (2002, 122–4) suggests for Indonesian elites in general, prone to the impact of rapidly changing socio-economic conditions which bring other types of associations – ethnic, political, religious – to the fore and demand swift transformations of the elite in order for them to persevere. Nonetheless, a charismatic and popular leader can maintain a prominent position throughout successive transformations. Anderson's (1990, 21–3) analysis of the Javanese concept of power shows it as concrete, homogeneous, constant in quantity and without inherent moral implications. Although Anderson focused on Java, his findings can be applied to Pasir as well. Not only has Javanese cultural dominance spread Javanese values throughout Indonesia, Pasir has for centuries been inhabited by a large Javanese minority. A leader in possession of power could thus maintain authority regardless of his actions.

This idea gains depth once a historical context is added. The Malay word for sultanate, *kesultanan*, means little more than 'being in the condition of having a sultan'. In the sultanates, power was linked to the person of the sultan (Milner 1982, 8), making most fiefs absolute autocracies in which the ruler's word was law.[4] The sultan, however, was rarely directly involved in direct governance. His task lays in the correct application of tradition in the domain (Milner 1982, 94–111), while an elite of nobles and members of the royal family formed the actual administration. Whereas the actions of this elite could damage the sultan's popularity and cause his subjects to migrate to better places, the sultan's inherent quality of personal power would remain in place.

Whereas the remnants of these auras of authority may still shimmer around the descendants of Indonesia's former sultans, others attempting to rise on the tide of present day decentralization still had to obtain them. Regional autonomy widened and diversified access to authority, and created space for distinctly local factors. Power and authority could still be attained by the normative rules of official government elections and appointments, but the local potential of ethnicity, custom and religion provide a second set of pragmatic rules often influencing the outcome to a considerable extent.[5] Aspiring power brokers attempt to gain support from various local sources of power, creating a stronger and more absolute position by enlisting the full potential in a creative and dynamic manner which, however, enhances the uncontrollability of the process as well.

---

4 See Mabbett (1985, 14–23) for a more extensive discussion of Asian feudalism.

5 Normative and pragmatic rules are terms coined by Bailey (1969). Normative rules refer to the rules of the game, pragmatic ones to how to win.

The present power situation in many Indonesian districts lacks a dominant discourse. Aspiring authorities bring in a multiplicity of discursive elements that can come into play in various strategies. It is the usage made of these elements that make up the discourse and ensuing counter-discourse that shape the local constellation of law. The chronological development of this constellation in Pasir, and that of the fluctuations of power-constellations surrounding Pak Tur's claim, are what defined and eventually decided the claim's (il)legitimacy and the ensuing (lack of) success. The laws applied were instrumental to this decision and by no means independent.

Pak Tur and the Sultans of Pasir

Pasir is the southernmost district of East Kalimantan. With a territory of 11,600 square kilometres and almost 173,000 inhabitants it is sparsely populated. Geographically it consists of an extensive coastal plain bisected by various rivers and a mountainous hinterland. Extensive oil palm plantations as well as coal mining and extraction of oil make up the district's main economic sectors. These are all located in the coastal plain, where the majority of the population is concentrated. Pasir has been an immigration destination for hundreds of years but notably since Indonesian independence migrants from all over Indonesia have come to the district, independently or through government-sponsored programmes in search of land and work. Those people not working in the district's plantations or natural resource extraction are farmers or fishermen. The vicinity of the large city of Balikpapan guarantees a market for agricultural produce as much as for poultry, beef or fish. Ethnically diverse, the district has sizeable populations of Javanese, Buginese, Banjarese and Paserese; the latter being considered the original inhabitants of the area. Forming the majority in the sparsely populated mountains, the Paserese live intermingled with migrants in the coastal plain. Generally, Paserese and migrants live together without problems. All major population groups, including the Paserese, are Muslim Malay and intermarriage is common and frequent.

In the mountains, where the Paserese are the dominant population group, Paserese culture strongly resembles that of neighbouring Dayak groups.[6] Even though the people feel themselves connected to the Paserese of the plain through language and culture, their history is one of relative independence whereas the coastal groups have been under the influence of the sultanate for centuries.

A Paserese myth recounts how the Dayaks of Pasir wanted a single ruler to govern them and went looking for a suitable person outside of Pasir. When no one could be found, a foreign princess was sent into their midst by magical means. The

---

6 'Dayak' is used as an ethnic and religious distinction which designated the non-Muslim, non-Malay original inhabitants of Borneo, who generally live in the interior of the island (King 1993, 29–30).

princess married a Prince of Giri (Java), making it likely that Pasir's remote past is one of subservience to that kingdom (In 't Veld 1882).

From the sixteenth century onwards Buginese from Sulawesi married into the royal line, giving it a Buginese turn that would remain until the end of the sultanate (Assegaff 1982) and installing a strong orientation to southern Sulawesi. Thus Pasir's indigenous population was ruled by 'stranger-kings' (Henley 2004) which may have united and pacified the area at the time, but, as will follow, provided a powerful argument to those opposing Pak Tur's land claim.

From the second half of the nineteenth century onwards Pasir effectively became a Dutch protectorate, with the colonial government gradually taking over the sultan's authority. Colonial support often determined Pasir's rulers from the ranks of the intensely striving royal family. In 1896, the colonial government deposed Sultan Muhammad Ali on the pretext of supporting Banjarese rebels and banished him to Banjarmasin where he requested, and received, for himself and his descendants the right to provide for their livelihoods through the proceeds of the areas of Samuntai, Adang and Muru; three fertile coastal parts of Pasir (Assegaff 1982, 186–8).

After a period of turmoil and swift successions Sultan Chatiloeddin was elected to the throne from the midst of Pasir's heavily divided royal family in 1900 on the condition that Aji Nyesei, the son of one of his opponents, would be his successor.

Sultan Chatiloeddin preferred popularity to strong government and he regularly omitted to collect taxes, to the annoyance of the colonial government. A new political contract in 1902 strengthened the government's grip on Pasir, but led to rioting among Chatilloedin's adversaries in the sultanate's government. In 1907, Sultan Chatiloeddin proposed the colonial government to bring Pasir under direct colonial rule as his opponents in the royal family were steadily absorbing his authority. The proposal was enacted in 1908, under strong protest by opposing nobles (Eisenberger 1936, 88–9). The sultanate's main nobles, among them Chatiloeddin, Aji Nyesei and Pangeran Mantri (Chatiloeddin's brother), were paid indemnifications (Assegaf 1982, 209–10) and the territory of the Sultanate of Pasir was incorporated in the Dutch East Indies.

The fortunes of the royal family varied considerably. Aji Nyesei, Chatiloeddin's agreed successor, married into a family of Buginese traders and became a successful businessman who acquired property in Sulawesi, Kalimantan and Singapore. Chatiloeddin's adversaries, however, attempted to regain the position of Sultan of Pasir in a failed revolt in 1912, while Chatiloeddin and Pangeran Mantri were arrested as the secret leaders of a 1916 uprising. Chatiloeddin was banished to Java, Pangeran Mantri to Padang in Sumatra (Eisenberger 1936, 93, 96–8; and Assegaf, 1982, 219–27). Chatiloeddin remained in Java and eventually died in Cianjur. Pangeran Mantri died in Padang, but one of his sons returned to Pasir. There he married a great-granddaughter of Sultan Muhammad Ali and they had a son: Pak Tur.

Pak Tur was well known and respected in Tanah Grogot, Pasir's capital. A middle management civil servant with the district government, he was also the treasurer of one of Pasir's main indigenous peoples NGOs, the Paser Adat Foundation (*Lembaga Adat Paser*, hereafter LAP), which had its headquarters in the capital, and a member of several Muslim charitable organizations. While preparing his land claim, Pak Tur consulted these bodies. His seniors in the government and in the charities did not object, while the LAP board took the stance that the land claim was a private undertaking by one of its members and hence not their business. He also contacted some of the companies operating on the land to find out their stance on a change of landlord. Receiving mostly favourable results, Pak Tur was assured of the backing, or lack of objections, of a wide array of authorities and parties.

Two historic documents formed the base of Pak Tur's claim. The first was the map described in the introduction of this chapter, the second was a notification from 1898 in which the *Resident* confirms Sultan Muhammad Ali's right to the territories of Samuntai, Adang and Muru. Pak Tur, a descendant of Chatiloeddin through his father and of Sultan Muhammad Ali through his mother, claimed that land as his lawful inheritance. It was a substantial claim. The government estimated the land to cover some 1,160 square kilometres of prime coastal land, which equalled around 10 per cent of the district's territory or 22 per cent of its fertile coastal zone. It contained agricultural plots, villages and houses, large-scale plantations and mining operations. It was, in short, of considerable social and economical importance to the population and the economy of the district.

Pak Tur took a realistic approach to the possible results. In his opinion, the land concerned covered some 300,000 hectares. Claiming all of this would definitely lead to trouble with the population and the government so he decided to leave out all land in use by local villagers, roughly half of his claim. A further 40,000 hectares were used by a state palm oil enterprise and hence out of boundaries as well. This would leave him some 110,000 hectares, which he intended to develop together with the district government on a 30 per cent (Pak Tur) – 70 per cent (government) base.

Pak Tur's first attempt to get formal recognition of his heritage claim dates from the early eighties. He claims that the district government of that time was willing to endorse his claim in exchange for the financial equivalent of six cars. Pak Tur did not have that money and decided to leave the project for the time being.

With the arrival of decentralization and the increased government attention for the interests of the local population Pak Tur decided to revive his claim. In early 2002 he sold 15 hectares of forest land, part of his claim, to a third party. When in September 2002 two other persons started to cultivate the land and claimed it to be their property, Pak Tur instituted a lawsuit against these two with Pasir's district court, charging them with land theft. The court accepted Pak Tur's map and documentation as evidence of his right to sell the land and sentenced the perpetrators to a suspended prison sentence.

One of the two defendants, whom we shall call Pak Tio, disputed the court's verdict. Pak Tio was of royal descent as well and claimed to have documentation proving his ancestors' ownership of the land. Remote relatives, Pak Tur and Pak Tio thus were united in maintaining the continued validity of the sultanate's rights to the land, but disagreed on who had the strongest claim. The local population was divided, some contesting the claim and arguing local adat rights to the land. Although neither Pak Tur nor Pak Tio agreed to those, Pak Tio was first to respond and did so by publicly denouncing the existence of other traditional rights other than those of the sultanate. In the fall of 2002 Pak Tio and five of his relatives filed a lawsuit against Pak Tur and against 93 families living on the land Pak Tio and his relatives claimed ownership of, altogether some 15,000 hectares.

To the relief of many, the district court found Pak Tio's documentation insufficient. During the court's session Pak Tur requested to have his claim judged separately from Pak Tio's to have its validity again confirmed, but this was refused. The court rejected Pak Tio's claim because of his poor evidence, but remained silent on the validity of Pak Tur's documents. Both parties were dissatisfied, although Pak Tur felt that his claim was implicitly recognized.

Pak Tio then brought the case before the East Kalimantan court of appeal which, in February 2003, fully endorsed the ruling of Pasir's district court without adding new considerations of its own. On the request of Pak Tio, the district court secretary then sent the case to the Supreme Court in Jakarta in late August 2003. As this court had a considerable backlog, no decision had been taken at the time of writing. However, the Supreme Court's pending decision is of great importance to Pak Tio, Pak Tur, the villagers working and living on the land, and to the district government which could lose authority over ten per cent of its best land.

While awaiting the decision of the Supreme Court, Pak Tur filed another claim with the district court in November 2004. Farmers from the village of Janju, which fell within the boundaries of the area Pak Tur claimed, were clearing new fields on forest land. Pak Tur, considering unused forest lands part of his land claim sent them word that they were trespassing and that he would press charges if necessary. When his warning did not have the desired result, he sued 67 of the village's families for 120 hectares. The land issue was becoming serious, but the court case took a rather unexpected turn. During the second court session Pak Tur's legal representative quit for undisclosed reasons while Pak Tur himself remained absent at the third, fourth and fifth sessions. His continued absence led the court judges to declare that his claim could not be maintained, but not without including the conclusion that the plaintiff had apparently lost his desire and was no longer serious about his claim in their conclusion.

That the claim could not be maintained under such circumstances was clear, yet the conclusion that Pak Tur was no longer interested was not. He could have withdrawn the case or made his desire to discontinue known in another way. Pak Tur did not want to drop the case of his own accord. Another interpretation of the sultans' rights, this one by opponents, was the cause.

Favourable Circumstances?

After President Suharto's more then thirty years of authoritarian rule the decentralization laws brought unexpected and unfamiliar laws to the regions. Law 22/1999 on regional government and Law 25/1999 on the fiscal balance between the centre and the regions redefined relations between the central and regional governments. Law 22/1999 decentralized considerable administrative powers to the district level government but did not include precise definitions of these powers (Ray and Goodpaster 2003, 75–7), while Law 25/1999 allowed for a greater percentage of local revenue to benefit the region.[7] District government interpretations' of their new powers basically went unchecked, resulting in highly diverse legislation and local circumstances throughout the nation (Schulte Nordholt and Klinken 2007) among other things due to differences in regional resources and ethnic make up.[8]

Almost from the beginning critics and observers feared that the potential for change provided by decentralization would see regional government captured by local elites (Malley 2003; and Dasgupta and Beard 2007) consisting of local bureaucrats (Rohdewohld 2003; and Hadiz 2004), army officers (Mietzner 2003; and Rinakit 2005) or even the regional underworld (Wilson 2006). Ethnicity proved a uniting factor. Whereas *masyarakat adat*, or 'adat communities', strove for the recognition of customary (adat) rights to land and natural resources by the government (Li 2000; and Sakai 2003), organizations positioning themselves as *putra daerah*, or 'son of the region' tended to aim for an economic or politically privileged status of the indigenous group over newcomers (see usage in Duncan 2007; and Schiller 2007). Whereas Pak Tur sought to associate his claim with Pasir's largest adat NGO, he found Pasir's main *putra daerah* organization opposing him.

Indonesia's Sultans: Lost and Returned

The role of sultans and other indigenous rulers was gradually diminished when the colonial government strengthened its grip at the end of the nineteenth century, largely transforming the position of sultan into a solely ceremonial and customary function without administrative authority. In the eyes of Indonesia's population, however, the indigenous rulers were closely associated with the

7 Law 22/1999 gives a negative definition of the powers of the district government by stating what fields remain under the central government's authority. These include among others international politics, defence, justice, monetary and fiscal policy, and religion (Jaya 2003).

8 Laws 32/2004 on Regional Administration and 33/2004 on the Fiscal Balance were later issued as replacement laws of Laws 22/1999 and 25/1999. These limited the powers of the regions by expanding provincial authorities and elaborated the powers that remained with the central government.

Dutch colonial authorities. When the 1945 national revolution ended the colonial period, indigenous feudalism followed in its wake (Langenberg 1982; and Lucas 1991). After Indonesian independence the legal system no longer held a place for privileged sultans or kings.

Article 131 of the Provisional Constitution of 1950 stipulated that autonomous governance of areas of Indonesia had to be confirmed in a national law, while sultans and aristocrats were stripped of their lands.[9] The 1960 Basic Agrarian Law decreed that the national interest should be protected by limiting large landownership (Article 7) and that all land has a social function which supersedes individual interests (Article 6). It also instructed the establishment by law of a maximum size of land property (Article 17), and the formal registration of all land tenure (Article 19).[10]

In practice, preservation of large estates did occur in areas where the owners could muster political support (Tjondronegoro 1991, 21–3) and in fact still exists (see *Suara Merdeka*, 17 April 2007). The popular view of sultans as extensions of the colonial government denied them such support in newly independent Indonesia. Although the former royal families remained people of social standing, many had to find a job outside of the royal environments. After hundreds of years, the era of sultanates thus appeared to have ended with Indonesia's independence.

However, since the fall of Suharto, sultans have been returning to the fore in local politics. As autonomy focuses on the districts, which outside of Java often are former kingdoms or sultanates, these pasts are often invoked as symbols of district unity and identity. Klinken (2004; 2007, 163) shows the attractiveness of sultanist symbols by arguing that they evoke place as much as hierarchy. Sultans unite, ethnically, culturally or both, and are representations of the 'social capital' of the group. They symbolize integrative age-old customs that give identity and meaning to the local in modernity. Sultans are authoritative symbols of local legitimacy. They are not only *putra daerah* par excellence who legitimate the rights of an ethnic group in an area, but in a wider context they symbolize the area's history and its social uniqueness.

---

9 As none such laws existed at the time, sultanates were thus essentially made into illegal arrangements. The single exception to this was the Sultan of Yogyakarta, whose support of the Indonesian Independence movement was recognized in Law 3/1950 which declared Yogyakarta a special region province (*propinsi daerah istimewa*) and gave the sultan authority in the province's regional affairs. When Indonesia's original 1945 constitution replaced the 1950 provisional constitution, Article 18 of the 1945 constitution confirmed Article 131 of the provisional constitution. A few years later law 1/1957 was passed which further limited the potential authority of sultans. Article one of this law required special regions, such as Yogyakarta, to have a government of seven people, making an individual sultan a minority whose ideas and policies could be controlled and countered by the other six members.

10 Law 56/1960 allows for plots of between 5 to 20 hectares (Article 1), depending on population pressure, while the Minister of the Interior's regulation 6/1972 (Article 2) limits farm land to 2 hectares, building land to 0.2 hectares.

Examples of the legitimizing symbolism of sultans are the revival of Malay sultanates in West Kalimantan (Sambas, Pontianak), which, as Davidson (2003, 85–6) shows, form a counterweight to rival Dayak *putra daerah* claims in that province and the ethnic and religious rallying points offered by the Sultanates of Ternate and Tidore in the bloody North Maluku power struggles of 1999 (Klinken 2001, 5–7, 16, 25–6; 2007, 157).

A more peaceful and unifying usage of sultanist symbols takes place in the district of Kutai Kartanegara, which borders Pasir to the north. In 2001, the district head crowned Sultan H. Aji Muhammad Salehudin II as Sultan of Kutai Kartanagara, thus reviving the 'oldest kingdom of Indonesia' (for instance, *Tribun Kaltim* 1 November 2007).[11] In the view of the district head, the sultan was deemed a worthy and essential trait of Kutai Kartanegara's identity while the royal ceremonies and the splendour of a newly built palace were hoped to generate extra tourism to the district.

Yet the reinstitution of the sultanate is given other reasons as well. Kutai Kartanegara is among the richest districts of Indonesia. The district is rich in oil, coal and natural gas, and has a limited timber industry. When oil was discovered in 1902 the revenues almost instantly made Kutai's sultan one of the richest persons of Indonesia (Magenda 1991). In 2000 popular elements in Kutai's coastal zone campaigned to became a new district independent from Kutai Kartanegara. Possessing extensive natural gas and oil reserves, the new district would be economically well off. It is argued that Kutai Kartanegara's district head revived the sultanate to prevent partitioning of the district which so far seems to be effective.

The sultan's position is mostly symbolic, although district officials publicly seek his council in matters of importance (see *Kaltim Post* 20 September 2002; 29 May 2003; and 19 December 2004). The sultan is paid a wage from the district revenues, which is determined by the district head. It is hoped, however, that the revenues from tourism will in time suffice to provide for the sultan's expenses (*Kaltim Post* 30 September 2002).

At the national level, various sultans have formed the *Forum Komunikasi dan Informasi Keraton se-Nusantara* (Indonesian Palaces Communication and Information Forum), a group whose meetings often coincide with the *Festival Keraton Nusantara* (Festival of Indonesian Palaces) at which representatives of Indonesia's royal families gather to discuss royal matters and enjoy performances of palace arts and culture. Consecutive meetings saw the sultans become more adept in speaking to the press and building up a political position. While the Sultan of Ternate stated in 2002 that what the sultans really wanted was to have their lands back (Klinken 2004), the 2004 meeting saw various representatives arguing for a return to politics and a position for the sultans in the government system (*Jakarta Post* 4 October 2004). At the 2006 meeting the representatives vowed to uphold the unity of the Indonesian Republic and recommended that a law be made

11 For an extensive discussion of events in Kutai, see Mahy (2005).

to formally arrange the position of communities pertaining to adat law, sultanates among them (*Tempo Interaktif* 12 September 2006).

The Sultan of Ternate may have spoken his mind thoughtlessly in 2002, but his remark unveiled an essential point. In 2003, the Sultan of Kutai Kartanegara referred to the ancient borders of the sultanate to legitimate his demand for 3.3 trillion rupiah from the Kutai Prima Coal (KPC) company that operates a mining plant in the neighbouring district of Kutai Timur.[12] However, the sultan's claim was opposed by the 'Grand Sultan' of Kutai, an individual who based himself on his lineage and historic documentation to argue that he was the actual guardian of Kutai's adat lands and natural resources (*Kaltim Post* 25 August 2003). The 'media-launched' Sultan of Kutai Kartanegara, the Grand Sultan felt, only had authority over the palace culture. The adat land of Kutai he argued, such as the land that KPC operated on, had traditionally been under the governance of his family. The 68-year-old Grand Sultan intended to undergo a DNA test to prove his descent, should this be required (*Kaltim Post* 23 September 2003).

Yet betting on status and descent to gain more then ceremonial recognition remained a gamble. In 2001, two members of Kutai's royal family basing themselves on inherited documents claimed ownership of land in central Tenggarong, the capital of Kutai Kartanegara. The case went as far as Indonesia's Supreme Court, which ruled in their favour. Nonetheless, the local office of the National Land Agency (NLA) refused to draw up a certificate of ownership (*Kaltim Post* 4 December 2002). Officials stated that the land superseded the maximum size allowed for individual property and hence ignored the Supreme Court's ruling.[13]

Nonetheless, royal descent can be profitable. Employees of KPC told me how their company had informally settled the matter with the sultan and grand sultan of Kutai Kartanegara to avoid time-consuming legal processes that could endanger their operation.

Royal descent can also bring unexpected inheritance. A branch of Pasir's royal family owned a stretch of prime land in Singapore through Aji Nyesei, the heir-apparent turned trader. Most members of this branch actually live in Singapore, but some remained in Pasir. Recently the land was needed for city development and the government of Singapore paid a compensation based on contemporary land prices. The money was shared among the relatives, turning a few individuals in Pasir into instant rupiah multimillionaires. Several bought new cars or motorbikes; one could afford a handsome house, a new car and quit his job.

---

12 At the time around 348 million euros or 386 million US dollars.

13 The non-implementation of court judgments is common throughout Indonesia. See, for instance, Benda-Beckmann, K. von (1984, 118–39) on opposition to district and Supreme Court decisions in West Sumatra; Benda-Beckmann and Benda-Beckmann (1994, 238–9) on a Supreme Court decision in Ambon; and Pompe (2005, 462–4) on local opposition in North Sumatra to a Supreme Court decision.

The Role of Indigeneity in Pasir

As an ethnic group, the Orang Paser have risen to prominence in the district following decentralization. Various NGOs claiming to represent the adat interest of the Paserese population have presented themselves, of which two, the aforementioned LAP and the PBA-PDS (*Pertahanan Benuo Adat – Paser Dayak Serumpun*; Defence of our Adat – Dayak Paser Branch, hereafter PBA) have gained the ear of the government.[14] Supporting Orang Paser in land conflicts and devoting themselves to furthering Paserese identity in the district the two organizations have appropriated Paserese adat and identity as their field of expertise. The leaders of the LAP and PBA are intense rivals, both resenting and denying the other's knowledge and status and both blackening the other's reputation.

Most of the LAP's leadership stems from the district's government apparatus, while its head is a descendant of Sultan Muhammad Ali. Following the promulgation of a district regulation on the relation between the government and adat organizations the district government has affirmed the LAP as its official NGO counterpart, declaring that all NGOs wishing to address the district government need to do so through the LAP. The organization is moderate, undertaking to represent the adat interests of all living in Pasir, including migrants with their own non-Paserese adat.

By contrast the PBA only concerns itself with the interests and adat of the Paserese. Their leader, a retired police sergeant, maintains good contacts with the local police and military forces but not with the district government. The PBA associates itself with Dayak organizations from elsewhere in the province rather than with the government and prefers to present itself as an independent organization. The members have elected its leader as '*entero*' supreme adat leader of Pasir, a newly invented position which has been received with enthusiasm among the Paserese of the coastal plain. As much Paserese adat lands in that area was given out by the government to migrants and plantation companies, the PBA's pleas for *putra daerah* rights and a return of adat land find an enthusiastic audience.

The PBA and LAP are not on speaking terms and ignore each other's existence as much as possible. The PBA refuses to acknowledge the LAP's government position and refuses to initiate contact with the organization. As a consequence they have no direct lines of communications to the district government.

Both organizations hold different views on Pasir's history and the role of the sultanate. The LAP position is that the sultanate was a legitimate power in Pasir and governed all of its population. By contrast, the PBA maintains that the sultans were Buginese from Sulawesi who invaded Pasir and were foreign to its people and culture. In their view the sultanate is a black chapter of oppression and Buginese colonialism in Pasir's history.

---

14 Which shows among others in the recent (2007) name change of the district from Indonesian 'Pasir' to 'Paser' and the adoption of a new motto in Paserese.

The return of sultans throughout Indonesia and the prominent role of indigeneity in Pasir form the background to Pak Tur's land claim. As a member of the LAP's board, Pak Tur was certain that this organization would not oppose him, while his connections in society and the government could lend support to the implementation of a positive court decision. He did not expect much opposition from the PBA, which maintained an aloof isolation, or of any other social movements since he would not, or so he claimed, demand the return of any land in use by the population. Maintaining that his rights would not interfere with the social circumstances in the district, Pak Tur lodged his claims, which ended with the result discussed above. The reasons follow below.

The Claim in Society

While in court, details of Pak Tur's and Pak Tio's claims reached the ears of society. Both parties were blackening the other's name and spreading wild and ugly rumours about their opponents. Among the farmers living on the disputed land the notion arose that two potential sultans were fighting in court, assisted by allies in the government and the district's business circles, over who owned the farmers' land. When the court would reach a decision, the story went, the farmers would almost certainly be cleared from the land. When contacted by alarmed villagers, the LAP was unwilling to get involved but the PBA, who hitherto had displayed little activity in this part of Pasir, rose to the occasion. While parties awaited the decision of the Supreme Court, the PBA set about organizing itself and making its stance known. In early 2004 the PBA leader, claiming extensive knowledge of the adat of Pasir, passed what he maintains was an adat sentence on Pak Tur in a public PBA meeting. The verdict, called *temberau*, resembled an official warning. It instructs someone to stop what they are doing or face the consequences. Pak Tur did not react and a few weeks later a second adat sentence was passed: *peondang*, anyone could beat-up the sentenced person with approval of the adat community. By now, Pak Tur was opting for a dialogue with the PBA, which the latter persistently refused. They informed him that the next step would be *penirak bombai*: anyone wanting to kill Pak Tur would have the adat community's full consent. Pak Tur decided to temporarily move to Balikpapan, but maintained his claim.

In August, when Pak Tur instigated the Janju claim, the farmers who considered the land as adat land belonging to their community, approached the PBA for assistance.

The 23 September saw some 400 farmers and PBA members gather in front of the district head's office, carrying banners denouncing all claims by sultans' descendants. The PBA leader had informed his police contacts beforehand and riot police barred the entrance to the office. A PBA spokesperson quickly pointed out that no demonstration was taking place but an adat ceremony of which the mainly Javanese police officers obviously had no knowledge. Gongs were beaten, fires were lit and the PBA leader performed magic spells. Those knowledgeable of Paserese adat knew that the ritual was to cleanse a house of evil spirits. The message was quite clear.

The PBA leader was invited to discuss the matter with the district head, a Buginese from Sulawesi, and several senior officials. The next day East Kalimantan's main newspaper reported that the district head had voiced his concern and his interest in local adat, while his staff had pointed out that it was impossible for one person to own so much land (*Kaltim Post* 24 September 2004). Unfazed, Pak Tur retorted in the same newspaper three days later (*Kaltim Post* 27 September 2004). He stated that he had never been consulted on the land clearings and the villagers could have known about his rights. The land, Pak Tur stated, had been the private property of Sultan Muhammad Ali and hence was his by inheritance. He announced that he would refer the case to the district court, which he did in November, as described above.

Then one of Pak Tur's houses burned down. According to the official report a neglected fire in a neighbour's backyard was to blame, but on the street people spoke of magic. Not just any magic; renowned Paserese black magic that was invoked during the demonstration a few weeks earlier. The PBA neither confirmed nor denied it, but their leader's star was on the rise. Summoned to a meeting with the district government, the PBA leader explained that according to the adat of Pasir the sultans, whose ancestors were migrants, never owned any land in Pasir. They were guests, nothing else. Valid law had always been Paserese adat, to which even the sultan had to adhere.

The district government drew up a request to the Supreme Court to treat the case with urgency and added the PDA's recommendations as those of an authoritative adat leader. Pak Tur, as mentioned above, seemed to have lost heart and did not show himself in Tanah Grogot. He awaited the Supreme Court's conclusion in Balikpapan. The Supreme Court replied to the district government's request that the court intended to consider the case in due time. However, contacts at the Supreme Court ensured Pasir's officials by telephone that the Supreme Court judges read the district court's decision as stating that Pak Tur's claim is not acknowledged in any case, and neither is Pak Tio's. Whatever the Supreme Court will rule, it seems unlikely that it will favour the descendants of Pasir's sultans.

Concluding Remarks: Controlling Law's Spatialization

Regaining a sultanate with just an old map and a handful of documents is a fairytale story. Popular support was close to non-existent. Pak Tur's attempt lacked the unifying element that reinstalled sultans had provided in the local contexts of war-torn West Kalimantan and Maluku, and that was thought to have prevented partitioning of the district in Kutai Kartanegara. Support for reinstalled sultans is most likely in areas where a crisis makes sultans unifying symbols, but Pasir was not in crisis. Second, Pak Tur desired only the privileges of the sultan, not the public and ceremonial parts that position him as an authority in society. Although

Pak Tur had carefully generated acceptance, if not sympathy for his version of Pasirese customary rights among the district's influentials, he had not rallied supporters among the rest of the population.

Pak Tur's plan, initially supported by the new availability of positions of power in local elites, was thwarted in the first place by just this circumstance. Having ensured the approval of the elite in the capital he omitted to seek the support of the rural population although his claim concerned land in the countryside. Pak Tur's carefully constructed discourse of sultan's customary rights was countered by the PBA when they hijacked the LAP's role as the local guardians of indigenous peoples rights and fielded a militant *putra daerah* counter-discourse of dynamic and active Pasirese customary law, the knowledge of which they expertly monopolized. The PBA acknowledged that the sultans had held sway over the Buginese settlers in and around its capital, but that authority did not pervade to include the indigenous Paserese who had their own customary laws. They saw the sultanate as a colonizing power, foreign to Pasir and the Paserese. The PBA's highly personal implementation of 'anti-sultanate Pasirese customary law', which forced Pak Tur to give up a court case and leave Pasir for an uncertain period of time, met with considerable appreciation of the rural Paserese population.

The PBA was most successful in altering their arguments to the location. Overt threats with a veneer of adat were uttered among supporters, while an anti-sultan demonstration became an 'adat ceremony' to placate (or more likely confuse) police officials. Staging the 'ceremony' in front of the district head's office served its purpose in talking round the district government: they recognized the PBA as a hitherto unknown but legitimate adat authority at the expense of the LAP's influence, thus confirming the PBA's success in altering the constellation of Pasir's law-giving authorities.

Nonetheless, Pak Tur is not beaten. The non-local Supreme Court could decide in his favour and the LAP, who had maintained a neutral stance so far, could engage the PBA's monopoly on adat and support Pak Tur through fielding a contesting version of adat. Yet like customary law, national law is subject to discourse and counter-discourse in Indonesia's regions. The district court's initial decision overlooked the maximum size of a plot of land an individual may own under Indonesian law; an error the district government made sure the Supreme Court is aware of. Nonetheless, even a Supreme Court decision can be overruled by local legal arrangements, as shown in the final Kutai Kartanegara example, if local authorities deem it necessary.

Since decentralization, the spatialization of law in Indonesia has emerged as a potent tool for acquiring and maintaining power at the regional level of government. The proposition of regional cultural and customary arguments as locally valid law makes for a large and dynamic legal diversity among the nation's hundreds of regions. Pak Tur's main mistakes were that he enlisted only urban support and that he formulated the substantiation of his claim after successful examples from neighbouring regions. Pasir proved to have a different power constellation and to require its own discourse of law.

References

Anderson, B. (1990) *Language and Power. Exploring Political Cultures in Indonesia*. Ithaca and London: Cornell University Press.

Assegaff, A.S. (1982) *Sejarah Kerajaan Sadurangas Atau Kesultanan Pasir*. Pemerintah Daerah Kabupaten Tingkat II Pasir, Tanah Grogot.

Bailey, F. (1969) *Strategems and Spoils: A Social Anthropolgy of Politics*. Oxford: Blackwell Publishers.

Benda-Beckmann, F. von and Benda-Beckmann, K. von (1994) 'Texts in Context: Historical Documents as Political Commodity on Islamic Ambon' in W. Marschall (ed.) *Texts from the Islands: Oral and Written Traditions of Indonesia and the Malay World*. Bern: Ethnologica Bernensia 4, pp. 223–43.

Benda-Beckmann, K. von (1984) *The Broken Stairways to Consensus. Village Justice and State Courts in Minangkabau*. Dordrecht: Foris Publications, KITLV Press.

Bromley, N. (2003) 'From "what?" to "so what?": Law and Geography in Retrospect' in J. Holder and C. Harrison (eds) *Law and Geography*. Oxford: Oxford University Press, pp. 15–33.

Dasgupta, A. and Beard, V.A. (2007) 'Community Driven Development, Collective Action and Elite Capture in Indonesia'. *Development and Change*, 38(2): 229–49.

Davidson, J. (2003) 'The Politics of Violence on an Indonesian Periphery'. *Southeast Asia Research*, 11(1): 59–89.

Duncan, C. (2007) 'Mixed Outcomes: The Impact of Regional Autonomy and Decentralization on Indigenous Ethnic Minorities in Indonesia'. *Development and Change*, 38(4): 711–33.

Eisenberger, J. (1936) *Kroniek der Zuider – en Oosterafdeling van Borneo*. Banjarmasin: Drukkerij Liem Hwat Sing.

Hadiz, V.R. (2004) 'Indonesian Local Party Politics'. *Critical Asian Studies*, 36(4): 615–36.

Henley, D. (2004) 'Conflict, Justice and the Stranger King: Indigenous Roots of Colonial Rule in Indonesia and Elsewhere'. *Modern Asian Studies*, 38(1): 85–144.

In 't Veld, S.G. (1882) 'Legende over het Ontstaan van het Vorstenhuis van Pasir'. *Tijdschrift voor Indische Taal-, Land-, en Volkenkunde*, 27: 557–9.

Jakarta Post (2004) 4 October, *Sultans Want Return to 'Good old Days'*.

Jaya, W. (2003) 'Fiscal Decentralisation and its Impacts on Local Government Revenue in Indonesia' in M. Sakai (ed.) *Beyond Jakarta, Regional Autonomy and Local Societies in Indonesia*. Adelaide: Crawford House Publishing, pp. 38–56.

Kaltim Post (2002) 20 September, *Giliran Syaukani Dibersihkan*.

Kaltim Post (2002) 30 September, *Dianggarkan. Sultan Muspida Plus. Syaukani: Kalau Ingin Sejahtera Jangan Duduk Saja di Keraton*.

Kaltim Post (2002) 4 December, *BPN Diperingatkan Tak Bikin Sertifikat. Persoalan Tanah Rapak Mahang Tenggarong Muncul Lagi.*

Kaltim Post (2003) 29 May, *Kesultanan Netral.*

Kaltim Post (2003) 25 August, *Grand Sultan Angkat Bicara Soal Tanah KPC.*

Kaltim Post (2003) 23 September, *Permintahan Berlebihan.*

Kaltim Post (2004) 24 September, *'Ganti Saja Pasir dengan Kerajaan' Ratusan Warga Tanah Grogot Resah karena Digugat Ahli Waris Sultan Paser.*

Kaltim Post (2004) 27 September, *Bukti Kepemilikan Surat Residen 1898. Pak Tur Jelaskan Tanah di Desa Janju.*

Kaltim Post (2004) 19 December, *Sultan Kirim Surat ke Mendagri. Minta Penunjukan Penjabat Bupati Ditinjau.*

King, V.T. (1993) *The Peoples of Borneo*. Oxford: Blackwell.

Klinken, G. van (2001) 'The Maluku Wars: Bringing Society Back In'. *Indonesia*, 71: 1–26.

Klinken, G. van (2004) 'Return of the Sultans'. *Inside Indonesia*, 78 at www.insideindonesia.org.

Klinken, G. van (2007) 'Return of the Sultans: The Communitarian Turn in Local Politics' in J.S. Davidson and D. Henley (eds) *The Revival of Tradition in Indonesian Politics. The Deployment of adat from Colonialism to Indigenism*. London and New York: Routledge, pp.149–69.

Langenberg, M. van (1982) 'Class and Ethnic Conflict in Indonesia's Decolonization Process: A Study of East Sumatra'. *Indonesia*, 33: 1–30.

Li, T.M. (2000) 'Articulating Indigenous Identity in Indonesia: Resource Politics and the Tribal Slot'. *Comparative Studies in Society and History*, 1: 149–79.

Lucas, A. (1991) *One Soul One Struggle: Region and Revolution in Indonesia*. Sydney: Allen and Unwin.

Mabbett, I. (1985) *Patterns of Kingship and Authority in Traditional Asia*. London: Croom Helm.

Magenda, B. (1991) *East Kalimantan. The Decline of a Commercial Aristocracy*. Ithaca, New York: Cornell University.

Mahy, P. (2005) 'Gateways to Power: Adat and Modernity in Kutai Kartanegara, Indonesia', unpublished honours thesis, Australian National University.

Malley, M. (2003) 'New Rules, Old Structures and the Limits of Democratic Decentralisation' in E. Aspinall and G. Fealy (eds) *Local Power and Politics in Indonesia; Decentralisation and Democratisation*. Singapore: Institute of Southeast Asian Studies, pp. 102–18.

Mietzner, M. (2003) 'Business as Usual? The Indonesian Armed Forces and Local Politics in the Post-Soeharto Era' in E. Aspinall and G. Fealy (eds) *Local Power and Politics in Indonesia; Decentralisation and Democratisation*. Singapore: Institute of Southeast Asian Studies, pp. 245–58.

Milner, A.C. (1982) *Kerajaan: Malay Political Culture on the Eve of Colonial Rule*. Tucson: The University of Arizona Press.

Musson, A. (2005) 'Introduction' in A. Musson (ed.) *Boundaries of the Law. Geography, Gender and Jurisdiction in Medieval and Early Modern Europe*. Hants: Ashgate Publishing Limited, pp. 1–6.

Pompe, S. (2005) *The Indonesian Supreme Court: A Study of Institutional Collapse*. Ithaca: Cornell University.

Ray, D. and Goodpaster, G. (2003) 'Indonesian Decentralisation' in D. Kingsbury and H. Aveling (eds) *Autonomy and Desintegration in Indonesia*. London and New York: RoutledgeCurzon, pp. 75–96.

Rinakit, S. (2005) 'Decentralization and the Military' in M. Erb, P. Sulistiyanto and C. Faucher (eds) *Regionalism in Post-Suharto Indonesia*. London and New York: RoutledgeCurzon, pp. 75–86.

Rohdewold, R. (2003) 'Decentralisation and the Indonesian Bureaucracy: Major Changes, Minor Impact?' in E. Aspinall and G. Fealy (eds) *Local Power and Politics in Indonesia; Decentralisation and Democratisation*. Singapore: Institute of Southeast Asian Studies, pp. 259–74.

Sakai, M. (2003) 'Regional Responses to Resurgence of Adat Movements in Indonesia' in M. Sakai (ed.) *Beyond Jakarta. Regional Autonomy and Local Societies in Indonesia*. Adelaide: Crawford House Publishing, pp. 245–69.

Schiller, A. (2007) 'Activism and Identities in an East Kalimantan Dayak Organization'. *The Journal of Asian Studies*, 66(1): 63–95.

Schulte Nordholt, H. and Klinken, G. van (2007) *Renegotiating Boundaries. Local Politics in Post-Suharto Indonesia*. Leiden: KITLV Press.

Suara Merdeka (2007) 17 April, *56% Asset Indonesia Dikuasai Hanya 1% Penduduk.*

Tempo Interaktif (2006) 12 September, *Gowa jadi Tuan Rumah Festival Keraton 2008.*

Tjondronegoro, S. (1991) 'The Utilization and Management of Land Resources in Indonesia, 1970–1990' in J. Hardjono (ed.) *Indonesia: Resources, Ecology, and Environment*. Oxford and New York: Oxford University Press, pp. 17–35.

Tribun Kaltim (2007) 1 November, *Ikapakarti Kunjungi Sultan Kutai.*

Watson, C.W. (2002) 'The Changing Nature of Elites in Indonesia today' in C. Shore and S. Nugent (eds) *Elite Cultures. Anthropological Perspectives*. London and New York: Routledge, pp. 110–26.

Wilson, I. (2006) 'Continuity and Change: The Changing Contours of Organized Violence in Post-New Order Indonesia'. *Critical Asian Studies*, 38(2): 265–97.

Chapter 6
Contested Spaces of Authority in Indonesia

Franz von Benda-Beckmann and Keebet von Benda-Beckmann

Introduction

The recent spatial turn in the social sciences has also spawned an interest in the relations between law and space.[1] In most studies in the emerging legal anthropological geography of law, spatial metaphors are used that refer to social spaces and boundaries, to fields, rooms or places in which law is made, reproduced, used and sanctioned.[2] These studies have engendered important insights, but they have rarely examined the grounding of social spaces in physical space. They also pay relatively little attention to the legal construction of spaces and the ways in which legal relationships and rights are localized in physical space. Moreover, the complexities arising from the coexistence of legal orders that constitute different and often contradictory legal spaces have been largely neglected. As a consequence, the spatial references are often ambiguous, and interrelationships between social and physical spaces are rarely problematized.[3] As we have argued earlier (Benda-Beckmann and Benda-Beckmann 1991), looking for law in society then remains a bit like a game of blind man's bluff.

We argue that the grounding of social spaces, social relations and institutions, in physical space and the role of law in these processes deserve more attention. We substantiate these more general points by comparing two regions within Indonesia, West Sumatra and the island of Ambon, regions that have particularly well-documented, post-colonial histories. In both regions, important changes occurred in local people's access to productive resources and village citizens' rights. They show some characteristic differences within and between the regions, in the extent to which colonial law has affected categories of economic and political spaces, and in the spatial grounding of social stratification. These differences cannot fully

---

1 See the introduction to this volume for a more comprehensive discussion of the literature. We thank Anja Sing for correcting our English.

2 Examples are: semi-autonomous social fields (Moore 1973); rooms and landscapes (Galanter 1981; 1983); structural places (Santos 1985); and external/internal influences (Kidder 1978).

3 See Benda-Beckmann and Benda-Beckmann (1991); and Benda-Beckmann, F. von (1999; 2001). A prominent example of such ambiguity between field and space is Bourdieu's notion of 'field'. Ultimately, field is no more than a spatial metaphor (Bordieu and Wacquant 1992, 97; and Voell 2004, 78–80).

be explained by differences in traditional social structures and the coexistence of state law and local customary law, in Indonesia referred to as adat or adat law. Rather, we shall argue that the histories of incorporation into the colonial state, settlement policies, as well as the specific ways political and economic rights are localized within villages and the ensuing localized forms of social stratification are critical factors that help explain differences in access to productive resources and village citizens' rights. For both regions, we discuss some of the implications of the competing bodies of law that lead to a quite distinct spatial grounding of property categories and related authority structures. The coexistence of different legal orders, as the Ambonese case tells us, is not confined to the generally discussed coexistence and competition of customary law with state law. It can also concern different versions of customary law.

The examples will also show that attempts of states to eliminate existing customary laws often fail. Old forms of customary law may have a much higher degree of continuity than one might expect from the claims of validity made by state law. As the Ambonese example illustrates, this also goes for the continuity of older and politically weaker versions of adat in coexistence with adat law versions that have been largely standardized and used by the administration and courts of the state. As a consequence, we find complex constellations of legal pluralism with very different ways of constructing space and positioning rights and authority within space. This has important implications for the degree of 'permanence' of places as constructed by different bodies of law (Harvey 1996, 261). This in turn leads to differences in acquiring control over land (Blomley 1994; and Forman 2006). These different spatial constructions as embodied in legal categories and regulation provide sets of resources that become part of the repertoire for 'spatial idiom-shopping' that can be mobilized against each other by a variety of actors in the pursuit of their respective economic and political objectives.[4] To echo Santos' (1987) notion of interlegality, people interact in a context of 'interspatiality'. How individuals operate in such a constellation not only depends on power differentials in general, but also on the specific location of individuals and their rights. As we will show, the location of rights, obligations and authority in physical space may in fact be an important explanatory factor for variation in the working of law and the relationships between different segments of the village population.[5]

4 See Giddens (1979; 1985); and Löw et al. (2007, 63). For illustrations see Orlove (1991); and Benda-Beckmann and Taale (1996). For a particularly vivid illustration from Costa Rica, see Brooijmans (1997).

5 See also Long and Roberts (1984, 4). In Benda-Beckmann and Benda-Beckmann (1998), we have discussed the importance of the socio-spatial localization of the personnel and resources of the state apparatus for understanding regional variation in state-village relationships.

On the basis of these considerations, we discuss two major issues.[6] The first concerns the competition over authority arising from the differential spatial localization of political and economic rights and obligations through different legal orders. The second issue concerns the consequences of the differential grounding of rights and obligations in physical space for social stratification and power relations. We will investigate the rights to land and political authority as they are localized within what is generally glossed over as 'local communities' in order to understand how overlapping legal orders create hierarchies of localities within local communities.

We shall first discuss the complex property system that has developed on the island of Ambon and show some of the tensions and conflicts arising out of the multiple resource spaces and political authority. Then there follows a discussion of the socio-political consequences of variation in settlement patterns for the relationships between the Ambonese population and Butonese immigrants. In the next section, we turn to Minangkabau in West Sumatra where we start with an analysis of what we call the geographies of political authority. We first discuss the Minangkabau property system and how it was affected by incorporation into the Dutch East Indies and by the Indonesian state. We then focus on the resurgence of social differentials that were thought to have all but disappeared, but turned out to re-emerge as an unintended outcome of decentralization policies.[7] In the final section, we shall draw some conclusions about the tensions arising from the varied ways in which space is embodied in legal categories and for the negotiation of property and citizens' rights within a stratified population.

Multiple Resource Spaces and Political Authority on Ambon

The island of Ambon was one of the earliest strongholds of the Dutch colonial empire. The region, known as the Spice Islands, was subject to intense competition among European and regional powers. After the Dutch East India Company (*Vereenigde Oost-Indische Compagnie* VOC) had brought the island under its control in the first half of the seventeenth century, it forced the mountain population to leave their settlements and settle at the coast amid clans that had migrated to the island and had settled at the coast prior to the VOC. It also imposed a new political and economic organization. However, older forms of adat organization have remained politically important up until the present day and exist side by side with, but distinct from, the new organization by the Dutch that was also labelled adat. These two types of adat have produced quite distinct localizations of resource

6 Based on a number of earlier publications, see Benda-Beckmann, F. von (1985; 1999; 2001); and Benda-Beckmann and Benda-Beckmann (1991; 1994a; 1998).

7 For more detailed accounts see Benda-Beckmann and Benda-Beckmann (2006; 2007a; 2007b).

rights and socio-political space.[8] The differences in spatial constructions that gave rise to major conflicts developed within the wider category of adat law.[9]

Prior to their relocation to the coast, the indigenous population, the Alifuru, lived in hamlets in the hills, close to water sources and at places suitable for defence. Their political and social organization was based upon patrilineal clans and clan associations.[10] Their property regime made a fundamental distinction between rights to vegetation and rights to the land on which it grew. Ambonese cultural and legal thought was primarily concerned with vegetation, especially sago palms and other trees, and less with the land in the sense of a demarcated space on the surface of the earth. Consequently, people had no clear 'land rights'. Clans held political control and exploitation rights over large tracts of the uncultivated forest[11] and cultivated tree gardens,[12] and they gradually extended their zone of influence to secure their members' subsistence up to a point where they were met with the expansion of clans from a neighbouring settlement. The zones of influence, and their boundaries, in general were not thought to demarcate division of land but primarily of vegetation used for food and housing; clearly demarcated boundaries between these zones of political and economic influence were rare. Neighbouring villages left a border zone open, which people from both sides could cultivate, and by which they established more specific property rights.

The second basic distinction in property categories was that between wild and cultivated vegetation. Clans or clan associations that politically controlled the area held primary rights to all wild trees, in particular sago, and other vegetation on their territory and this could be used by all its members. With the first cultivation, the cultivator established individual rights to the cultivated vegetation in their garden (*perusa*), while the wild vegetation within the garden remained under control of the clan or clan association. After the death of the original cultivator, these individual rights devolved to the heirs and became inherited property (*pusaka*).

Perusa and *pusaka* were inherently temporary rights. The original cultivators and their heirs kept these rights as long as there were visible signs of cultivation. If all signs of cultivation had disappeared the area was open for new cultivation by other members of the group holding the general rights. Each tree garden (*dusun*) therefore usually contained vegetation at different stages of development.[13]

8 See Benda-Beckmann and Taale (1996); and Benda-Beckmann, F. von (1999).

9 The conflicts between adat and state law conceptualizations of property rights have not been a major source of conflict in this part of Ambon (see Benda-Beckmann, F. von 1999).

10 This section is based on Holleman's (1923, 40) detailed analysis of the original ideas about space and boundaries of these mountain people.

11 Moluccan: *wesi*, Indonesian: *ewang*.

12 Moluccan: *wasi*, Indonesian: *dusun*.

13 See Ellen (1978) for the Nuaulu. See also Taale (1990); and Brouwer (1996). The spatial localization of sago palm property was even more complex due to the characteristics of the reproduction of sago palms, which establish offshoots often in several meters

At the same time, these gardens were regarded as a distinct category of land. Since inheritance followed bilateral patterns, over time people from different clans could acquire rights to the garden as such or to specific trees within a garden. After a few generations, the groups that controlled larger territories, in which these tree gardens were located, no longer coincided with the individuals or groups of heirs having rights to specific gardens or trees.

The Dutch administration brought fundamental changes in the political and legal structures. Instead of the Alifuru clan structure of the hills, the new coastal villages (*negeri*) became the basic spatial and political units for the colonial administration. The Alifuru population lost the privileged position they had had in the mountains, and came under the rule of the coastal clans, who now claimed title to the new position of village head. The Dutch also introduced new notions of territoriality and property rights that were rather different from the original notions of the Ambonese population. The residential areas of the coastal *negeri* became the political and conceptual centres and introduced a new conceptual framework for ecological resource spaces.[14] They introduced clearly defined boundaries between coastal villages, based upon the notion of the village territory (*petuanan*) and cross-cutting older territorial and political divisions. Some clans even came to live in one village while having their land in another village.

Throughout the period of Dutch colonial rule, the government borrowed heavily from what they regarded as adat to shape their political–administrative structure of the *negeri*. Thus, over a period of three and a half centuries of colonial domination they developed, in collaboration with adat law scholars and courts, an official and standardized version of Central Moluccan adat law. According to this, the village territory as a whole is under control of the village government (see Map 6.1). It consists of two major legal categories of land, village land (*tanah negeri*) and clan land (*tanah dati*). Village land includes all the land covered by wild vegetation and falls under the right of avail of the village. The patrilineally structured clan-segments, *dati,* were the basic units for administration, *corvée* labour, and forced clove production. As compensation, the government 'gave' them clan lands for the subsistence needs of their members over which the clan-segment had a right of avail.[15] Upon cultivation, land would obtain the status of inherited land (*tanah pusaka*) for the heirs of the cultivator. Bringing village land under the legitimate control of clan or inherited property groups would render the right of avail latent. The right of avail would only revive should the property group have become extinct. In that case it could be reallocated to other members of the village or the clan. On the basis of this adat law doctrine, the village council today claims the right of avail over *all* uncultivated forests in the higher parts of the village territory.

---

distance. Over time, sago palm stands can invade other people's property spaces (see Benda-Beckmann, F. von 1990a; 1999).

14 See Ohorella (1993, 157).

15 On *dati* see Holleman (1923, 56, 64, 109); and Fraassen (1972, 39).

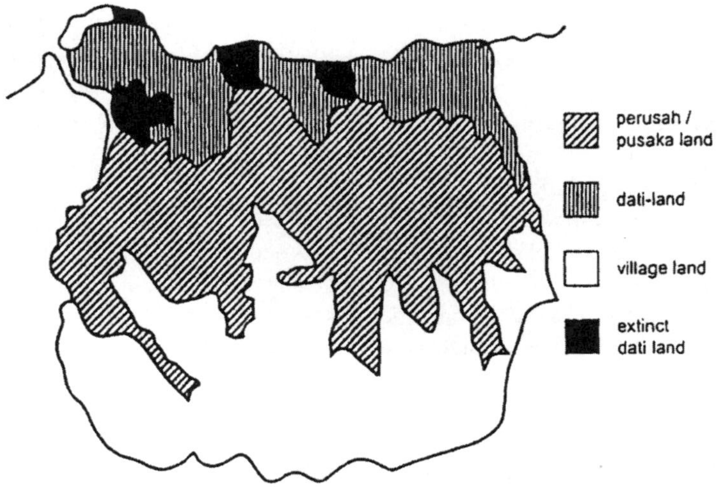

Map 6.1 The legal status of land according to adat law

Source: *Remaking Maluku*, in D. Mearns and Chris Healey (eds). Centre for Southeast Asian Studies, Darwin: Northern Territory University.

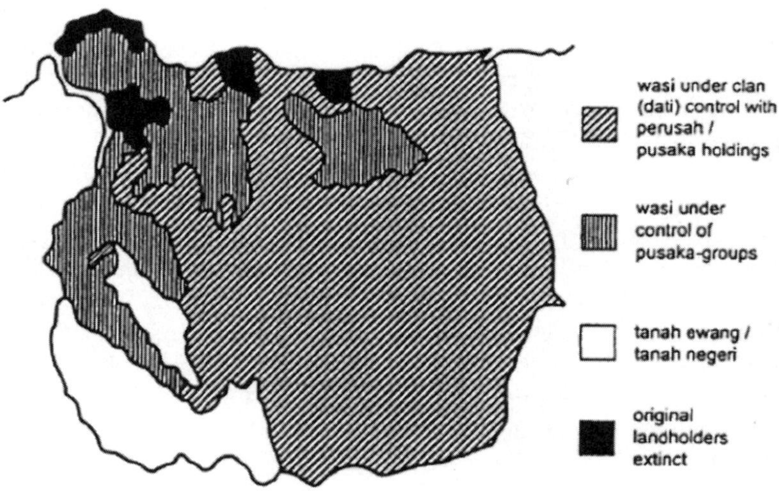

Map 6.2 The legal status of land according to village adat

Source: *Remaking Maluku*, in D. Mearns and Chris Healey (eds). Centre for Southeast Asian Studies, Darwin: Northern Territory University.

Despite the fact that this colonial 'standard' adat law is dominant, it has not entirely suppressed the historically older forms of socio-political control over vegetation and land. The clans originally living in the mountain villages have largely maintained control over their pre-colonial clan land. They base their claims on a version of adat that does not deny the position of village government but severely restricts the size of the territory under control of the village government and the extent of its rights. In this 'pre-colonial'[16] adat version, only uncultivated forest falls under the direct control of the village council. Therefore, only this can have the status of village land under standard adat law. All the other land is tree garden land, either under the control of a clan as clan gardens or as inherited gardens of inherited property groups of variable genealogical depth. Clan land loses its status and acquires the status of inherited property after it has been occupied for more than five generations. As Map 6.2 shows, most tree gardens in the village territory are considered to have the status of inherited property. These basic differences still shape everyday social practices and conflicts in the area. The coexistence of the different versions of adat law gives rise to three major types of conflict.

First, the same resources on the village territory can be defined as village land, clan land or inherited property. Depending on the definition, different groups are entitled to claim socio-political control and allocation rights over the same property. Maps 6.1 and 6.2 show how the different status of land and controlling units were conceived in Hila in the mid-1980s according to standard adat law and pre-colonial adat. A typical conflict would revolve around the question of whether a tree garden is clan land, in which case it would devolve patrilineally, or whether it is inherited property, which devolves bilaterally. The village population and their leaders mobilized the two variants of adat strategically. For example, the village government might claim control over clan land of an extinct clan on the basis of pre-colonial adat while the users would emphasize that the line of heirs was not extinct because the land is inherited property.

Second, the scope of socio-political authority over resources is contested. Standard adat law requires the consent of village government authorities, the village head or the village forester, to open up new tree gardens on village land, but such consent is not required according to pre-colonial adat.

Third, there are additional problems of authority because there is no complete congruence between village membership and holding property rights within the village. Mountain clans kept their original rights to tree gardens when settling in a coastal village, even if the land was assigned to another village. Moreover, given the bilateral inheritance of inherited property, persons often have rights to inherited tree gardens within another village. While the actual use is left largely to relatives in the village in which the land is located, others can assert their rights at any time and this regularly leads to disputes.[17]

16 Pre-colonial is used here in the sense that it refers to that period; not in the sense of being unaffected by later developments. There is, for example, more emphasis on rights to land than previously, see Benda-Beckmann and Benda-Beckmann (1994a; 1994b); and Benda-Beckmann and Taale (1996).

17 On the development in Hila and illustrations of disputes, see Benda-Beckmann and Benda-Beckmann (1994a; 1994b); Benda-Beckmann and Taale (1996); and Benda-Beckmann, F. von (1999).

Thus, political and administrative spaces related to the various categories of land rights introduced in earlier historical periods have lingered on after they have been superseded by new law. And they have continued to be relevant till the present, coexisting, intertwined, and yet distinct. In fact, during the turmoil of 1999, many conflicts resulting from this constellation have been revived (Benda-Beckmann, K. von 2004). The importance of the respective versions of adat law in decision-making processes has varied historically depending on the relative power of their respective protagonists. In matters concerning the village as a whole, the coastal clans were privileged in that they were entitled, with the endorsement of the government, to furnish the village head. The clan council retained a predominantly ritual role for the village as a whole, and here the mountain clans were still important. But the council also retained economic and political control over clan land.

Socio-political Consequences of Differential Localization of People and Rights in Ambonese–Butonese Relationships

The conflicts discussed in the previous section concerned old mountain clans and immigrated clans who had settled before the Dutch and were regarded as part of the Ambonese population. New problems occurred as a consequence of the later waves of immigration from Buton, an island group at the south-eastern tip of Sulawesi, that started at the end of the nineteenth century.[18] Relations between the population groups oscillated between cooperation and contestation. The different versions of adat rights and authority became a relevant factor in the relationships between the Ambonese population and the Butonese. However, the nature and outcomes of conflicts were also shaped by the settlement patterns of Butonese immigrants and the localization of their rights within villages.

The Butonese had come as guest labourers in the clove harvest. In some villages they lived interspersed with the Ambonese population, but in others, such as Hila, they were allocated land at the border of the neighbouring village, far from the Ambonese settlement, where they formed a buffer zone to fend off encroachment from the neighbours. Later groups were settled closer to but still separate from the Ambonese settlement. As Map 6.3 shows, the Butonese settlements form social, political and economic enclaves on the territory of Hila, the hamlet (*kampung*) furthest from the Ambonese village core being the oldest one.

---

18 This section is largely based on Benda-Beckmann, F. von (1990b); Benda-Beckmann and Benda-Beckmann (1991); and Benda-Beckmann and Taale (1992). The situation described here refers to the mid-1980s before the fall of the Suharto regime and before the violent conflict of 2000 put a stop to this immigration, and many have left the island since. See Benda-Beckmann, K. von (2004).

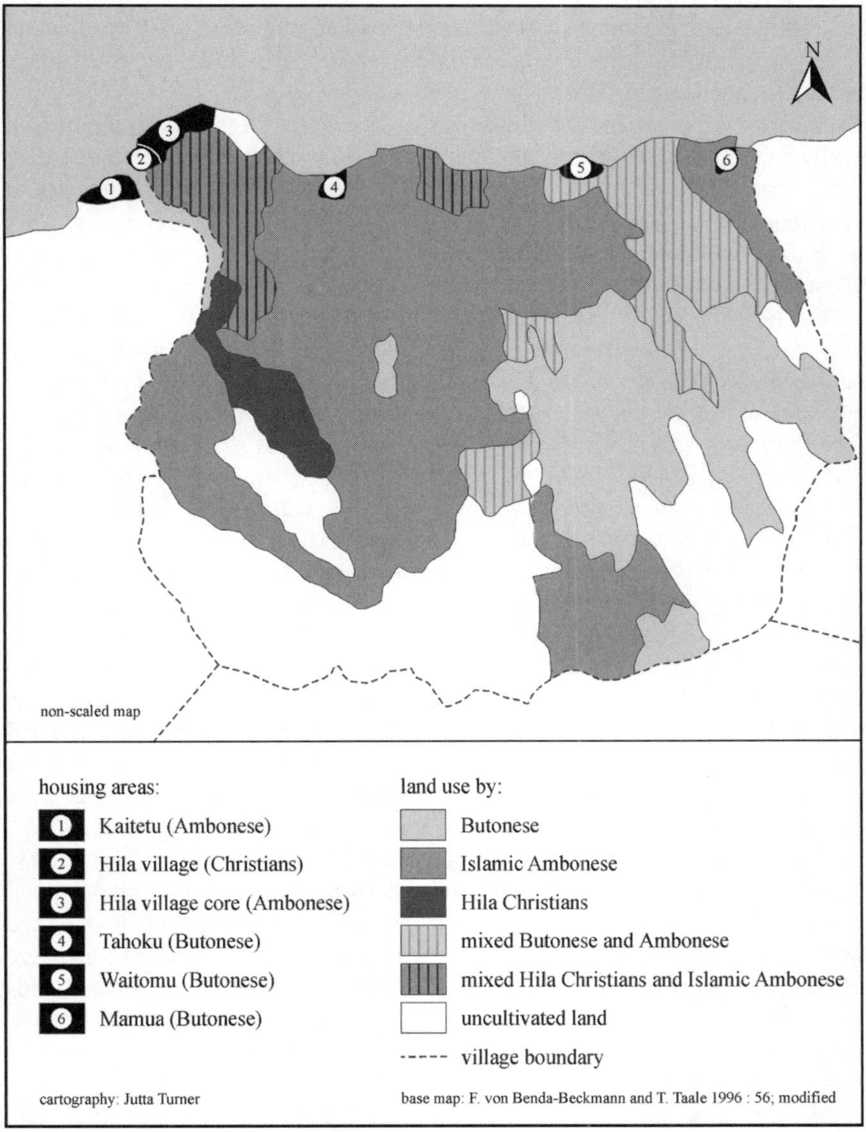

Map 6.3 Housing areas and land use in Hila

Source: *Social Security Between Past and Future*, Franz von Benda-Beckmann. Münster: LIT Verlag.

The first source of conflict concerned citizens' rights and participation in elections of village heads. To regulate their internal affairs, the Butonese have their own hamlet administration. In terms of the local adat constitution, however, they only have limited political and economic rights. This had implications for the election of the village head who is mayor according to state legislation, but adat village head at the same time. While the *Undang-Undang tentant Pemerintahan Desa* (Law of Local Government) Number 5 of 1979 granted all villagers with official residence in the village for a minimum of half a year voting rights for the election of the village head, the Ambonese adat constitution granted such rights only to those incorporated into the system of clans and clan associations. Butonese were not incorporated and therefore were in practice excluded from the village head elections.

The significance of the specific spatial location of people and rights transpires when we compare the relationships between Ambonese and Butonese in Hila with that of villages on Ambon with a different settlement history. In Hila, the political and economic subordination of the Butonese had been maintained well into the late 1980s. Until then, the district officials charged with the supervision of the elections, for instance, did not dare intervene on behalf of the Butonese on the issue of voting rights for the village head. When the voting rights of the Butonese were finally recognized in the 1988 elections, this was due to a political manoeuvre by one of the Ambonese candidates who enrolled the support of the Butonese in order to win the elections. This then led to an en bloc recognition of voting rights of all Butonese in Hila. In the villages of Tulehu and Seith, by contrast, there was no clear-cut spatial segregation of Butonese immigrants in separate hamlets. In these villages, the voting rights of some Butonese people had been recognized much earlier. However, voting rights were not granted en bloc but to individual Butonese who 'behaved like an Ambonese'.[19] And Butonese who were recognized as behaving as an Ambonese were also allowed durable property rights to trees and houses, which Hila had long resisted against.

The Butonese were also largely subject to the Ambonese adat property rights regime that did not allow them to cultivate permanent crops, and prohibited them from planting clove and nutmeg trees. This prohibition gradually dissolved in the 1960s when a clove and nutmeg boom started, and many new plantations were opened up on uncultivated land, mainly with Butonese labour. They planted trees on Ambonese land under the agreement that the plantation would be partitioned when the trees would start producing, after approximately six years. The economic boom rendered uncultivated land economically important and the legal status of the land, on which lucrative trees were planted, became a source of intense conflict. Most new plantations were located in the border area between Hila and its neighbouring village with which Hila had been engaged in many disputes about rights to land and trees. New cultivation is only allowed with the consent of the 'lords of the land', and here the distinction between pre-colonial adat and standard adat and their different localizations of rights discussed earlier re-emerged. Thus, the Butonese who planted new trees were usually confronted with a host of conflicting claims: of different sets of inherited property groups, of clan and

19 Ohorella (personal communication) and (1993). See also Hospes (1996).

village heads, both of Hila and of the neighbouring village. According to standard adat, the village head was the highest authority to give permission for cultivation, but according to pre-colonial adat, it is the heads of the mountain clans on whose territory the new plantations are located. The Butonese quickly learned to turn the ensuing uncertainties to their advantage. They would typically express readiness to split up the clove trees or the clove harvest with the rightful owners, but demand that the question to whom the land or the trees belong be sorted out first, knowing that this would take much time. Until then they would keep the trees for themselves. During the 1980s, Butonese also started to invoke state law to escape from the subordinate position under Ambonese adat law and turned to the village government for permission to cultivate gardens and plant more permanent crops. The village government profited from these arrangements because of the fees they received for these licences and because they could bind an important electorate.

Geographies of Political Authority in Minangkabau

While the major historical fault line that created two sets of adat with quite distinct ways of localizing authority and property rights occurred in Ambon in the seventeenth century, major spatial differentiations in West Sumatra, the homeland of the Minangkabau, occurred only in the late twentieth century. The major differences in localization of rights did not occur within the realm of adat but between adat and state law. When the Dutch incorporated Minangkabau into the colonial state in the early nineteenth century, the political organization of the Minangkabau in their *nagari*, village or village republic, had been well established and the Dutch did not deem it necessary to resettle the population as they had done on Ambon. Instead, they built their administration more or less on the existing territorial political organizations. While colonial administrators and judges also reinterpreted adat concepts of property considerably, the *localization* of these rights was not fundamentally different from the adat territorial units. This changed when the Indonesian government introduced a uniform administration to village administration in 1983. This created a misfit in the geographies of local authority that seriously undermined adat authority. When the government reverted to the *nagari* organization in 2000, the reunification processes engendered new political struggles that were largely shaped by the spatial location of political and economic rights in the *nagari*.

Adat rules of local authority reflect a layered system of matrilineal kin groups and residence, according to which various rights and obligations are anchored in localities of different size nested within the village territory (Benda-Beckmann and Benda-Beckmann 1978). A person's social and legal persona is located where his or her matrilineage is located, but what the relevant locality is depends on the kind of rights. For one's highest political rights, the relevant locality is the territory of the *nagari*, the traditional village, made up of its constituting matrilineages. These political rights entail the right to be represented in the village council and the right to participate in the commons located within the village territory. Each lineage has a male representative who has the authority to manage disputes and who represents the lineage at the higher levels of authority: the clan, the neighbourhood and, the village. However, a person's economic rights and obligations, and some of the lower level political rights, are located in that part of the village, where the original core of the lineage property and the lineage house are located. Post-marital residence is uxorilocal.[20] Women are born and continue to live on the property of their lineage, while men move into the house of their wives. Most lineage property is located in the sector of the village where the lineage is located according to adat, but lineages may also have property in other parts of the village, for example, where ancestors brought new land under cultivation. Married men usually work on the lineage property of their wives, which falls under the control of their wife and her matrilineal relatives. Husbands are respected in the house of their wives, but they have no economic or political rights in decision-making processes in their wives' lineage. Their political rights and rights to inherited property are located in the part of the village where their lineage is localized. Nowadays, some married couples live neo-locally and many work on rented, pawned or bought land, which is considered the joint property of the couple. This does not change their residence rights in adat terms and the house is considered the house of the wife.

The colonial and Indonesian state adopted the *nagari* as the basis for local government. Initially, land taxation followed the matrilineal structure for land taxes, which was collected from the matrilineages and paid by the lineage head. However, the state administration focused more and more on the actual residence of people. For census, house taxes and voters' registration, married men were counted where they lived, in the house of their wives, on the lineage land of their wives. This shift complicated the differential social, economic and political residence within the *nagari*, but it did not really undermine the adat authority structure. Marital residence, property holding and decision-making authority were regulated by the parallel normative orders of adat and state government within the same political unit pertaining to the same territory, the *nagari*. The state recognized this double structure and provided for participation of adat authorities within village government.

This changed in 1983 when the government introduced in West Sumatra the nationwide local government reform of 1979. For various reasons, the provincial government decided to divide the *nagari* into several much smaller *desa* villages.[21] These *desa* were purely state administrative units without any adat participation in the village government organization. In their attempt to create as many *desa* as possible, village wards were converted into *desa*. Over time, several of the

20 The *nagari* used to be strictly endogamous until the endogamy rule was abolished for men in 1950 and for women in 1954. But in the mid-1970s, endogamy still was the statistical rule (95.2 per cent for men and 93.6 per cent for women. See Benda-Beckmann, F. von (1979, 102).

21 On the process of decentralization and reorganization of village government in West Sumatra, see Benda-Beckmann and Benda-Beckmann (2001; 2007a; 2007b).

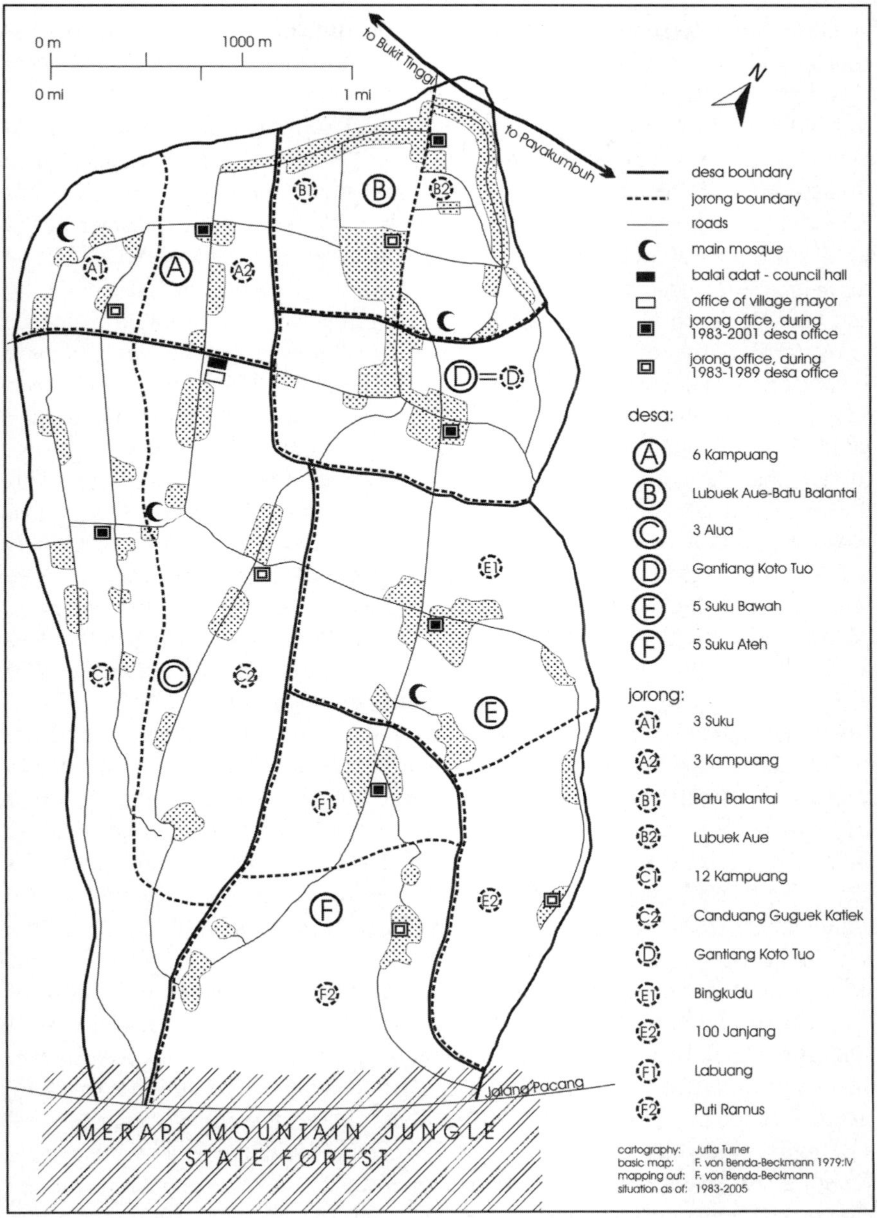

Map 6.4 ***Nagari* Candung Kota Lawas**

Note: The map is also reproduced in *Decentralisation and Regional Autonomy in Indonesia* (2008), by C.J.G. Holtzappel and M. Ramstedt (eds). Singapore: Iseas.

smallest wards were combined into more effective units. For example, *Nagari* Candung Kota Lawas, where we have done research since the mid-1970s, was first divided into 11 *desa*, which later were recombined into six (see Map 6.4).

The multiplication of villages intended to boost the provincial fiscal basis turned out to produce problematic side effects because it created a misfit in the geography of authority of the *desa* administration and the *nagari*. Authority relations according to adat still played a role, certainly in the day to day management of land, kinship affairs, ceremonies and disputing processes. The unifying force of the *nagari* organization had lost most of its strength because its adat authority had been detached from state authority. *Desa* authority was based on residence in the territorially defined *desa*. It was strictly administrative and was no longer supported by adat structures. Moreover, the adat authority of adat functionaries and their economic and administrative residence were now frequently located within two different *desa*. Three *desa* heads in the *Nagari* Candung Kota Lawas, for example, did not originate from the *desa* in which they were *desa* heads. This did not affect their administrative tasks so much, but their relations with adat authorities within the *desa* were uneasy. Day to day economic and property affairs had to be managed by adat authorities at the level of the lineage whose lineage property was located within the *desa*. A *desa* head 'coming from a different *desa*' would not be readily involved. The result was that in case of disputes, the *desa* head would be close by, but he might not have the adat authority required to deal with the dispute, while the relevant adat authority might live in a different *desa*. Under the *nagari* structure, the links between the two lines of authority had been problematic and controversial, yet they had to some extent supported each other. In the *desa* structure, these links had been severed because the spatial organization of authority of *desa* heads and adat leaders 'did not belong together'. Adat authority suffered most, and many positions of adat functionaries had become vacant for lack of interest. Village government had turned into the lowest extension of a highly centralized state administration and its authority was hardly rooted within the village itself.

The most recent local government reform that started after the demise of the Suharto regime in 1998, largely redressed this severance of adat and state authority. The province of West Sumatra returned to the *nagari* as the lowest level of state government within their old territorial boundaries (Benda-Beckmann and Benda-Beckmann 2006; 2007a; 2007b). Once again, state village authority and adat authority are linked. The scaling up that occurred with the return to the *nagari* structure presents us with a paradox. The *desa* was close to the population but the village government was exclusively focused on the higher levels of administration. The larger *nagari* territory has made village government more remote from its population, but the village government is now forced to pay more attention to village internal matters and the needs of its population. In order to generate their own revenues, it has to negotiate access to property on its territory with adat leaders who also claim authority.

Adat authority also shows some paradoxical features. Many lineages and clans have filled vacant adat offices, but many of the new adat leaders live and work outside the village and have very limited knowledge of village life and adat. They are elected because of their good connections in the urban centres, and villagers expect them to mediate in services from the government. These new adat authorities affirm their localization within the village by frequent visits, participation in decision-making, either in person or by mobile phone. They also have to watch closely over the property rights of their lineage or clan and defend these if necessary against claims by the village government. Thus, with the renewed geographical fit between adat and state authority, adat authority has expanded its scope within and beyond the village, while the village government has expanded into village internal matters. Village government and adat authority compete in both village external connections, through which services for the village are mediated, and village internal property affairs. Here the differences in spatialization of authority between adat and state law give rise to conflicts.

Space and the Resurgence of Social Differentials

In most *nagari*, this reunification of *desa* into *nagari* went relatively smoothly, but in some this was accompanied by enduring and violent conflicts, especially in villages with sizable populations of 'newcomers', that is Minangkabau who had settled later in the village, descendants of former slaves and a few Javanese transmigrant communities (see Benda-Beckmann and Benda-Beckmann 2007a; 2007b). According to adat, they had a lower status than the old settler lineages. But the way this worked out depended on the specific location of these people within the village.

Political, social and economic incorporation into a *nagari* was based on the matrilineal structure. Persons who wished to settle on the territory of an existing *nagari* had to become part of one of the lineages. If their clan was represented within that *nagari*, the migrants would be incorporated into a matrilineage of that clan; otherwise they would become part of a (putatively) related clan. The patron lineage or the village authorities would assign them a place to live and land to cultivate. From then on the new citizens would stand in a patron–client relationship with those who had given them land. After slavery was abolished in the 1860s, former slaves were incorporated into *nagari*, but their descendants remained dependent on their original masters and had an even more pronounced inferior social and political status within the village than other newcomers. While the descendants of the lineages who originally founded the *nagari* usually live in the village centre and had the best areas of irrigated rice land, newcomers, descendants of former slaves and transmigrants were often given land in the more marginal and remote areas of the village, such as the slopes higher up the mountains or in border zones with neighbouring *nagari*. In the course of time some of these settlements developed into more or less separate wards. While the history of incorporation may go back as far as 250 years, none of these 'newcomers' are full citizens in the adat sense, and they do not enjoy full political and economic rights. The territory on which they live is usually part of founding lineages' or clans' inherited property, which has been 'given' to them under adat terms. While this property has the status of inherited property for the newcomers, it remains under some residual rights of control of the original holders and the rights of the original lineages have to be recognized by the newcomers. Their property and political rights within these wards are relatively strong because of their separate location, but their political rights pertaining to the village as a whole are weak. For these, the newcomers depend on their patron lineages and their respective heads.

Under the *desa* structure, these more separate wards of newcomers often became independent *desa* and the ties of patronage lost meaning. The founding lineages had regarded the *desa* system as an infringement on their rights, but since adat had lost much of its political clout anyway, the issue was not further pursued.[22] With the return to the *nagari* and the ensuing rise of adat authority and interest in village resources, the old status differences re-emerged. The 'newcomers' resented this, but they responded differently. The Javanese, though located in separate wards, willingly adjusted to the new village structure in order not to stir ethnic resentment. Minangkabau newcomers living together in a relatively separate space reacted most forcefully. Suspicious of the revival of adat authority and fearing the potential loss of their independence, they lobbied with the state administration for the establishment of their own *nagari*. Those living interspersed with the original settlers could not use the separate location to establish their own independent village.

Thus, the persons of lower adat status that were least integrated had the weakest political rights at the *nagari* level, but their economic and political rights within their wards and clans were relatively strong as a result of the separate location. By contrast, those living interspersed with the founding lineages were better integrated and suffered less from inferior political rights at the *nagari* level. But their political rights within the wards, clans and lineages were in effect weaker than those living in separate wards.

Conclusions

Categorizations entailed in political, kinship and property regimes have important implications for the way in which law attaches authority to legally defined spaces. This is in particular the case where positions of authority over people and resources, and relations towards these authorities, are legally constructed by different legal orders. Since these constructions embody social, economic,

22 In several villages such attempts to gain independence go back more than a century and the history is riddled with violence. See Adatrechtbundel (1913, 74); Benda-Beckmann, F. von (1979, 259); and Benda-Beckmann and Benda-Beckmann (2001; 2007a; 2007b).

political interests and, status and power differences, they are a source of potential conflicts once confronted with alternative definitions of space and localizations of rights. Many of the current conflicts over property and local authority have roots in pre-colonial legal constructions of rights and authority introduced by the colonial state. The two examples presented in this chapter show that the time of incorporation and the settlement policies of the colonial power were important factors for the construction of space and the associated authority within adat. In Ambon, incorporation occurred very early in colonial history and was accompanied by a displacement and resettlement of the original population. Radical changes in adat introduced by the colonial state were over time appropriated by the Ambonese population as the dominant valid forms of adat, without, however, fully relinquishing older versions of adat. Minangkabau settlement patterns were hardly affected by colonial incorporation that took place at a much later stage, and the Minangkabau did not develop two clearly distinct bodies of adat law, each with their own characteristic constructions of space. Both in West Sumatra and Ambon, older legal categorizations of space have lingered on and retained some of their political and economic force despite attempts of governments to replace them. Over time, they came to coexist with later adat versions and with those of the state legal system itself. These form a legal repository that may remain dormant but which in times of rapid economic or political change, such as the incorporation into the colonial state, an economic boom or a decentralization policy, may be revitalized and used as a resource in political and economic struggles. Since the economically most important legal categories of space often do not coincide but tend to cross-cut and overlap, this gives rise to conflict and uncertainty, and for some the possibility for negotiation.

We have also seen that the localization of a population has important consequences for the ways in which economic and political rights can be negotiated. Both the Ambon and the Minangkabau examples have shown that adat norms of village citizenship continue to exist side by side with state norms. In both regions, adat laws distinguish between original settlers and newcomers who are assigned a lower status with less political and economic rights. The examples have also shown that a population of lower status operates quite differently and shapes its relations with the dominant and higher positioned population differently, depending on whether they live interspersed with the higher status population or whether they live in separate locations. These examples illustrate how important it is to look at rights and other social relationships as located in space, and that the spatial localization of political and economic rights is an important factor in explaining village internal relationships and responses to state policies of village organization. Such a geography of political and economic rights thus provides additional insights that cannot be derived from general statements about the validity of law, whether this is adat or state law, nor from an analysis in terms of social categories and networks or semi-autonomous social fields. Our analysis suggests that too strong a focus on metaphorical references to space conceals the importance of a geography of law that focuses on space in a more literal way. This implies close attention to legal constructions of space in the physical environment and to the spatial–temporal permanence of political and legal places, however fluid and temporary their boundaries may be.

References

Adatrechtbundel XI (1913) 's-Gravenhage, Martinus Nijhoff.

Benda-Beckmann, F. von (1979) *Property in Social Continuity: Continuity and Change in the Maintenance of Property Relationships through Time in Minangkabau, West Sumatra*. The Hague: Martinus Nijhoff.

Benda-Beckmann, F. von (1985) 'Some Comparative Generalizations about the Differential Use of State and Folk Institutions of Dispute Settlement' in A. Allott and G.R. Woodman (eds) *People's Law and State Law: The Bellagio Papers*. Dordrecht: Foris, pp. 187–205.

Benda-Beckmann, F. von (1990a) 'Sago, Law and Food Security on Ambon' in J.I. Bakker (ed.) *The World Food Crisis: Food Security in Comparative Perspective*. Toronto: Canadian Scholars' Press, pp. 157–99.

Benda-Beckmann, F. von (1990b) 'Ambonese Adat as Jurisprudence of Insurgence and Oppression'. *Law and Anthropology*, 5: 25–42.

Benda-Beckmann, F. von (1999) 'Multiple Legal Constructions of Socio-economic Spaces: Resource Management and Conflict in the Central Moluccas' in M. Roesler and T. Wendl (eds) *Frontiers and Borderlands: Anthropological Perspectives*. Frankfurt, Berlin, Bern, New York, Wien: Lang, pp. 131–58.

Benda-Beckmann, F. von (2001) 'On the Reproduction of Law: Micro and Macro in the Time-Space Geography of Law' in W. Fikentscher (ed.) *Begegnung und Konflikt – Eine kulturanthropologische Bestandsaufnahme*. München: C.H. Beck Verlag, pp. 119–31.

Benda-Beckmann, F. von and Benda-Beckmann, K. von (1978) 'Residence in a Minangkabau Nagari'. *Indonesia Circle*, 15: 6–17.

Benda-Beckmann, F. von and Benda-Beckmann, K. von (1991) 'Law in Society: From Blindman's-buff to Multilocal Law'. *Living Law in the Low Countries*, Special Issue of *Recht der Werkelijkheid*. Amsterdam: Vuga, pp. 119–39.

Benda-Beckmann, F. von and Benda-Beckmann, K. von (1994a) 'Property, Politics and Conflict: Ambon and Minangkabau Compared'. *Law and Society Review*, 28: 589–607.

Benda-Beckmann, F. von and Benda-Beckmann, K. von (1994b) 'Texts in Context: Historical Documents as Political Commodity on Islamic Ambon' in W. Marschall (ed.) *Texts from the Islands: Oral and Written Traditions of Indonesia and the Malay World*. Bern: Ethnologica Bernensia 4/1994, pp. 223–43.

Benda-Beckmann, F. von and Benda-Beckmann, K. von (1998) 'Where Structures Merge: State and Off-state Involvement in Rural Social Security on Ambon, Indonesia' in S. Pannell and F. von Benda-Beckmann (eds) *Old World Places,*

New World Problems: Exploring Resource Management Issues in Eastern Indonesia. Canberra: The Australian National University, Centre for Resource and Environmental Studies, pp. 143–80.

Benda-Beckmann, F. von and Benda-Beckmann, K. von (2001) 'Actualising History for Binding the Future: Decentralization in Minangkabau' in P. Hebinck and G. Verschoor (eds) *Resonances and Dissonances in Development: Actors, Networks and Cultural Repertoires*. Assen: Van Gorcum, pp. 33–47.

Benda-Beckmann, F. von and Benda-Beckmann, K. von (2006) 'Changing One is Changing All: Dynamics in the Adat–Islam–State Triangle' in F. von Benda-Beckmann and K. von Benda-Beckmann (eds) *Dynamics of Plural Legal Orders. Special Double Issue of the Journal of Legal Pluralism and Unofficial Law Nrs. 53–54/2006*. Berlin: Lit, pp. 239–70.

Benda-Beckmann, F. von and Benda-Beckmann, K. von (2007a) 'Between Global Forces and Local Politics: Decentralization and Reorganization of Village Government in Indonesia' in C. Antons and V. Gessner (eds) *Globalization and Resistance: Law Reform in Asia since the Crisis*. Oxford-Portland: Hart, pp. 141–68.

Benda-Beckmann, F. von and Benda-Beckmann, K. von (2007b) 'Ambivalent Identities: Decentralization and Minangkabau Political Communities' in G. van Klinken and H. Schulte Nordholt (eds) *Renegotiating Boundaries. Local Politics in Post Suharto Indonesia*. Leiden: KITLV Press, pp. 417–42.

Benda-Beckmann, F. von and Taale, T. (1992) 'The Changing Laws of Hospitality: Guest Labourers in the Political Economy of Rural Legal Pluralism' in F. von Benda-Beckmann and M. van der Velde (eds) *Law as a Resource in Agrarian Struggles*. Wageningse Sociologische Studies 33. Wageningen: Landbouwuniversiteit, pp. 61–87.

Benda-Beckmann, F. von and Taale, T. (1996) 'Land, Trees and Houses: Changing (Un)certainties in Property Relationships on Ambon' in D. Mearns and C. Healy (eds) *Remaking Maluku: Social Transformation in Eastern Indonesia*. Darwin: Centre for Southeast Asian Studies, NT University. Special Monograph no. 1, 1996, pp. 39–63.

Benda-Beckmann, K. von (2004) 'Law, Violence and Peace Making on the Island of Ambon' in M.-C. Foblets and T. von Trotha (eds) *Healing the Wounds. Essays on the Reconstruction of Societies after War*. Oxford and Portland Oregon: Hart Publishing, pp. 221–39.

Blomley, N.K. (1994) *Law, Space, and the Geographies of Power*. New York: Guilford.

Bourdieu, P. and Wacquant, L.J.D. (1992) *An Invitation to Reflexive Sociology*. Cambridge: Polity Press.

Brooijmans, W. (1997) 'The Plains of Tortuguero: Tropical Paradise or Paradise Lost?' in F. von Benda-Beckmann, K. von Benda-Beckmann and A. Hoekema (eds) *Natural Resources, Environment and Legal Pluralism*. Special Issue of *Law and Anthropology* 9, pp. 258–301.

Brouwer, A.R. (1996) 'Sustainability and Social Security in Central Moluccan Resource Management' in D. Mearns and C. Healey (eds) *Remaking Maluku: Social Transformation in Eastern Indonesia*. Special Monograph no. 1. Darwin: Centre for Southeast Asian Studies, pp. 64–79.

Ellen, R.F. (1978) *Nuaulu Settlement and Ecology: An Approach to the Environmental Relations of an Eastern Indonesian Community*. Verhandelingen KITLV no. 83. The Hague: Martinus Nijhoff.

Forman, G. (2006) 'Law and the Historical Geography of the Galilee: Israel's Litigatory Advantages during the Special Operation of Land Settlement'. *Journal of Historical Geography*, 32: 796–817.

Fraassen, C.F. Van (1972) Ambon-Rapport, Doktoraalskriptie, Stichting W.S.O., Werkgroep Studiereizen Ontwikkelingslanden.

Galanter, M. (1981) 'Justice in Many Rooms'. *Journal of Legal Pluralism*, 19: 1–47.

Galanter, M. (1983) *Reading the Landscape of Disputes: What We Know and Don't Know (and Think We Know) about our Allegedly Litigious Society*. Wisconsin: Institute of Legal Studies, University of Wisconsin.

Giddens, A. (1979) *Central Problems in Social Theory*. London: Macmillan.

Giddens, A. (1985) 'Time, Space and Regionalization' in D. Gregory and J. Urry (eds) *Social Relations and Spatial Structures*. London: Macmillan, pp. 265–95.

Harvey, D. (1996) *Justice, Nature and the Geography of Difference*. Oxford: Blackwell Publishers.

Holleman, F.D. (1923) *Het Adat-grondenrecht van Ambon en de Oeliasers*. Delft: Molukken Instituut.

Hospes, O. (1996) *People that Count. Changing Savings and Credit Practices in Ambon, Indonesia*. Amsterdam: Thesis Publishers.

Kidder, R.L. (1978) 'Western Law in India. External Law and Local Response' in H.M. Johnson (ed.) *Social System and Legal Process*. San Francisco: Jossey-Bass, pp. 155–80.

Long, N. and Roberts, B. (1984) *Miners, Peasants and Entrepreneurs: Regional Development in the Central Highlands of Peru*. Cambridge: Cambridge University Press.

Löw, M., Steets, S. and Stoetzer, S. (2007) *Einführung in die Stadt- und Raumsoziologie*. Opladen und Farmington Hills: Uni-Taschenbücher Verlag.

Moore, S.F. (1973) 'Law and Social Change: The Semi-autonomous Social Field as an Appropriate Subject of Study'. *Law and Society Review*, 7: 719–46.

Ohorella, M.G. (1993) *Hukum adat mengenai tanah dan air die pulau Ambon dan sumbangannya terhadap pembangunan hukum agraria nasional (UUPA) dan undang-undang lainnya*. Universitas Hasanuddin, Ujung Pandang. PhD dissertation.

Orlove, B.S. (1991) 'Mapping Reeds and Reading Maps: The Politics of Representation in Lake Titicaca'. *American Ethnologist*, 18(1): 3–38.

Santos, B. de Sousa (1985) 'On Modes of Production of Law and Social Power'. *International Journal of the Sociology of Law*, 13: 299–336.

Santos, B. de Sousa (1987) 'Law. A Map of Misreading: Toward a Post-modern Conception of Law'. *Journal of Law and Society*, 14: 279–302.

Taale, T. (1990) 'Looking for a Livelihood in Hila: Continuity and Change in Land Use and its Implications for Social Security in an Ambonese Village', Unpublished Masters Thesis.

Voell, S. (2004) *Das nordalbanische Gewohnheitsrecht und seine mündliche Dimension*. Bamberg: Curupira.

Chapter 7
The New Global Legal Order as Local Phenomenon: The Special Court for Sierra Leone

Gerhard Anders

> The recent establishment of international criminal tribunals … has given an impetus to the evolution of a body of international criminal law proper and we can now look forward to the formation of a fully-fledged body of law in this area.
>
> (Antonio Cassese 2003, 724)

International law derives its authority from its superior position vis-à-vis the nation state. In textbooks on international law it is common to represent the domestic legal order of the nation states at a lower level than the international legal order, which encompasses the various national legal orders. This notion of a hierarchical relationship between the global and the national is at the core of legal and political science approaches to international law, arguably best exemplified by Kelsen's (1934) theory of law. It also informs representations of the quickly expanding field of international criminal law which invariably place the international war crimes tribunals in The Hague and Arusha above national courts. This verticality is crucial to the legitimacy of these tribunals. They are promoted as impartial adjudicators of large-scale human rights violations and war crimes committed in regions where courts are either not functioning or deeply compromised by particularistic interests.

The image of international criminal law as universal and far removed from the entanglements of national politics is also reinforced by television broadcasts of trials against Milosevic, Lubanga Dyilo or Taylor. Customarily they take place in sterile high-tech courtrooms that remind one of nondescript conference rooms to be found in multifunctional office buildings all around the world. Because of their anonymity these courtrooms evoke associations with Augé's (1995) 'non-places', airport lounges and shopping malls. Such a representation of international criminal justice, however, would be oblivious to the fact that the international criminal tribunals constitute places with their own myths of origin, internal order and social relationships. The nondescript courtrooms in The Hague and elsewhere are merely a façade designed to project an image of international criminal justice as being aloof and universal, without being rooted in particular places or environments.

This chapter collapses the common juxtaposition of local place and global space by drawing on ethnographic evidence gathered at the Special Court for Sierra Leone. It argues that, in spite of its apparent universality and remoteness from local concerns, international criminal justice, as global legal order in general, is made and instantiated in particular places ranging from boardrooms in New York and Washington to the tribunals in The Hague, Arusha and Freetown. This angle owes much to recent legal anthropological scholarship on the global–local nexus transcending the binary opposition between the global human rights discourse and its local production and appropriation (Wilson 1997; Merry 2001; 2005; and Goodale 2006). Merry (2001, 129), for example, argues that 'the global is itself constituted by various locals'. In these sites individuals and groups participate in the production and reproduction of ideas about international justice by pursuing their careers and designs. Abstract ideas, as Dezalay and Garth (1996, 3) point out in their study of transnational commercial arbitration, are 'closely tied to the activities of individuals and groups, who thereby give concrete meaning to the abstraction'. Hence, this chapter presents an ethnography of one of the places where a new global legal order is in the making.

The Special Court for Sierra Leone is an ad hoc international war crimes tribunal seated in Freetown. Three trials have been conducted in Freetown and one against Charles Taylor, the most notorious of the accused, in The Hague. Unlike the other tribunals the Special Court is a so-called hybrid tribunal established by the United Nations on request of the government of Sierra Leone.[1] It is funded through voluntary contributions of a number of governments and its mandate is limited to those 'bearing greatest responsibility' for war crimes and crimes against humanity committed during Sierra Leone's civil war. The Special Court was explicitly set up as an alternative to the International Criminal Tribunal for the Former Yugoslavia (ICTY) in The Hague and the International Criminal Tribunal for Rwanda (ICTR) in Arusha which were perceived as being too slow, too expensive and too far removed from the people in whose name justice was being sought. The Special Court was promoted by its proponents as 'mean and lean' alternative, distributing justice expeditiously as one of the employees of the Office of the Prosecutor (OTP) pointed out to me. From the outset the Special Court has been the site of national contests and debates although legally it is not part of the national polity and the domestic legal system.

---

1 The court is referred to as a hybrid because the government nominates a minority of the judges and the deputy chief prosecutor while the Secretary General of the UN appoints the other judges, the chief prosecutor and the registrar. The Special Court applies both international humanitarian law and domestic criminal law. In spite of its hybrid character it is an international criminal tribunal outside or rather above the national justice system. See the decision on preliminary motion on lack of jurisdiction – illegal delegation of jurisdiction by Sierra Leone by the appeals chamber (SCSL-04-14-PT-102, 25 May 2004). See also the Sierra Leone Supreme Court decision on the validity of the Special Court for Sierra Leone on 14 October 2005, which confirmed the international character and constitutionality of the Special Court.

But what is the relevance of the spatial dimension of international criminal justice? Why does place matter? To approach international criminal justice from below, from the places where it is being made and from where it is disseminated, enables us to transcend the Manichean dualism that informs both proponents and critics of international war crimes tribunals. The former, mostly international jurists, imagine a world of threatening chaos and factional strife that can only be overcome by the establishment of a cosmopolitan legal order limiting the sovereignty of the nation state and guaranteeing the rights of the individual. In order to achieve this global order the proponents of international criminal justice call for an end to impunity of heads of states and warlords who misuse their authority and commit war crimes and crimes against humanity. They hail the international war crimes tribunals as milestones in the development of universal legal order in the tradition of Kant's eternal peace (Robertson 2002; and Cassese 2003).

The critics, on the other hand, denounce them as sophisticated show trials, primarily serving the West's political agenda. They see international criminal justice as merely one of a whole bundle of interventions ranging from humanitarian to developmental, aimed at pacifying volatile regions. Their assessment of international war crimes tribunals and humanitarian interventions in general is diametrically opposed to the idealistic view. Instead of a global legal order they see the advent of a military–humanitarian apparatus which serves 'to link transnational forms of domination over local political practices' as, for example, Pandolfi (2003, 369) argues. She interprets the 'humanitarian–military complex' as quasi-colonial regime and global industry that has 'eliminated the other social partners involved in the conflict from the game' (Pandolfi 2003, 381). Drawing on Foucault, Kelsall (2004) makes a similar argument in his study of the Special Court for Sierra Leone. He argues that interventions by 'the machinery of international criminal justice' is 'part of a larger developmental complex that de-politicizes new political formations rendering them amenable to technical solutions' (2004, 8). Pandolfi's and Kelsall's view echoes a by now well-established fundamental critique of development discourse in general (Ferguson 1994; and Escobar 1995).

Pandolfi and Kelsall are certainly right in highlighting a trend towards bureaucratization of humanitarian interventions. Their observations regarding the convergence of military and development interests are also confirmed by recent studies on the topic (Duffield 2001; and Abrahamsen and Williams 2007). Their representation is nevertheless flawed: they succumb to the same dichotomization as the proponents of the global order they criticize. Whereas the latter identify global legal order superseding national jurisdictions as the only remedy against leaders who spread chaos and violence, Pandolfi and other critics imagine a monolithic and all powerful global apparatus resembling in many ways a colonial regime that legitimizes its interventions with lofty rhetoric and disregards local concerns and needs. Both positions, however, fail to appreciate the local production of global discourses such as humanitarianism or international justice. Proponents of global justice are not able to account for forces that shape these war crimes tribunals and the environment affecting them in often subtle and unforeseen ways. Critics, on the other hand, fail to see the often precarious and contested position of these institutions that bear little resemblance to the efficacious and monolithic machines as they are represented. Furthermore, critics such as Pandolfi do not explain the general reluctance of the 'international community' to intervene in crisis regions like Darfur and Rwanda. While she conducted research in the Balkans, where a large-scale humanitarian intervention took place, there was only a little effort to intervene in the civil wars in Sierra Leone and Liberia that had raged since the early 1990s.

This chapter aims at elucidating the concrete processes influencing the field of international criminal justice and maps the local conditions and the external influences that have impinged upon the Special Court for Sierra Leone and the trials being heard there. This does not imply that justice is being compromised by political pressure; the aim is rather to contribute to a more nuanced understanding of the forces that shape the field of international criminal justice (Hagan 2003; Hagan et al. 2006; and Anders 2007). The first section of this chapter will deal with the symbolism of the physical presence of the Special Court. The second one provides a summary of the trials. The third and the last section sketch the court's international environment and the influence of the domestic political landscape.

The Arrival of International Criminal Justice in Freetown

Looking down on the city centre of Freetown from the surrounding hills one cannot fail to notice a collection of blue-roofed buildings on a large area south of the high-rise buildings of the city centre and the national stadium. These buildings are laid out like army barracks easily identifiable from the air. Seen from above the large compound with its symmetric layout dominates this part of the city bordering a crowded residential area and various government buildings.

The complex resembles a fortress, surrounded by a high wall with watchtowers commanding the adjacent neighbourhoods and streets. As everybody in Freetown knows, these buildings house the Special Court for Sierra Leone. Alongside the Mammy Yoko Hotel at the tip of the Freetown peninsula, where the headquarters of the UN[2] is located together with the offices of the various international organizations, it is one of the visible signs of the interest the group of mainly Western states usually referred to as 'international community' takes in a country still haunted by the spectres of civil war. The Special Court for Sierra Leone constitutes the legal dimension of the international response to the atrocities committed during the civil war between 1991 and 2001, it was created pursuant to

2 Since 2004 the UN has been reducing its presence and in 2006 the United Nations Mission in Sierra Leone (UNAMSIL) was replaced by a much smaller mission, the United Nations Integrated Office for Sierra Leone (UNIOSIL) numbering only a few hundred UN officials and a contingent of UN peacekeepers securing the compounds of the UN and the Special Court.

Security Council Resolution 1315. It commenced its operations in July 2002 and has the mandate to hold those accountable who bear 'the greatest responsibility for serious violations of international humanitarian law and Sierra Leonean law committed in the territory of Sierra Leone since 30 November 1996'.[3]

Until January 2003, when the registry moved to the present site in Freetown, the court led a somewhat nomadic existence. First hearings were held at temporary facilities in Bonthe, a town on the relatively isolated Sherbro Island off the coast at 150 kilometres distance from Freetown, where the accused where held in a temporary detention facility. The judges' plenary meetings were held at various locations in Freetown and London. This changed when the site in Freetown was developed as the First Annual Report of the President of the Special Court for Sierra Leone points out:

> In January 2003, the New England site near central Freetown was occupied by the Registry. As the Registry became operational in a densely populated, central area of the city, the reality of the court, both physically and psychologically, became apparent to the surrounding community (Annual Report, 23).

The completion of the detention facility and the stationing of UN troops guarding the compound raised the visibility of the court according to the annual report. Visibility further increased when the first hearings were conducted at the site in Freetown.

Although hearings on motions had been conducted by the Trial Chamber previously, in November 2003 the Appeals Chamber conducted the first hearings in the temporary courthouse within the New England site. These hearings focused both national and international attention on the Court and marked the Court as a functioning judicial institution (Annual Report, 23).

The link between the physical place, the buildings in Freetown, and the quality of a 'functioning judicial institution' is interesting. Offices, a courthouse, a detention facility, the infrastructure and a perimeter are all necessary preconditions for the trials against those responsible for the crimes against humanity and war crimes; the purpose of the Special Court.

The first annual report informs the reader that the court 'developed a previously barren 11.5 acre site in Freetown, building offices, a detention facility, a temporary courthouse and … the courthouse itself' (Annual Report 2002–2004, 5). The site where the court was built, however, was not really 'barren'. There used to be the headquarter buildings of the Prisons Service, living quarters for Prisons staff, a soccer field and a lawn tennis court. The area served also for political rallies and military parades. The Prisons headquarters was burnt down during the invasion of Freetown by the rebels of the Revolutionary United Front (RUF) and the Armed Forces Revolutionary Council (AFRC) in January 1999. This was part of the

3 Article 1(1) of the Agreement between the United Nations and the Government of Sierra Leone on the establishment of a Special Court for Sierra Leone.

strategy of the rebels who saw itself fighting against a corrupt regime, to destroy the symbols of state power.[4]

It is significant that the court occupies a site of government buildings destroyed in the attack on Freetown in January 1999. This attack on the capital finally succeeded in attracting the attention of the international community and the international media, which had ignored the conflict as long as it 'only' affected Sierra Leone's hinterland. The location of the court on a site previously occupied by government buildings symbolizes the transformation of sovereignty in Sierra Leone. The destruction of the government buildings at the hands of the rebels made the international intervention necessary and created the conditions for the insertion of international agencies in Sierra Leone's national space. This, however, was not part of the 'humanitarian–military apparatus' hidden agenda as Pandolfi would argue, but the long delayed hesitant and under funded reaction of the 'international community' to stop the disintegration of the state in Sierra Leone. Consequently, the UN and the Special Court for Sierra Leone did not replace functioning state institutions but rather filled the void left by the destruction of the state apparatus during the civil war.

The Trials

The Special Court for Sierra Leone was promoted as an alternative to both the ad hoc tribunals in The Hague and Arusha and the ICC. It was supposed to be cheaper and swifter in dispensing justice, and more in tune with the needs of victims and the people of Sierra Leone. Therefore, it was designed as a separate institution to be financed by voluntary contributions, operating within a limited period of time and located in Sierra Leone. The financial constraints and political pressure to be 'lean and mean' as staff in OTP recalled during my fieldwork has had effects on the jurisdiction of the court, the operation of OTP and the conduct of the trials heard at the Special Court.

Most notably the court's mandate is limited to those individuals bearing the 'greatest responsibility' for the crimes committed during the civil war and its temporal jurisdiction is limited to crimes committed after 30 November 1996, the date of an ill-fated peace agreement between the then newly elected government and the RUF. Both limitations have been widely criticized because it meant that many perpetrators of war crimes would not be prosecuted and countless crimes had been committed prior to 1996. Although it was never officially confirmed it is a public secret that the limitation of the court's jurisdiction was aimed at saving time and keeping costs low. I will return to this point in more detail in the following section.

4 On the history of the conflict, see Keen (2005); and Gberie (2006). See also Richards (1996).

The limitation to individuals who held positions of authority was aimed at keeping the number of trials to the absolute minimum unlike the ICTY and the ICTR who have no such restriction and in principle have the mandate to try all individuals who committed 'serious violations of international humanitarian law' (Article 1 Statute ICTY and ICTR). Therefore, the court indicted and tried only a small number of individuals alleged to be leaders of the various warring factions. In 2003 the prosecutor indicted 13 individuals of which 11 stood or are currently standing trial. Two of them died of natural causes in the court's custody. So far two trials have been concluded. The trial against three leaders of the AFRC, a group of soldiers that toppled the democratically elected government in 1997 and who had been accused of countless atrocities against the civilian population, started in March 2005 and was concluded in June 2007 when the three accused were found guilty and sentenced to prison sentences of respectively 45, 55 and 55 years. The judgment was confirmed by the court's appeals chamber in late 2007. The trial against the leaders of the Civil Defence Force (CDF), a pro-government militia also known as *Kamajors* accused of committing crimes while fighting against the AFRC and RUF, started in March 2004 and was concluded in August 2007. One of the accused, the CDF leader Sam Hinga Norman, died on 22 February 2007 while undergoing medical treatment in Senegal. The other two accused were found guilty in August 2007 and sentenced to respectively seven and eight years. The trial chamber's majority judgment was overturned by the appeals chamber in a majority decision which raised the sentences to respectively 15 and 20 years in May 2008. The trial against three leaders of the RUF commenced in June 2004 and is still being heard by Trial Chamber I in Freetown. The defence expected to conclude its case by June 2008 and the judgment is expected by the end of 2008. The trial against former warlord and Liberian president Charles Taylor started in June 2007 and is currently being heard in The Hague on the premises of the International Criminal Court (ICC) where the trial has been moved due to security concerns. Taylor is charged with 11 counts of war crimes and crimes against humanity committed by members of the AFRC and RUF in Sierra Leone who acted on his orders or were at least aided and abetted by Taylor according to the prosecution.

The International Environment

The establishment of the Special Court had been a protracted process commencing with a letter of the government of Sierra Leone to the Secretary General of the UN in June 2000 requesting the establishment of an international criminal tribunal. The next significant date had been 14 August 2000, when the Security Council passed resolution 1315 authorizing the establishment of an international tribunal to try the leaders of the warring factions for war crimes and crimes against humanity committed during the civil war in Sierra Leone. On 16 January 2002 the UN and the government signed the *Agreement between the United Nations and the Government of Sierra Leone on the Establishment of a Special Court*. The court officially began its operations on 1 July 2002. The judges were sworn in on 2 December 2002 and the prosecutor filed the first eight indictments during a meeting in London in March 2003. The court has two trial chambers (three judges each, two appointed by the UN Secretary General and one by the government of Sierra Leone) and one appeals chamber (five judges, three appointed by the UN Secretary General and two by the government). The first trial chamber commenced work in May 2004 and the second trial chamber in March 2005. The court is expected to wind down after the trial against Taylor is completed, according to the court's completion strategy, in late 2009.

The court's hybrid character and its establishment in Sierra Leone reflected the debate on international criminal justice during the late 1990s. In the late 1990s, following the establishment of the two first ad hoc tribunals, the ICTY and the ICTR, a fierce and often polemical debate was fought over the best avenue towards establishing international criminal justice. Basically there were two competing models. On one hand, there were those governments and non-governmental organizations which rallied for the establishment of a permanent criminal court with universal jurisdiction and, on the other, there were governments led by the US and several US NGOs arguing that international tribunals should be only temporary ad hoc institutions dealing with specific situations.

The US government promoted the Special Court for Sierra Leone as an alternative to both, a permanent international criminal court and the ICTY and ICTR, which were perceived as too expensive and too slow. Pierre-Richard Prosper, then US ambassador-at-large for war crimes, expressed this position in a presentation to Congress on 28 February 2002 arguing in favour of ad hoc tribunals and criticizing the ICTY and ICTR as too slow, too expensive and too far removed from the lives of those in whose name justice is sought. When the request of the Sierra Leone government was discussed in the UN Security Council and the UN Secretary General's Office, the US and Britain took the lead in developing the court's set-up. Ambassador Prosper participated in the negotiations leading up to the establishment of the Special Court and was one of the key people in the planning process.[5]

Unlike the ICTR and the ICTY, the Special Court for Sierra Leone is not part of the UN structure but has been established as 'sui generic independent institution having its legal basis in an agreement between UN and government'. It is supported by several UN member states which have set up the so-called Group of Interested States (GIS). From the outset the Special Court has been hampered by financial constraints and has lived 'from hand to mouth' as the second registrar Munlo put it. Unlike the other international criminal tribunals, which are funded through the regular UN budget, the Special Court has relied on voluntary contributions of UN member states, the GIS. Originally a budget of US$114.6 million over three years had been drawn up but this was reduced to US$57 million in June 2001. In the

5 Interview with ambassador Prosper in New York City, 4 December 2007.

subsequent years the Special Court was struggling to secure funding and had to reduce costs from US$34 million in the first year to US$25 million in the fiscal year 2005–2006. At one point the court was forced to seek financial support from the UN and secured a so-called Subvention Grant of US$20 million for 2005. Financial insecurity continued to dominate the court's operations throughout 2006 and 2007. The transfer of Taylor's trial to The Hague posed a heavy burden on the court's budget and the acquisition of funds continued to be a major challenge (UN 2007). Although these amounts would seem considerable from the perspective of the court's critics and the Sierra Leone public, many of whom have to survive on less than a dollar a day, they are dwarfed by the other international criminal tribunals. The ICTR has an annual budget of about US$90 million and the ICTY's annual budget is well over US$100 million.

The court's financial constraints that have been a direct consequence of the Security Council's 'tribunal fatigue' (Scheffer 1996, 34) were responsible for the long duration of the CDF and RUF trials and partly for the delayed appointment of the second trial chamber. Since there was only one trial chamber in 2004 this trial chamber had to hear two trials. Consequently, the trials have not been significantly shorter than those heard at the ICTY and ICTR.

The most important consequences of the desire of the 'international community' to save costs and time have been the limitation to 'those who bear greatest responsibility' and to crimes committed after 30 November 1996. This decision has forced OTP to indict only a relatively small number of individuals who are believed to be the leaders of the warring factions. This meant that many others would not be held accountable since at the national level an amnesty was granted to all who had committed crimes during the civil war. It also resulted in a somewhat one-dimensional view of the conflict which assumed very clear hierarchies and quasi-military organization with a few individuals at the top. The evidence presented in court, however, has painted a more muddled and complex picture and in all three trials the defence has challenged the view that it is possible to identify the accused as those bearing indeed the greatest responsibility for crimes and war crimes committed during a long and dynamic conflict.

Another important limitation of the court's jurisdiction is the explicit exclusion of foreign military personnel from prosecution. Article 2 of the Special Court's statute provides that 'transgressions by peacekeepers … shall be within the primary jurisdiction of the sending state'. In 1997 the regional organization ECOWAS[6] deployed troops to Sierra Leone to defeat the AFRC and RUF rebels who had forced President Kabbah's government into exile in Guinea. This contingent was called ECOMOG[7] and consisted mainly of Nigerian personnel. ECOMOG was succeeded by UNAMSIL in October 1999. Although ECOMOG was designated as peacekeeping mission it constituted in fact one of the warring factions fighting on behalf of the democratically elected government. ECOMOG peacekeepers

6 Economic Community of West African States.

7 Economic Community of West African States Monitoring Group.

committed numerous human rights violations and war crimes such as summary executions of suspected rebels (Keen 2005, 244–7; and TRC Report 2004 Vol. 2, 87–8). Even though they are held responsible for less than one per cent of the crimes committed during the war (TRC Report 2004 Vol. 2, 38) it is noteworthy that the Security Council and the governments involved in the establishment of the Special Court went to great lengths to protect peacekeepers from prosecution by the Special Court.

The court's principal supporters have also been its main contributors. The US government, the court's strongest supporter, contributed a third of the budget in the court's first year (US$5 million in 2002–2003), almost half in 2006 (US$13 million) and again more than a third in 2007. Other countries that have contributed significantly are the Netherlands, Canada and Britain. These countries have also played an important role in the management of the Special Court. Following a suggestion from several members of the Security Council who took an interest in the Special Court for Sierra Leone, notably Britain and the US, a Management Committee was formed 'to assist the court in obtaining adequate funding, provide advice on matters of Court administration and be available as appropriate to consult on other non-judicial matters' (Annual Report 2002–2003, 30). The Management Committee comprises representatives of the US, Britain, the Netherlands, Canada, Nigeria, Lesotho, Sierra Leone and functionaries of the UN secretariat (Mochochoko and Tortora 2004).

The court's independence from its main sponsors, in particular the US government, has been hotly debated both within and outside the court. From the very beginning there was gossip about US influence on OTP and its operation. The first Chief Prosecutor David Crane and the first chief investigator Alan White had been affiliated with US military intelligence services. They were soon joined by several lawyers who had worked in the US military and had prior experience with war crimes prosecution, such as former Air Force lawyer Brenda Hollis. More recently a former Chief Federal Prosecutor and United States Attorney was appointed Chief Prosecutor and Brenda Hollis was appointed senior trial attorney in the trial against Taylor.

Crane[8] and Prosper[9] confirmed that these appointments were indeed the result of the interest taken in the Special Court by circles in the US government, in particular the State Department, who were keen to promote an alternative to both the ad hoc tribunals in The Hague and Arusha and a permanent international criminal court. To conclude, however, that OTP is an extension of the US government would be wrong. Although the appointment of senior staff certainly is a political decision reflecting the support of the US this does not necessarily mean that they received orders from their government. First Chief Prosecutor David Crane was adamant that he acted as representative of an international tribunal striving to see justice

8 Interview with David Crane in Utrecht, 11 June 2008.

9 Interview with ambassador Prosper in New York City, 4 December 2007.

done on behalf of the victims of the civil war.[10] Lawyers like Stephen Rapp or Brenda Hollis were not only chosen because they were US citizens or had worked for the Pentagon but also because they had extensive experience in international criminal tribunals. Rapp had served as senior trial attorney for six years at the ICTR, leading the prosecution in the 'media trial', and Brenda Hollis had served in the prosecution team in the trial against Tadic at the ICTY. Especially with regard to financial and logistical support, which has not always been forthcoming, the American prosecutors often have had to lobby in Washington on the court's behalf. Most recently, for example, Rapp had to exercise pressure on the US government through the media, the UN and international NGOs to commit more funds to the Special Court (UN 2007).

While US influence has attracted most attention it is important to note that a number of other governments have taken a keen interest in the operation of the court, most notably Canada and Britain. Britain, the former colonial power, is Sierra Leone's most important donor funding a range of institutional reforms including the restructuring of the judiciary reform and the police force. Together with other Commonwealth countries, most notably Canada, Britain is also funding a long-term military assistance programme. Whether this political engagement is linked to economic interests as Richards (2004) suggests is a difficult question to answer. Although it is correct that since the 1990s British and Canadian companies have been active in the diamond mining sector in Sierra Leone and continue to do so, there is no direct evidence for a causal relationship between British or Canadian support for the Special Court and these private enterprises.

With regard to staff composition, nationals from Commonwealth countries are by far in the majority. British and Canadian citizens especially have occupied and continue to occupy a number of important positions in the Special Court. The first chief of prosecutions was Canadian and the Canadian government seconded a contingent of the Royal Mounted Police to the Special Court. Other important positions at the court were held by British and Australian citizens, especially in OTP and the registry. The first deputy prosecutor, for example, Desmond de Silva, is a British national who was nominated by the government of Sierra Leone. The second deputy prosecutor was an Australian who had worked for the ICTR in Arusha. The first registrar, Robin Vincent, used to work in the British court administration and important positions in the registry were held by British and Australian nationals. There are also a considerable number of Africans working mainly in the registry. Since 2006 more Africans have been hired. As of 31 December 2006 there were eight Nigerians, eight Tanzanians, four South Africans and five Ghanaians, mainly in the registry. This was due to the policy of the second registrar, a Malawian, and the principal defender, a Nigerian, to employ more Africans in order to expose more Africans to international criminal justice.

To see these people as mere proxies of their respective governments would be too simplistic. Relatively high numbers of individuals from specific countries may

10 Interview with David Crane in Utrecht, 11 June 2008.

stem from a variety of reasons. The eight Tanzanians who worked for the court illustrate this well. All of them had worked as security guards at the ICTR in Arusha and were pursuing an international career in this field. The Canadian interest in the Special Court and the ICTR, for example, is at least partly motivated by Canada's involvement in the failed UN missions in Somalia and Rwanda as Judge Boutet, a former Canadian Judge Advocate General, pointed out.[11] The language of the Special Court and the adversary system, in combination with Sierra Leone's colonial past, make it a more obvious choice for people from Commonwealth and Anglophone African countries seeking employment in an international organization. For Africans pursuing an international career the Special Court is an important point of entry. The UN Secretary General has emphasized the importance of the court for the region and has promoted the employment of people from ECOWAS member states and sub-Saharan Africa in general. This reading is also supported by the fact that only very small numbers of Dutch or German nationals have worked at the Special Court although both countries have provided substantial financial support to the court.

Another important influence is the assemblage of various international NGOs supporting international justice. NGOs have been at the forefront in the struggle for international criminal justice and the 1998 Treaty of Rome probably would never have materialized without the unrelenting efforts of a broad and transnational coalition of NGOs often pushing unwilling governments. Many employees of the court have been affiliated with this movement and used to work for international NGOs such as Human Rights Watch (HRW) and No Peace without Justice and often find employment in an international organization or NGO after their contract at the court ends. NGOs have played an important role at every stage of the Special Court intervening in the debate on its establishment, monitoring the trials and issuing statements on issues such as funding of the court and the location of Taylor's trial. Representatives of No Peace without Justice advised the government of Sierra Leone and the Special Court and the representative of Human Rights Watch in Sierra Leone, Corinne Dufka served as advisor to OTP in 2003. Reports of Medécins sans Frontiers and other NGOs documenting war crimes and human rights violations have been used extensively by OTP.

The Court in the National Political Landscape

The court is also part of Sierra Leone's political topography. The court has to be situated in relation to the other transitional justice mechanism in Sierra Leone, the Truth and Reconciliation Commission (TRC). The commission was explicitly established to 'create an impartial historical record of violations and abuses of human rights and international humanitarian law related to the armed conflict in Sierra Leone' (TRC act section 6(1)). Its final report including a set

11 Interview with Justice Boutet in Freetown, June 2006.

of recommendations for the government was published in October 2004.[12] The parallel operation of two transitional justice institutions proved to be difficult and their relationship was often characterized by tension and competition. This had mainly two reasons. First, both institutions relied on voluntary contributions and competed for the limited funding made available in the Western donor countries for transitional justice in Sierra Leone. In the end the Special Court was more successful attracting initial funding of US$56 million, less than half of what originally had been budgeted, whereas the TRC eventually was pledged only US$4 million, also less than half of what initially had been budgeted (Schabas 2003, 1039–40). Second, because of their parallel operation and debates about the scope of the amnesty granted under the Lomé-Agreement, a peace deal signed on 7 July 1999, many people in Sierra Leone did not perceive the two institutions as separate entities with complementary mandates and therefore were not sure where the boundary between those who would be granted amnesty and those facing prosecution would be drawn. In practice both institutions often had difficulties in delineating the respective mandates and tasks (TRC Report 2004 Vol. 2, 17–18; and Shaw 2005).

Apart from its relation to the TRC the court itself has been a site of national politics. One of the ways it is integrated into the national political landscape is by way of its national staff. Many of the court's employees are Sierra Leone nationals, and constitute the majority of the court's employees (180 out of 306 as of 31 December 2006) and although most of them hold junior positions the importance of employment by the Special Court for highly qualified Sierra Leoneans should not be underestimated. At the time of writing (May 2008) three of the eleven judges were Sierra Leonean nationals, Justice Thompson in Trial Chamber I and Justice King and Justice Kamanda in the appeals chamber. The other judge appointed by the government of Sierra Leone is Lussick, a Samoan, in Trial Chamber II. Kamanda's predecessor in the appeals chamber was Geoffrey Robertson, a British barrister who had been nominated by the government of Sierra Leone. Justice King has played a prominent role in the appeals chamber. Before Kamanda's appointment in 2008, King was the only judge of the appeals chamber who resided in Freetown and was twice elected president of the court by his fellow judges (May 2006–May 2007 and May 2007–May 2008).

The Special Court has been attracting considerable interest from the country's legal profession and a good portion of Sierra Leone's tiny population of lawyers have been working at the court. The first prosecutor David Crane went to great lengths to recruit Sierra Leoneans for OTP and it largely due to his efforts that three trial attorneys are Sierra Leonean nationals. The national element is more conspicuous in the defence teams. Each of the nine defence teams (excluding Taylor's team, consisting mainly of British lawyers) included lawyers from Sierra Leone and two defence teams were led by Sierra Leoneans (first and third accused in the CDF trial).

12 The final report is available at www.trcsierraleone.org.

The court's origin lies in a conflict in the national political landscape in May 2000. On 7 July 1999 the warring factions had signed a peace agreement in Lomé under heavy international pressure. This agreement provided for the sharing of power with the RUF, disarmament and an amnesty for all combatants. Foday Sankoh and other members of the RUF became ministers in the new government and took residence in Freetown while RUF forces continued to occupy territories in the north and the east of the country where they ill-treated the civilian population and took hundreds of UN peacekeepers hostage. When a peaceful demonstration gathered at Sankoh's residence in Freetown on 8 May 2000, to urge him to respect the terms of the Lomé Accord, his bodyguards opened fire on the crowd and killed 23 demonstrators. After this incident the government arrested Sankoh and a number of RUF members for the murder of the demonstrators.[13]

President Kabbah and then Attorney General Berewa seized the opportunity and sent a letter to the Secretary General of the UN requesting the establishment of a joint national–international court 'to try and bring to credible justice those members of the RUF and their accomplices responsible for committing crimes against the people of Sierra Leone and for taking of UN peacekeepers as hostages'. This was welcomed by the UN Security Council and the UN Secretary General who were concerned about the fate of the UN mission to Sierra Leone, UNAMSIL, which was in severe difficulties at the time. The RUF, however, was not the only group accused of having committed atrocities against the civilian population; there had also been serious allegations of human rights violations raised against the CDF, a pro-government militia fighting against the RUF in alliance with ECOMOG troops.

During the preparation of the Security Council resolution there was intense lobbying by several international human rights groups, most of them based in the US, as exponents of the movement for the advancement of international criminal justice to expand the court's mandate to include all parties in the conflict. HRW, for example, expressed concern:

> That a possible dominant role in the court by Sierra Leonean authorities could lead to political manipulation of the process leading to biased prosecutions and inadequate protections for persons standing trial before the tribunal … The job of bringing the perpetrators of international crimes to justice must reside with the international community.

The Security Council heeded these protests by HRW, Amnesty International and other NGOs and passed resolution 1315 establishing an international court to prosecute all bearing 'greatest responsibility'. The court implemented this provision when it indicted the leaders of the CDF alongside those of the RUF and the AFRC. This stance is in line with the practice of international criminal tribunals seeking to increase their legitimacy by trying representatives of all factions in

13 On the events surrounding 8 May 2000, see TRC Report (2004 Vol. 3A, 364–448).

armed conflicts, with the notable exception of international troops. Impartiality and political neutrality are at the core of the movement to advance international criminal justice aiming at establishing the rule of law and is deemed a necessary precondition for reconciliation in the post-war development.

President Kabbah, a former UNDP functionary, aimed at increasing his legitimacy and getting rid of the threat posed by the RUF when he sent the letter to the Secretary General of the UN. An international tribunal would focus the interest of the UN, Europe and the US on Sierra Leone. The national jurisdiction, apart from its difficulties stemming from ten years of civil war, would not have enjoyed the same legitimacy as an international tribunal. Earlier trials against alleged participants in the coup against Kabbah's government on 25 May 1997 were widely seen as mere show trials and did not increase the government's legitimacy. On the contrary, according to the report of the Truth and Reconciliation Commission it was the execution of 24 officers of the Sierra Leone Army on a beach near Freetown on 19 October 1998 that further radicalized the RUF and AFRC leadership.[14] It should also be noted that several representatives of the NGO No Peace without Justice served as advisors to the Sierra Leone government during that time and pushed for an international war crimes tribunal. No Peace without Justice was part of an alliance of international NGOs lobbying for the establishment of an international war crimes tribunal and an end to the impunity of political and military leaders generally.

Political conflicts and splits in Sierra Leone have affected the court in manifold ways. Most importantly it was a political conflict that eventually led to the establishment of the Special Court. The unravelling of the power-sharing agreement between government and RUF after the 8 May 2000 incident created sufficient momentum within Sierra Leone to push for an international war crimes tribunal. After its establishment the court continued to be contested in Sierra Leone. The CDF trial has been highly controversial in Sierra Leone for the accused are considered heroes by large parts of the population, especially among the Mende ethnic group in the south-east of the country where the CDF had its main power base. In their eyes the CDF defended their communities against attacks from the rebels.[15] Consequently, many

---

14 During a state of emergency following the reinstatement of Kabbah's government in March 1998, three trials against 59 persons charged with treason in connection with the coup in May 1997 were heard at magistrate's courts in Freetown and one court martial against 38 soldiers who allegedly participated in the coup. Thirty-two accused were found guilty in the trials heard at the magistrate's courts and 31 of them received the death sentence. In the court martial 34 officers received the death sentence (judgment handed down 12 October 1998) and 24 were executed by firing squad on a beach near Freetown whereas the sentences against the remaining ten were commuted to life imprisonment. While the appeals against the magistrate court's ruling were pending all accused escaped during the invasion of Freetown in January 1999 (TRC Report 2004 Vol. 3A: 307–16).

15 Interestingly this popular view is shared by the dissenting opinion of the Sierra Leonan judge in the trial chamber who acquitted the accused because they had fought for a legitimate purpose, the restoration of democracy. It is noteworthy that both Sierra

people were disappointed when Norman, then deputy defence minister, was arrested on 10 March 2003 and put on trial. This fed into a wider sense of disenchantment within the ruling Sierra Leone People Party (SLPP) and many opposed Solomon Berewa's candidacy for the 2007 election, former Attorney General and later vice-president, who was Kabbah's preferred successor for party leadership. They supported Charles Margai, son of the country's second president and SLPP stalwart but after intense internal haggling Berewa was chosen as presidential candidate. Margai responded by forming his own political party, the People's Movement for Democratic Change (PMDC) with him as presidential candidate.

These events on the national political stage were directly linked to the CDF trial since Charles Margai acted as lead counsel for the third accused. His political campaign in the east benefited greatly from the fact that he defended members of the CDF against charges that were in the eyes of many Sierra Leonans politically motivated. The political conflict between him, Kabbah and Berewa overshadowed the trial especially in 2006 when the PMDC stepped up its campaign against Kabbah's government and the SLPP. The defence lawyers carried this controversy into the courtroom when they filed a motion to subpoena the president to testify in court because they argued that the president had been in fact Norman's superior. During the civil war president Kabbah also held the post of defence minister and commander-in-chief. In 1996 he appointed Norman, who had been coordinating the fight of the *kamajors* against the RUF, deputy defence minister with the task to organize the resistance against the RUF. The prosecution, however, neither indicted him nor called him as a witness, arguing that Kabbah, who was most of the time in exile in Guinea, was only nominally Norman's superior and did not exercise effective control over the CDF leaders who meanwhile had formed a 'criminal enterprise' without Kabbah's knowledge. This was disputed by the defence lawyers who wanted to call Kabbah as a witness in an attempt to elucidate the relationship between him and the accused. Kabbah dismissed this as a political move aimed at slandering him in the run-up to the 2007 elections and the defence, in turn, filed a motion to subpoena him. Eventually the trial chamber decided on that motion, rejecting it on the grounds that the president's testimony was not necessary for the conduct of the trial.[16] This decision was upheld in the appeals

Leonan judges in the appeals chamber also dissented, one acquitting the accused and one arguing in favour of lower sentences for the same reasons as the dissenting judge in the trial chamber. See the dissenting opinions attached to the trial chamber's judgment of 2 August 2007 (SCSL-04-14-T-785) and the appeals chamber's judgment of 28 May 2008 (SCSL-04-14-A-829).

16 'The chamber finds that the applicants' arguments either fail to demonstrate that the proposed testimony would materially assist the cases of the … accused (the "purpose" requirement) or alternatively fail to show that the proposed testimony is necessary for the conduct of the trial (the "necessity" requirement).' Decision on Motions by Moinina Fofana and Sam Hinga Norman for the Issuance of a subpoena *ad testificandum* to H.E. Alhaji Dr. Ahmad Tejan Kabbah, President of the Republic of Sierra Leone, 13 June 2006 (SCSL-04-14-T).

chamber. To many people in Sierra Leone this was a political decision aimed at supporting Kabbah but ironically it was the court's very concern to be dragged into national politics that motivated these decisions rather than political influence from the government.

Suspicions against the court were raised again when Sam Hinga Norman died on 22 February 2007 in a military hospital in Senegal while undergoing medical treatment. Among supporters of the PMDC and the Mende it was widely believed that Norman was murdered. There was nothing to support these allegations; the autopsy showed that Norman died of natural causes after a routine operation.[17] Norman's death came as a shock to the court since the case was concluded and the judgments were being drafted. This meant that there would be no verdict against him and that only two relatively minor figures were eventually convicted in August 2007.

Even the other two trials against the RUF and AFRC leaders have been interpreted as politically motivated by many Sierra Leoneans. Since independence in 1961, the SLPP had been regarded as promoting the interests of the Mende elite in the south-east by people in the north. Consequently there was considerable distrust in the north when the SLPP government took office after winning the elections in 1996. The RUF enjoyed sympathies in some parts of the north because some perceived of the RUF as protector against a Mende conspiracy to acquire absolute control over the country. Many soldiers were also hostile to Kabbah's government and the CDF militia and it has been argued that their fear of the SLPP and CDF was the main motive for the AFRC coup in May 1997.[18] As a result, the establishment of the Special Court and the trials against the leaders of the RUF and AFRC were perceived by many Sierra Leoneans, especially in the north and the army, as a move by the SLPP and the Mende to strengthen their grip on the state apparatus. These people did not perceive the trial against the CDF leaders as a sign of the court's impartiality as was intended by the UN Security Council but rather as an attempt by the president to get rid of a political rival within the SLPP. The national political landscape shifted after the August 2007 parliamentary and presidential elections when Ernest Bai Koroma, the candidate of the All People's Congress (APC), won and the APC achieved the majority in parliament. President Koroma visited the Special Court in February 2008 and promised the continuing support of the government but he will have to tread very cautiously since he draws his main support from the north and had appealed directly to former RUF fighters for support during his election campaign.

---

17 Special Court of Sierra Leone Press Release, 'Autopsy Shows Sam Hinga Norman Died of Natural Causes', 28 March 2007.

18 See TRC report (2004 Vol. 3A, 234–42). See also Keen (2005, 197–203).

Conclusions

The main argument advanced in this chapter is that place matters in international criminal justice. In spite of its appearance as universal and trans-local it is made and instantiated at particular places. These places have a particular history and are embedded in specific power relations that need to be investigated. Anthropology, relying on in-depth fieldwork, in the tribunals and other relevant places, could contribute to a better understanding by studying the complex interplay of external political influences and the tribunals' internal dynamics. The analysis presented here suggests a much more contested and ambivalent field than critics and proponents assume. Whereas the latter paints an evolutionary narrative of the development of a cosmopolitan world order, the former denounce international criminal justice as thinly disguised neocolonialism. Both fail to appreciate that international criminal law, in spite of its universal and abstract character, is the product of concrete social processes in specific localities contested both nationally and globally.

In conclusion the Special Court has been subject to many competing influences. Decisions by a number of governments shaped the court and influenced it during its operation. The court was established at the request of the government of Sierra Leone. During the negotiations, US government representatives played a major role in fashioning the court as alternative to both the ad hoc tribunals and a permanent international criminal court. The US government continued to be one of the court's major supporters and a number of US nationals were employed in leading positions, especially in OTP. Other governments, most notably Canada and Britain, have also rendered logistical and financial support and monitored the court's operation through the Management Committee. Governments have not been the only international actors exercising influence. International NGOs, such as No Peace without Justice and HRW, have played an important role at the court. Their influence has been directly through lobbying and campaigning and, probably even more important, indirectly by shaping individuals who work at the court and setting the agenda in the debate on international criminal justice at a global scale.

Within Sierra Leone the court has been both the subject and site of often intense political debates. These debates are structured by the competition between a number of political actors that emerged during the civil war such as the SLPP, president Kabbah, Charles Margai and the APC. This rivalry has to be considered against the background of Sierra Leone's post-colonial history in which the Mende elite has been pitted against the north and regional divisions have led to an intense feeling of distrust between the different ethno-political factions. These fissures have affected the trials and the popular perception of the court to a considerable extent. This necessarily brief sketch shows that the Special Court is the product of both international and national debates, and subject to a wide range of influences. Hence, it is neither above particularistic interests nor is it part of an all powerful neocolonial global regime.

References

Abrahamsen R. and Williams, M.C. (2007) 'Introduction: The Privatisation and Globalisation of Security in Africa'. *International Relations*, 21(2): 131–41.

Anders, G. (2007) 'Follow the Trial: Some Notes on the Ethnography of International Criminal Justice'. *Anthropology Today*, 23(3): 23–6.

Augé, M. (1995) *Non-Places: Introduction to an Anthropology of Supermodernity*. London: Verso.

Cassese, A. (2003) 'International Criminal Law' in M.D. Evans (ed.) *International Law*. Oxford: Oxford University Press, pp. 721–56.

Dezalay, Y. and Garth, B. (1996) *Dealing in Virtue: International Commercial Arbitration and the Construction of a Transnational Legal Order*. Chicago: University of Chicago Press.

Duffield, M. (2001) *Global Governance and the New Wars: The Merging of Development and Security*. London: Zed Books.

Escobar, A. (1995) *Encountering Development: The Making and Unmaking of the Third World*. Princeton: Princeton University Press.

Ferguson, J. (1994) *The Anti-Politics Machine: 'Development', Depoliticization, and Bureaucratic Power in Lesotho*. Minneapolis: University of Minnesota Press.

Gberie, L. (2006) *A Dirty War in West Africa: The RUF and the Destruction of Sierra Leone*. Bloomington: Indiana University Press.

Goodale, M. (ed.) (2006) 'In Focus: Anthropology and Human Rights in a New Key'. *American Anthropologist*, 108(1): 1–83.

Hagan, J. (2003) *Justice in the Balkans: Prosecuting War Crimes in the Hague Tribunal*. Chicago: Chicago University Press.

Hagan, J., Levi, R. and Ferrales, G. (2006) 'Swaying the Hand of Justice: The Internal and External Dynamics of Regime Change at the International Criminal Tribunal for the Former Yugoslavia'. *Law and Social Inquiry*, 31(3): 585–616.

Keen, D. (2005) *Conflict and Collusion in Sierra Leone*. Oxford: James Currey.

Kelsall, T. (2004) 'Politics, Anti-politics, International Justice: Notes on the Special Court for Sierra Leone', Paper Presented at the Conference 'Settling Accounts: Truth, Justice and Redress in Post-conflict Societies'. Harvard University, 1–4 November 2004.

Kelsen, H. (1934) *Reine Rechtslehre*. Aalen: Scientia Verlag.

Merry, S.E. (2001) 'Crossing Boundaries: Methodological Challenges for Ethnography in the 21st Century'. *PoLAR: Political and Legal Anthropology Review*, 23(2): 127–34.

Merry, S.E. (2005) *Human Rights and Gender Violence: Translating International Law into Local Justice*. Chicago: University of Chicago Press.

Mochochoko, P. and Tortora, G. (2004) 'The Management Committee for the Special Court for Sierra Leone' in C. Romano, A. Nollkaemper and J.K. Kleffner (eds) *Internationalized Criminal Courts and Tribunals: Sierra Leone, East Timor, Kosovo and Cambodia*. Oxford: Oxford University Press, pp. 141–56.

Pandolfi, M. (2003) 'Contract of Mutual (In)Difference: Governance and the Humanitarian Apparatus in Contemporary Albania and Kosovo'. *Indiana Journal of Global Legal Studies*, 10: 369–81.

Richards, P. (1996) *Fighting for the Rainforest: War, Youth and Resources in Sierra Leone*. London: James Currey.

Richards, P. (2004) 'The Return of Great Britain to Sierra Leone'. *African Geopolitics*, pp. 15–16.

Robertson, G. (2002) *Crimes against Humanity: The Struggle for Global Justice*. London: Penguin.

Schabas, W. (2003) 'The Relationship between Truth and Reconciliation Commissions and International Courts: The Case of Sierra Leone'. *Human Rights Quarterly*, 25: 1039–40.

Scheffer, D.J. (1996) 'International Judicial Intervention'. *Foreign Policy*, 102: 34–51.

Shaw. R. (2005) *Rethinking Truth and Reconciliation Commissions: Lessons from Sierra Leone*. United States Institute of Peace Special Report no. 130. Washington DC: United States Institute of Peace.

Sierra Leone Truth and Reconciliation Commission (2004) *Witness to Truth: Report of the Sierra Leone Truth and Reconciliation Commission*. Accra: GPL Press.

Special Court for Sierra Leone (2004) *First Annual Report of the President of the Special Court for Sierra Leone for the Period 2 December 2002–1 December 2003*. Freetown.

United Nations (2007) *Press Conference by Prosecutor for Special Court for Sierra Leone*. Department of Public Information, News and Media Division, New York.

Wilson, R.A. (ed.) (1997) *Human Rights, Culture and Context: Anthropological Perspectives*. London: Pluto Press.

Chapter 8
The Myth of the Transparent Table: Reconstructing Space and Legal Interventions in Scottish Children's Hearings

Anne Griffiths and Randy F. Kandel

Scales of Projection: Law and Space

In our chapter we analyse the spatialization of law in a micro context, that of local children's hearings in Glasgow. These hearings are bounded in time (lasting on average from 40 to 50 minutes) and space (being located round a table in a room in a local authority building). They nonetheless encapsulate a far-ranging regulatory repertoire. This spans international conventions, such as the United Nations Convention on the Rights (UNCRC) of the Child; European Convention on Human Rights and Fundamental Freedoms (ECHR); and national legislation in the form of the Children (Scotland) Act 1995, as well as local norms that govern the everyday lives of children and families that appear before them. The differing scales that feature in this context oscillate between more abstract formulations of rights and social realities. As Scott (1998, 44) has observed in relation to maps, their value lies in their 'abstractions and universality'. The same can be said of law (Santos 1987; 2002) where international and national legislation follow the same principles. How these principles acquire meaning, however, raises questions about the factors that come into play when they are applied in more concrete local settings. For Scott (1998, 46) notes that such abstractions 'are always far more static and schematic than the social phenomena they presume to typify'.

Our chapter highlights how hearings represent both legal and social spaces that intersect in a whole variety of ways, sometimes overlapping, sometimes in contestation with one another depending on how they are mobilized by participants during proceedings. Thus space forms an integral part of social relations (Giddens 1984; 1985; and Lefebvre 1991) that frame the physical and social setting within which the legal domain of hearings are constituted, drawing on the perceptions, knowledge and experiences of those social actors who bring it into being and whose participation is shaped by their understandings of the world that exists beyond hearings, both real and imagined. Such an analysis is in keeping with scholarship that has challenged the notion that law can be separated out from space and vice versa (Blomley 1994).

Our discussion of these issues is based on research carried out on children's hearings in Glasgow from 1997–2000.[1] This covered interviews with 40 children's panel members (about 10 per cent of panel members serving in Glasgow at that time), 25 safeguarders, 25 social workers, 25 parents and 132 children,[2] as well as observations of 34 hearings. Our chapter focuses on three hearings[3] that highlight everyday spaces that represent sites of tension, embodying ambiguous interpretations of danger and safety to be found at home, at school and on the streets. These foreground key spaces where young people may find themselves at risk, or alternatively, in a more secure environment. The characteristics that give rise to these perceptions of 'danger' and 'safety' take on different meanings for participants at hearings. Given the lack of facilities in the areas where many young people live, the streets are often the only space that is readily available to them. What represents risk to panel members, for example, hanging about on street corners, may not have the same associations for young people for whom they represent a place for socializing with others of their own age, embodying a positive interactive space for them. How notions of danger and safety are constructed is important because they form an integral part of assessing behaviour that forms a significant component in reaching legal decisions about what is in the child's best interests.

This is especially salient given that many of the grounds for referral, such as falling into bad associations, being exposed to moral danger or failing to attend school are age specific and represent behaviour for which adults are held unaccountable. Distinguishing normal from deviant behaviour that puts young people at risk requires panel members to make judgements balancing children's developmental and decision-making capacities upheld by Article 5 of the UNCRC with their welfare. Unfortunately, it was a condition of our research access that we did not interview the children or families whose hearings we attended. This meant we could not engage in extended case studies but had to base our findings on observations from hearings along with comments derived from interviewees. Although drawn from a limited source, our observations are important because they reveal the multi-vocality of young people, families, social and other service workers and panel members. This is significant because 'by joining multilocality to multivocality, we can look "through" these places, explore their links with others, consider why they are constructed as they are, see how places represent people, and begin to understand how people embody places' (Margaret C. Rodman, *Empowering Place*).

---

1 This formed part of a comparative research project from 1997–2000 on 'The Child's Voice in Legal Proceedings' in Scotland and the US funded by the Annenberg Foundation and the British Academy.

2 For details, see Griffiths and Kandel (2000).

3 To protect the young people involved we have changed their names.

The Children's Hearings System

Hearings exist to deal with children under 16 who are in need of compulsory measures of supervision. Implemented in 1971,[4] on the recommendations of the Kilbrandon Committee,[5] children's hearings in Scotland represented a novel form of juvenile justice that permitted state intervention in the lives of children across a broad spectrum of circumstances. These include neglected or abused children, as well as those children who have committed offences or who are 'beyond the control of a relevant person' or who fail 'to attend school regularly without reasonable excuse'.[6] The system's underlying rationale was, and continues to be, that of a welfare perspective based on the best interests of the child. Currently regulated by Part II of the Children (Scotland) Act 1995,[7] the system has attempted to implement a more rights-based orientation based on international norms (Griffiths and Kandel 2004).

Children's hearings take the form of lay panels, consisting of three members who are unpaid volunteers who are not required to have legal qualifications. Referrals are made by a reporter who is employed by the Scottish Children's Reporter Administration (SCRA), a national body charged with the management and deployment of reporters throughout Scotland. Decisions, however, are made by panel members who must assess whether a child is in need of compulsory measures of supervision, and if so, what conditions, if any, should be imposed.[8] In doing so they must adhere to three overriding principles. The first is that the welfare of the child is paramount (s. 16(1)). This reflects a focus on welfare under Article 3(1) of the UNCRC that is enhanced under Scottish legislation. The second principle, that reinforces Article 12(1) of the UNCRC dealing with children's participation, provides that children must be able to express their views and have them taken into account, where sufficiently mature (s. 16(2)) with a presumption in favour of children aged 12 or over having sufficient age and maturity (s. 11(10)). Finally, the third principle states that there should be minimum intervention, that is, that a hearing should only make an order if it is better for the child that such an order is made than to make no order at all (s. 16(3)). This is in keeping with the idea of family autonomy in decision-making and with Article 8 of the ECHR dealing with respect for private and family life.

In applying these principles panel members have to fill in the substance of what they entail and where boundaries are to be drawn, for example, making decisions about what 'welfare' embodies in particular contexts and when the minimum

---

4 Under the Social Work (Scotland) Act 1988.

5 *Report on Children and Young Persons, Scotland*, Cmnd. 2306 (1964).

6 This is under s. 70 of the Children (Scotland) Act 1995 (CSA).

7 For a detailed discussion of the system, see Edwards and Griffiths (2006).

8 Under s. 70 the hearing has a wide range of powers including the power to make a residential supervision requirement placing the child in a foster or local authority home, or even, in secure accommodation.

intervention principle is to be discarded, on the basis of local knowledge. As our chapter will demonstrate, however, what form this knowledge takes is contested among participants. It comprises of competing interests that render any attempt to define the 'local' as a clearly defined sphere untenable. Such interests derive from differentially situated social actors who reveal how any notion of 'community' must entail recognition 'of the structural relations of power and inequality' (Gupta and Ferguson 1997, 14).

The aim of a hearing is to reach a decision that is in the child's best interests after an open and full discussion. Although a legal forum, every effort is made to encourage children and families to participate in proceedings by dispensing with unnecessary legal formalities. Taking consensus as the starting point for discussion hearings seek to avoid the adversarial nature of formal legal proceedings. Thus evidential and procedural requirements are less onerous than those operating in courts and while lawyers may be present they rarely appear. Panel members work hard at speaking directly with children and families. They believe this promotes a more open and frank discussion that is in keeping with international due process concerns that have been incorporated into Scottish law.

Despite these efforts children and young people's participation at hearings has always been problematic. This was highly evident from the hearings we observed. Many of the children we interviewed stated that they found them 'scary' as 'it's frightening to have to go and talk in front of lots of people' (Griffiths and Kandel 2000). Panel members also observed that while it is essential to hear a child's story about the circumstances giving rise to a referral directly from the child this is generally 'an uphill struggle'. Part of the problem derives from the fact that however egalitarian panels attempt to be there is always a power imbalance for children and families know that panels have the power to remove children from their home (although they rarely do so). The issue of class and status also add to this asymmetrical power relationship as most of the children in the system come from a different socio-economic group than that of the panel members despite great efforts to recruit from across a broad social spectrum.[9] In a series of publications (Griffiths and Kandel 2000; 2001; 2004; 2005; 2006; 2009; forthcoming) we have discussed how the power and control differentials, varying perspectives of all participants, complicated professional and familial roles, conflicting welfare and due process legal provisions and emotional strains of the hearings militate against an egalitarian, transparent dialogue and full information. Nonetheless, panel members strive for this and for them the table around which hearings take place not only encompasses a physical and social space but also represents a metaphor for the system.

9 A study of 1,155 children referred to the hearings system in Scotland in 1995 found that children primarily came from households characterized by social and economic disadvantage, see Waterhouse and McGhee (2002). Of the 40 panel members interviewed in our study out of around 300 members, serving Glasgow in 1997–1998, nearly all came from professional/management backgrounds. Only one panel member was a taxi driver (who owned his own business) and one was a secretary.

The Table as Place and Symbol

At children's hearings the formal and rigidly hierarchical space of the courtroom is replaced by a smaller room with a table and chairs. Thus the table is both the setting and the symbol for hearings. There are variations in the types of tables to be found in different locations. At Bell Street, where the reporters' Glasgow office is situated, the table in the meeting room is large, highly polished and somewhat reminiscent of a board room. In other more local settings in Glasgow tables are generally smaller and less formal. At Pollock, for example, hearings take place is in a small house that provides many social services and that is adjacent to a community hall which accommodates functions, such as old age pensioners' tea dances. Everyone here sits in armchairs around a large, low, round coffee table. In yet another venue, Rutherglen, the table is even smaller and the panel members dress less formally.

Sitting around a table is crucial for panel members who perceive of it as enhancing dialogue with families. From their perspective the conference or coffee table both symbolizes and invites an open conversation among all the participants. However, families do not necessarily view the table in this way. The spatial configuration around the table is instructive for in all of the 34 hearings we observed the three panel members sat together, almost always with the chair in the middle. Although nothing is said about who should sit where, families and children usually gravitate instinctively towards the other end of the table from the panel members, with the service providers in between. This positioning of participants reflects the power relations that are at work when one side of the table controls proceedings and the other side responds, trying to counteract this power by revealing as little as possible when the panel probe for information and only revealing what they perceive may be of benefit them. Thus what appears on the surface as an open, unhierarchical space becomes a site where the inequality in social relations is marked by the way participants position themselves. For as Blomley (1994, xiii) observes space like law 'has a direct bearing on the way power is deployed'.

Transgressing the Invisible Barrier – Jamies's Hearing

In this hearing, 13-year-old Jamie comes before the panel for minor offences including breaking a window, setting an aerosol can alight, stealing various goods and driving around with friends in a stolen car. In addition he regularly fails to attend school. He appears accompanied by his mother, his grandmother and his younger sister. On this occasion his mother is wearing a suit (which is unusual at hearings) but gives the impression that she has taken special care with her appearance for the panel. It is clear from the social background report circulated to the panel and Jamie's mother before the hearing that at the time of his offending behaviour he and his sister were living with their maternal grandmother. This was because his mother, who was addicted to heroin, was receiving treatment in a drug rehabilitation facility.

The issue for the panel is how to deal with Jamie's problems. The social worker and his day care worker have agreed beforehand that they want the panel to make a home supervision requirement allowing Jamie and his sister to continue residing with their mother. The discussion opens with the social worker's report presenting this option to the panel. Despite the family's problems the social worker explains 'there is plenty of support' because the grandmother lives nearby and the family is 'very loyal to Mum'. In favour of reintegrating the family, the social worker observes that Jamie was on the 'fringes of shoplifting' because he was 'depressed about his mother's situation' but that Jamie's problems are 'containable'. He also makes the point that Jamie's offending and truancy began while he was living with his grandmother, suggesting it was in response to his mother's circumstances.

One panel member, who is a nurse and who is observing the mother closely, directly accuses her of being under the influence of drugs in the hearing. Jamie's mother immediately denies this but from the glazed look in her eyes the accusation appears to be well founded. The panel member having observed this challenges the social worker's recommendation that supervision should be at home with the mother. The conversation between the two of them becomes very heated with the panel member stating, 'she [Jamie's mother] is obviously under the influence of something. Her eyes are pin point'. During this conversation Jamie becomes increasingly agitated and intervenes to say 'my mother's situation is not material'. His mother tells him to be quiet, remain polite and to let the panel be. However, as the questions continue he gets so angry and defensive on his mother's behalf that he jumps up and leans across the table shouting, 'I'm not going to listen to this' in a threatening manner. For a moment it appears as if he is going to hit the panel member. The reporter gets up and interposes herself between the panel member and Jamie and the moment of danger passes. Afterwards, however, the panel acknowledge that violence might have erupted and the reporter comments that she was still shaking when writing up the minutes. Jamie gradually backs down, looks sad and angry, and eventually starts to cry. What involves a palpably and potentially violent episode within the hearing arises in connection with the way in which an external space, namely the mother's home, is perceived by the different participants as a zone of relative safety or danger.

For the social worker it is important to view the home in the broader context of social networks. For him the 'informal care arrangements that have been in place over two years are such that Jamie and his sister are capable of going to Granny's if they come home and Mum is crashed out on the sofa on drugs'. From his perspective they can rely on a support network beyond Jamie's mother, for Jamie and his sister 'go to the grandmother's house on a daily basis' and the support of 'the neighbours and local networks on that street are sufficient [for their protection]'. In his experience 'these informal arrangements are very common in my line'. He considers 'that the risks on balance are that the children are safe'. For the social worker the main concern is to get Jamie off the street where he gets into trouble and back into attending school so that the emphasis should be on ensuring 'that he [continues to] attend school'.

The panel member who is a nurse, however, believes that the home is potentially dangerous for the children because of the mother's drug addiction that renders her 'not fit to care for you'. While she agrees that the streets are a dangerous place for Jamie and that school is good for him she thinks that if he stays at home this will be detrimental to him as he will continue to cut school in order to take care of his mother. She is also very angry with the social worker because she believes that he put her at risk by forcing her to address the mother's drug habit directly rather than raising it himself as she believes he should have done.

The chair and the reporter express the view, after the hearing, that the social worker did not raise the issue of addiction because he was afraid of damaging his relationship with the family with whom he has to work on an ongoing basis. They observe that he does not meet with the family at home but at his office, which they attribute to his fear of them, or rather, of Jamie. His attitude can also be explained on the basis that he believes that focusing on the mother's addiction would impact negatively on the decision to keep the family together which he considers to be in everyone's best interests.

From the mother's perspective, the panel member's questions and dialogue threaten her because her addiction may result in her children being removed from home. For Jamie, this questioning not only damages his mother's public image, but also raises fears about her ability to care for him and his sister. At several points during the hearing when he sees the specter of family dismemberment he loudly interjects, 'I can take care of myself.'

At the end of the hearing the decision is to continue Jamie's supervision on condition that he resides with his mother and attends day care. Ironically, what is conceived of as a place of safety appeared momentarily to become a place of danger. For the hearing that is intended to provide a non-threatening space for discussion almost becomes a place of violence. In this rather unusual case, the invisible barrier that exists between panel members and families becomes visible through the physical breach of space that Jamie's anger engenders.

Domesticating Aggression: Jimmy's Hearing

Jimmy's case has some similarities with that of Jamie. For 15-year-old Jimmy, like Jamie, has a problematic relationship with his mother who abandoned him when he was a baby leaving him in his grandmother's care. He also has a temper that has got him into trouble on several occasions in the past when he has assaulted people. This hearing represents one of many that Jimmy has attended. It represents a continuation from a previous hearing where he was sent under supervision to a residential school called Cardross. After assaulting one of the staff members there he was 'illegally' sent home. While at home he has been attending day care and the purpose of the hearing is to assess whether he should be sent back to Cardross or be allowed to continue residing with his grandmother.

Those present at the hearing include the usual core personnel, as well as Jimmy, his grandmother, his social worker, his key worker and his day care worker. Also present is a member of the Children's Panel Advisory Committee (CPAC) who is there to monitor the hearing in a supervisory capacity. The key issue in this case is how to deal with Jimmy's aggressive behaviour. This is expressly addressed by the social worker who, as in Jamie's case, is the first person to open up the dialogue after the chair has read the grounds for referral. According to his social worker:

> Jimmy comes across as having an aggressive character … He carries quite a temper … We're working on a plan but it requires Jimmy to work hard … He has had to be removed from the unit several times because of aggression. Jimmy, his grandmother, and I are trying to secure day care. It's his last chance for an education … [but he] … has jeopardized his group placement through intimidation.

In this hearing the panel appear to be much closer to Jimmy and his granny's socio-economic class than the previous panel were to that of Jamie and his mother. In addition, his social service providers appear to be more forthright than Jamie's social worker was in outlining Jimmy's situation. The whole tenor of this hearing represents an attempt by the panel to mediate Jimmy's relationship with his grandmother.

Jimmy's grandmother is deeply concerned about the situation but she does not directly express what is troubling her. Instead, she cloaks her own fear *of* Jimmy as fear *for* Jimmy himself. The two are easily conflated because the danger zones for Jimmy – in the flat with his friends (where they are liable to misbehave) or home alone where he gets bored and is prone to temper tantrums – are also dangerous for his grandmother as long as they are physically living in the same place. In addition there is also the fear of what might happen if Jimmy goes outside the home and on the streets with his friends.

The grandmother is obviously deeply concerned but hides her concern under the guise of requesting parenting advice which the chair readily accedes to. There is much talk about staying out late and being left home alone:

> C: Jimmy, why do you stay out late?
>
> J: Because I'm with my pals. She [grandmother] wants me to stay in every night and not do anything …
>
> C: Twelve's [midnight's] a pretty fair time to come, don't you think?
>
> J: I'm with my pals. Is that a big problem? I want to do what I want. Why is that a big problem? … My grandmother wants me to stay in when she is out herself … You haven't asked me what she is like … During the week I am usually in by eight and my grandmother goes to her old age pensioners' meetings … And she complains about me being out when she's not even there. [J's wearing a baseball cap and jacket. He pulls the collar of the jacket over his nose and hides his eyes in the collar as a way of avoiding the panel members].

> Gm: I always leave food for him when I am out ... I know it's not healthy to stay in the house all the time. But I'm worried sick. I can't handle it. I'm getting too old.
>
> C: Twelve o'clock seems fair ... Every home has got boundaries ... During the week he's in?
>
> Gm: Yes. It's weekends I'm worried about ... I'm not getting any younger.
>
> C: But he's getting older and more mature all the time. You've got to compromise.

The whole proceedings generate a discourse of threat and fear that is never tackled directly but rather elided by attempting to reach a compromise between Jimmy and his grandmother. This is couched in terms of what amounts to an appropriate sharing of responsibilities and duties given his age. Thus the panel endeavor to mediate compromise about how late Jimmy can stay outside, whether some of his friends can be in the flat and whether he should do household chores. They treat him as a normal adolescent and engage in homilies about teenage behaviour setting out appropriate boundaries and limits. However, the grandmother and everyone present know that Jimmy is violent. As the CPAC member commented after the hearing 'he's got monumental problems. He's not a normal fifteen-year-old'. Similarly, the reporter confides that 'his problems are more than just adolescence. He should have been removed from the family setting and been where boundaries are set. He goes berserk. He's been expelled from places dealing with small groups. He's much better since he's been at Cardross. He couldn't communicate at all before'.

It seems that wherever Jimmy is danger exists. He has been aggressive at home, in day care and in Cardross. The grandmother does not want her violent grandson to hang about with a group of troublesome kids whether at home or in the street. She hints that he and his friends have stolen the coins from the TV meter, and that at least one time, after some friends left, many things of hers were broken. However, she doesn't want Jimmy to be outside on the streets with his friends either because of what might happen. Jimmy, conversely, doesn't want to stay home after school because staying alone makes him bored, angry and sometimes violent. On the other hand, if his friends are at home with him their behaviour may incite violence. His grandmother worries about this noting that 'I won't allow his pals to come up. Because, [one time they did] and afterwards Jimmy smashed lots of things in the house and I had to pay to replace them.'

Thus, as in Jamie's case, the home represents a dangerous place for Jimmy and his grandmother but no one on this panel will directly confront this issue. Like Jamie, Jimmy would rather stay at home than return to Cardross. He also, like Jamie, stresses his need for freedom and independence. In both cases maintaining a balance in precarious situations is difficult given that neither family is willing to engage more actively with social services for Jamie's mother refuses to go to outpatient rehabilitation and Jimmy declines assistance with anger management because it's for 'crazy people'. The panel finally decide that Jimmy is to remain under supervision at his grandmother's home because, as the chair observes, 'the residential school is not for him. He doesn't want to be there. He and his grandmother need to work on things.' While Jimmy agrees to this his grandmother expresses some doubts asking, 'what if it falls through?'

Gendered Constructions of Space: The Vulnerability of Young Women

The next hearing focuses on the position of a young woman called Janice and highlights another danger zone that arises, that of potential sexual victimization, when young women socialize on the streets or in locations that are unknown to their parents. While the outside world represents a certain freedom for young people, for adults such as panel members, social workers and even parents, it also exposes them to the dark side of life involving alcohol abuse, drugs, underage sex, rape and prostitution. Young women are especially vulnerable and panel members often express their fears about these young women's vulnerability in terms of the coded language of moral danger. For panel members this creates somewhat of a dilemma where they deal with youngsters who are overtly sexualized and/or runaways. This is because they are aware that these young people may be seeking to escape from physical or sexual abuse at home. In these circumstances, normal associations of the home, as a place of safety, have to be suspended. Yet acquiring the evidence necessary to substantiate what is going on is almost impossible for panel members as children and their families often engage in a conspiracy of silence. The kind of difficulties panel member's face are highlighted by Janice's case.

Negotiating Boundaries: Janice's Hearing

Janice, a 14-year-old girl, has been before the panel several times because she has been staying out all weekend without letting her parents know where she is and without parental permission. The panel suspect that physical or sexual abuse may be the underlying cause of her behaviour and they have appointed a safeguarder to investigate Janice's situation and report back to them. Janice is tall, blond, physically mature and looks older than her age. She is sexually active (the social worker has given her the pill but the mother worries how that may intersect with her epilepsy medicine), and, until recently, had a boyfriend of the same age. The parents, who are divorced, seem to have withdrawn their emotional support. At a key point in the hearing her mother absolves herself from any responsibility for Janice's behaviour stating, 'I'm not her legal guardian … her father has custody.' Both mother and father agree that Janice, who has attempted suicide three times, is strong willed and appear to wash their hands of her.

The hearing opens with the safeguarder's report that states that Janice is in great danger, and that recommends her immediate placement in a residential school. However the panel members, who have little respect for the safeguarder because of what appears to be an inadequate report, disagree with the safeguarder's recommendations because they fear Janice will just run away from the school.

Their views are shared by Janice's social and intermediate treatment worker and her mother who states, 'She'll nae hack it' noting that she is a 'dangerous wee lassy' who reacts violently when her will is thwarted.

In dealing with Janice, the panel (as in Jimmy's hearing) attempt to provide a parenting lesson about rules and boundaries that is aimed at getting Janice to curtail her behaviour. However, unlike Jimmy's hearing, where they argued in favour of giving him more responsibility, they adopt the opposite approach with Janice who they characterize as being too immature to set her own limits. Yet in many ways Janice is maintaining the limits she sets for herself far better than Jimmy who cannot control his own aggression. Unlike Jimmy, Janice does stay at home during the week and goes to school. It is only at weekends that she absents herself from home. The problem is that the system believes that her limits are not appropriate given that the danger or safety of spaces in this context is intimately connected with a young woman's body and with her age and gender. Janice is adamant 'I want to do what I want' but the panel view this as inappropriate. They struggle throughout the hearing to get her to agree to stay at home at weekends or at least phone one of her parents to let them know where she is. Although Janice and her father participate vociferously at the hearing neither will say anything about what happens at her father's flat at weekends while Janice remains silent about where she goes and what she does. Those present who cannot get information from either of them desperately try to figure out what is going on.

> Chair to J: Is it right what they say that you won't go home?
>
> J: I won't go home weekends unless I've nowhere else to stay.
>
> Chair to J: Why won't you go home?
>
> Janice says nothing.
>
> Chair: Is there a reason we don't know about?"
>
> Mum: No.
>
> Social Worker: Janice has only been absent 3 weekends. I can't understand why Janice won't tell her father where she is and why her father would have a difficulty with this. Why can't Janice let her father know where she is? … Janice has played the game to a certain extent. I don't understand the problem.
>
> Chair to J: What's the big issue of letting your parents know where you are. You are making me wonder if you want to be put in a residential home. You're not accepting what we're saying.
>
> J: I don't want to go to a residential school. I hate people telling me what to do … I like school.
>
> Father and mother: To control her you need to chain her to her bed.
>
> Social worker: The crucial thing is to get Janice to communicate better with her mum and dad.

After going round in circles the panel finally persuade her father to agree to allow Janice out at weekends on the understanding that if she does not come home he will ring the police. This infuriates Janice who shrieks, 'Call the police? I go to school, I come home, I go to IT three times a week and I can't even go out at weekends. I can't even have a fucking life. What do you think I am. Fuck off the lot of you's!' (bangs fist on table and storms out).

After things have calmed down the panel decide that Janice will remain under a home supervision order at her father's because 'a residential placement will not address Janice's problem'. However a condition is attached to the order that requires her father to phone the police if she does not come home or ring him to say where she is at weekends. In order to monitor the situation an early review is called for in six to eight weeks time.

These three hearings demonstrate how decisions about what is in the child's best interests are reached on the basis of assessments about what constitutes safety or danger for young people in locations outside hearings. These locations represent both physical spaces and social settings that become intertwined in ways that render places like the home, the streets and school somewhat grey areas. For they embody ambiguous zones that can easily alter their characteristics by shifting from a more secure space to a potentially dangerous one at a moment's notice. How these spaces are interpreted and contextualized, in order to reach a legal decision, demonstrates that law 'cannot be detached from the particular places in which it acquires meaning and saliency' (Blomley 1994, 46).

This spatialization of law is complimented by the way in which the space within the hearing itself is processed. This is important because control exercised over who speaks when, and thus the sequencing of contributions, provides an effective mechanism for deciding what is to be included or excluded from the proceedings. This contributes to the 'closure of law and legal inquiry to outside influence' (Blomley 1994, Chapter 1). The sequencing of processual space is also intertwined with interpretations of body language that surface at panels, that assist panel members in forming their judgements, but that are never expressly acknowledged in hearings themselves. This goes together with coded messages that panel members may exchange with one another, discussed below. Thus what unfolds on the surface, in terms of dialogue and silence, must be deciphered through an understanding of the more hidden dynamics that underpin hearings.

Processing Space within Hearings: Management and Control

At the end of a hearing the panel members immediately give their decision to the child and family, one after another, stating their reasons for it. The decision of the majority is then recorded in writing. However, what appears to be a straightforward process has, in fact, proved to be somewhat contentious. This is because a number of the young people we interviewed interpreted the process as embodying decisions that were either predetermined before the hearing, or that were insufficiently reflected upon, due to the lack of a post-hearing caucus among panel members. They felt short-changed because of the lack of time allotted to panel members to meet in private (like judges) to reach their decision. Panel members, however, consider this process which differs from that of the courts, to be one of the jewels of the system because it is open and transparent. They consider the fact that it is based on a majority vote as representative of their independence and as militating against any collusion. As one member explained:

> I think the bottom line, the strength of the system, is that you've got three very different people, with different backgrounds, different expectations. And to allow one, maybe domineering person to try to persuade his or her colleagues what is right isn't the way we should be doing it. Each member makes their own decision and that's as valid as the others, and if it's a majority, then there's no problem.

Ironically, some young people feel dissatisfied because they only perceive the surface spontaneity that constitutes the public relations aspect of the system and not the less transparent backstage factors of earlier preparation, planning and procedural management that lead up to a decision. These include making notes beforehand based on social background and other reports and drawing up a list of options (that virtually every panel member we interviewed confessed to making) that are reassessed in the light of observations made during the hearing. Thus the decision is not as quick as it appears, nor is it as untainted by the influence of others as suggested. For there are ways in which the process may be shaped behind the scenes, for example, by the chair's control over the order in which panel members give their decision.

The chair who is always an experienced panel member has the responsibility for deciding who gives the first, second and third decision. It is considered best practice, and the training emphasizes, that the chair should be last to give the decision so that they can be the tie breaker if necessary. Similarly, because of the chair's authority, it is considered more appropriate for the chair to speak last because they might influence the other two panel members.

However, the chair is not obliged to go last and does not always do so. Of the 32 panel members who answered the question whether they had ever given their decision first as a chair only 15 denied doing so. A significant number of those that had done so observed that they summed up the position towards the end of the hearing. In effect this often proves decisive for the decision-making process. For by stating what they are going to decide the chair may have some influence over the other panel members who are still wavering or uncertain. As one interviewee observed:

> There have been occasions where I have felt that the way the hearing has gone and what has been discussed, that the decision should be a certain way and not been too confident that, that was what was going to happen, and therefore tried to maybe sum up and to put across the way I am thinking anyway and see what comes back.

Of the 17 panel members who had given their decision first as chairs, nearly all admitted that they had only done so on one or two occasions as they recognized that this was 'inappropriate' or at least 'discourteous'. Some of them, however, acknowledged that they had used the chair's prerogative to influence or control a decision. This was where they had an especially strong view and where they were afraid that if they left their decision until last the end result might not accord with what they considered to be in the child's best interests.

One gave this clarification:

> I knew this strong side member was thinking directly the contrary to what I wanted to happen. And I knew the other side member was wavering and was weak and could be persuaded … then [I] turn[ed] to this weaker one, and said 'And what's your decision?' and they agreed with me. [In] … this particular case I thought I can manipulate because I know there's a strong panel member here, and a weak one here, and I know I can get what I want if I do it this way.

Even if the chair goes last they have the authority to choose which other panel member goes first or second. Typically, they will ask one panel member to go first in one hearing and the other to give their decision first in the second hearing. Or, as one panel member observed, they might ask the panel member who is most 'determined or involved with the questioning' in a particular hearing to go first.

Yet, even if the chair is just choosing who goes first and second there is a potential ability to manipulate the hearing. One panel member told us:

> Certainly if you are sitting, particularly as chairman over here and I have been in situations where I know that the person, let's say on my left, is at odds with my view of a matter, okay, or is tending towards something that doesn't agree with my view of it, but the person on the right is tending to agree with my view of the matter, then I will tend to ask the person on the right to give their decision first in the hope that that might sway the person on the left to switch their decision. Otherwise you end up with a majority decision.

The chair also has the ability to jump into the second slot if they believe the second side member will follow the first side member's decision. As another panel member commented:

> I have heard of another case where the experienced person was in the chair and asked one person, it was actually a chap who trained with me … for his decision, which he gave. The experienced lady, who was in the chair, disagreed strongly with this decision and immediately intervened because she felt, probably correctly, that the rookie [new panel member] would have just followed suit.

Only five panel members stated that the first speaker could not or did not influence the others. Most panel members were highly aware of the possible influence of the first speaker. Indeed, ten panel members remembered having been swayed themselves by a prior speaker. One cautioned:

> That happened to me when I was a very new panel member. The other panel member was asked first and I wasn't terribly sure and went along with them and it was the wrong decision and I've never made that mistake again.

All panel members who spoke about new panel members brought up the subject of their greater vulnerability to influence by a previous decision-maker.

Thus panel members attempt to control the hearing through strategies involving the sequencing of speech and management of participation. It is not only the timing and order of decision-making that is relevant here but the order in which participants speak. There is no set order at panels which permit members to ask questions whenever they wish. However, given the difficulties of children's participation, they try not to break the hearing's flow by asking questions too frequently or that cover old ground. They do, however, give one another an indication of what they are thinking by the kind of questions that they ask.

Reconstructing Space: Legal Interventions

Through our observation and discussion of four hearings and interviews with participants at panels, we have highlighted the complexities that arise in spatializing law in children's hearings in Glasgow. For reaching a decision about whether or not a young person under 16 should be placed under compulsory measures of supervision involves making an assessment about the danger or safety of spaces, such as the home, school or the streets that that young person inhabits. This is in order to meet the welfare criteria that underpin the hearings' legal determination of what constitutes the best interests of the child.

In this process the table around which hearings are located represents both physical and social space which for panel members represents a metaphor for the system itself. This is one that embodies openness and transparency in its efforts to engage children and their families' participation in reaching a consensual decision. However, as we have demonstrated, this transparency is called into question by some young people who are skeptical about the decision-making process for the reasons discussed earlier. Not only that, but the basis upon which findings of danger or safety, and what amounts to the boundaries of acceptable or unacceptable behaviour, renders the process more opaque given that judgements are made on the basis of perceptions and understandings of spaces outside of the hearing. Such spaces have to be reconstituted within the hearing itself and contextualized from background reports, the participation of those present and through non-verbal communication, such as body language.

Mapping hearings onto these spaces through the perspectives of children and their families, panel members and relevant professionals reveals the multifaceted nature and ambiguity of their construction. For space in and of itself is never inherently safe or dangerous. How it is perceived and presented is structured in part by the roles attributed to it by participants that are never value neutral (Harvey 1996). Institutional and professional affiliations may shape participants' perceptions of space in such a way that the hearing comes to represent a variety of perspectives and agendas that, far from being complimentary, may in fact be at odds with each other (Griffiths and Kandel forthcoming).

In the three hearings there was wide disagreement on the facts and their meaning. In Jamies's hearing, the panel member and the social worker had different views about the mother's drug usage that clearly came from their professional orientations. The panel member, who was a nurse, based her approach on concerns arising from the mother's medical condition, while the social worker engaged with the broader social networks that he comes into contact with in his professional life. These represent different perceptions of what local space, namely the mother's home, entails. For the social worker it is embedded within a larger social matrix (Blomley 1994) that makes it sufficiently safe, in his judgement, for Jamie and his sister to remain there. Thus the boundaries of what was acceptable were much more widely drawn than those of the panel member for whom the space was more narrowly contained. For by focusing solely on the mother's behaviour, she saw it as a place that put the children at risk, although she was eventually persuaded to let them remain there.

Similarly, in Janice's hearing the safeguarder, whose remit is to focus on the child, interpreted Janice's absence from home, in space that was 'unknown', as involving drinking, using drugs and having sex, although she had no evidence of this and appeared to be relying on her imagination as to what was taking place given Janice's past history. Nonetheless, she formed the judgement that Janice should be put in a residential school immediately. Her view was at odds with that of Janice's social workers who wanted to work with the family to deal with her problems. Once again, perceptions of how to work with boundaries varied in determining whether or not to put Janice in a residential school.

Given that these kinds of consideration underpin assessments of what is in the child's best interests it is not surprising to find participants' overtly expressing, implying or deliberately ignoring certain features in their presentation of circumstances, including factors that may give rise to dangerous flashpoints in relation to themselves or others. Thus in Jimmy's hearing, the panel studiously avoid tackling his aggressive and violent conduct directly, but rather couch their discussions in terms of the need to address his adolescent behaviour, by trying to establish appropriate boundaries and limits. In this case their adherence to Article 5 of the UNCRC that promotes recognition of the child's developmental and decision-making capacities seems to totally ignore the realities of the situation. Indeed, the reporter made it clear after the hearing that in her view Jimmy should have been sent back to Cardross as the placement had benefited him. Her opinion was based on knowledge that is not accessible to panel members, as it is a feature of the system that they rarely deal with the same child twice, whereas reporters, as gatekeepers to the system, get to keep track of young people's progress. Such knowledge, however, cannot be relayed by the reporter to the panel at a hearing as they have to maintain a distance from proceedings because they are kept separate from the decision-making process. Thus the professional limitations placed on her constrained her from revealing this information at the hearing.

In this case the chair did most of the speaking at the panel and seemed determined to equate Jimmy with her own adolescent grandson, thus aligning his behaviour with that of a normal teenage boy. For example, she comments that 'my grandson is 16 and his room is a mess and he doesn't lift a finger. Where do they [adults] get these ideas of about this paragon of virtue?' It is possible that she was interpreting Jimmy's behaviour in line with her own conceptions of what being a teenager entails and the way they create their individual space, and thus contextualizing his actions as being just a little out of kilter with what is normal at that age. However, it is also possible that the adults present, including Jimmy's grandmother, considered that expressly focusing discussion on his violent and aggressive behaviour would breach the unspoken in family relations (namely abuse of his grandmother) that could not be repaired and that would prove counterproductive in these circumstances.

Families have their own code concerning behaviour, based on loyalty and perceptions about what it is appropriate to reveal to strangers or outsiders (Griffiths and Kandel 2004; 2005; 2006) that may lead them to being less than candid about what is going on in the spaces in which they live. Thus in Janice's case, neither she nor her father would allude to what was going on at his home at weekends that made her feel that she had to leave, although she and her father were otherwise actively vocal at the hearing. This put the panel at a disadvantage as they strongly suspected that her absence was due to some kind of abuse at home. Keeping silent can extend to other participants, such as the social worker in Jamie's case who colluded with Jamie's mother in skating over her ongoing drug addiction. For he was deliberately vague in his report where he acknowledged that there had been problems in the family but did not specify what they were, while the mother was in outright denial about her ongoing dependency.

What emerges from hearings are partial truths and silences. These call into question any notions of transparency in proceedings, for what emerges, is in fact, a mosaic of conspiracies, mysteries, understandings and misunderstandings that derive from the participants' varying positions with regard to participation in the decision-making process. These militate against an open dialogue. Thus, what unfolds on the surface must be understood in the context of more hidden factors that control and shape the legal proceedings. These include processing the space within the hearings themselves, through the timing and order of decision-making and through the order in which participants speak. For such timing and sequencing of information can influence decision-making about what is in the child's best interests in a powerful way. It also facilitates the exchange of coded messages as panel members pick up on each other's cues and subtle nuances of gesture that provide them with clues as to how their colleagues are thinking. More often than not this interpretive process also involves decoding families' dynamics, through paying close attention to their spatial configuration, body language and the sequencing of their speech or silences. Such maneuvers often result in panels reaching unanimous decisions. Thus law and space are intertwined in ways that reflect 'the field of power relations that links localities to a wider world' (Gupta and Ferguson 1997, 25) through an examination of how social actors map out material spaces, such as the home, the streets and school, in different, distinct and contested ways.

References

Blomley, N.K. (1994) *Law, Space and the Geographies of Power*. New York and London: The Guilford Press.

Edwards, L. and Griffiths, A. (2006) *Family Law*. Edinburgh: Thomson/W. Green.

Giddens, A. (1984) *The Constitution of Society: Outline of a Theory of Structuration*. Cambridge: Polity Press in association with Basil Blackwell, Oxford.

Giddens, A. (1985) *A Contemporary Critique of Historical Materialism Vol. 2. The Nation-state and Violence*. London: Polity Press.

Griffiths, A. and Kandel, R.F. (2000) 'Hearing Children in Children's Hearings'. *Child and Family Law Quarterly*, 3: 283–99.

Griffiths, A. and Kandel, R.F. (2001) 'Working towards Consensus: Children's Hearings in Scotland' in P. Foley, J. Roche and S. Tucker (eds) *Children in Society: Contemporary Theory, Policy and Practice*. New York/Basingstoke: Palgrave in Association with the Open University, pp. 121–32.

Griffiths, A. and Kandel, R.F. (2004) 'Empowering Children? Legal Understandings and Experiences of Rights in the Scottish Children's Hearings System' in S. Halliday and P. Schmidt (eds) *Human Rights Brought Home: Socio-Legal Perspectives on Human Rights in the National Contex*. Oxford and Portland, Oregon: Hart, pp. 231–55.

Griffiths, A. and Kandel, R.F. (2005) 'Localising the Global: Rights of Participation in the Scottish Children's Hearings System' in F. von Benda-Beckmann, K. von Benda-Beckmann and A. Griffiths (eds) *Mobile People, Mobile Law: Expanding Legal Relations in a Contracting World*. Aldershot/UK and Burlington/US: Ashgate, pp. 482–514.

Griffiths, A. and Kandel, R.F. (2006) 'Children's Confidentiality at the Crossroad: Challenges for the Scottish Children's Hearings System'. *The Journal of Social Welfare and Family Law*, 28(2): 137–52.

Griffiths, A. and Kandel, R.F. (2009) 'Half-told Truths and Partial Silence: Managing Communication in Scottish Children's Hearings' in F. von Benda-Beckmann, K. von Benda-Beckmann and A. Griffiths (eds) *The Power of Law in a Transnational World: Anthropological Enquiries*. Oxford: Berghahn.

Griffiths, A. and Kandel, R.F. (forthcoming) 'The Governance of Children: From Welfare Justice to Proactive Regulation in the Scottish Children's Hearings System' in F. von Benda-Beckmann, K. von Benda-Beckmann and J. Eckert (eds) *Rules of Law and Laws of Ruling*. Aldershot/UK and Burlington/US: Ashgate.

Gupta, A. and Ferguson, J. (1997) *Culture, Power and Place: Explorations in Critical Anthropology*. Durham and London: Duke University Press.

Harvey, D. (1996) *Justice, Nature and the Geography of Difference*. Oxford: Blackwell Publishers.

Lefebvre, H. (1991) *The Production of Space* (translated by D. Nicholson-Smith). Oxford: Blackwell Publishing.

Santos, B. de Sousa (1987) 'Law: A Map of Misreading. Toward a Postmodern Conception of Law'. *Journal of Law and Society*, 14(3): 279–302.

Santos, B. de Sousa (2002) *Toward a New Legal Common Sense: Law, Globalization and Emancipation*. London: Butterworths, LexisNexis.

Scott, J.C. (1998) *Seeing like a State: How Certain Schemes to Improve the Human Condition Have Failed*. New Haven and London: Yale University Press.

Waterhouse, L. and McGhee, J. (2002) 'Children's Hearings in Scotland: Compulsion and Disadvantage'. *Journal of Social Welfare and Family Law*, 24(3): 279–96.

Chapter 9

The Regulation of Commodity Exchange in Southern Africa during the Eighth to Fifteenth Centuries CE[1]

Edwin N. Wilmsen

In this chapter, I present more an exercise in epistemology than a completed case study and engage a social geography in order to map the processes by which law may have been fashioned to organize space in interior southern Africa during the eighth to fifteenth centuries. As will be seen, this region was at that time part of an early form of 'globalization' encompassing the entire Indo-Pacific province as well as the Islamic caliphates of the eastern Mediterranean. Although there exist a few documents pertaining to this larger province, there are no written records for or from this interior region until the beginning of the sixteenth century when the Portuguese captured the Swahili trading entrepôts on the east coast and began to penetrate into the interior; even these are sketchy. Other forms of evidence must be adduced to illuminate the social processes active in the interior in the centuries I am considering.

Premises

Material artifacts are a prime source of evidence for this task. Initially the products of human activity and later recovered by archaeological means, they can provide a firm basis from which to assess the trajectory of these social processes and the economic formations in which they functioned. This assertion while not, in itself, novel is still often dismissed by Euro-American common sense. Appadurai (1986, 4), drawing on Dumont (1980, 229–30), remarks on 'the powerful contemporary tendency to regard things as inert and mute, knowable only by persons and their words'; he notes, however, that this was not always so. Weiner (1992, 34–7) confirms how far not so: reading John Locke she finds that for him 'the boundaries between persons and things are not rigidly separate'. The basis for this finding is Locke's ([1690] 1980, original primes) thesis that 'yet every man has a "property" in his own "person" annexed [through] the "labour" of his body and the "work" of his hands'. Reading further, we find that Locke innumerated material as well as abstract property that a person annexes as ones own: material property is 'whatsoever

1 All dates are given as Current Era (CE) dates.

[a person] removes out of the state that Nature hath provided and left it in, he hath mixed his labour with it'; abstract property includes 'liberties and estates'. Weiner (1992, 34) says that these property relations were deemed so pervasive that Enlightenment philosophers 'modeled their claims for individual liberty after the way inalienable possessions [material as well as abstract] authenticated the rank and status of their owners'. This is a powerful platform from which to address the role of materials in fashioning and fostering social order.

Among archaeologists, Hodder (1982a; 1982b) has emphasized this active role of material artifacts, while Renfrew (1972; 1978) insists we cannot discuss such objects without attention to social concepts of value embedded in them. Nevertheless, many archaeologists – as well as many doubters of archaeology's capacity for social analysis – still have an underdeveloped comprehension of the anthropological principles needed to 'consider the intervening practices by which people actually negotiate, reproduce, and contest social order and authority' (Dietler 1999; 2001). To remedy this, Killick (forthcoming) urges an expanded archaeological 'study of the strategies of individuals, groups and institutions within societies, and of how structure emerges from their complex interplay'.

To engage with these strictures, I begin with a second assertion, one that may at first seem more novel and is surely contentious in some circles. This is that material artifacts have the same ontological status as words, and, marked by distinct intentions of their makers and users, are potentially as comprehensible as verbal documents; thus, they have communicative as well as utilitarian functions (Wilmsen 1994).[2] This perception derives ultimately from Locke followed by Marx and Engels ([1846] 1947, 16) who, in *The German Ideology*, wrote:

> The first historical act is thus the production of the means to satisfy [human] needs, the production of material life itself. And indeed this is an historical act, a fundamental condition of all history, which today, as thousands of years ago, must daily and hourly be fulfilled.

Central to Marxian thought is the proposition that human social relations are not primordial but are constructed by human agents through their labour, that human history and sociality are inextricably bound up with materials.[3] Note carefully the convergence with Locke.

---

2 We all know that words may be uttered either to inform or to deceive, to reveal or to conceal. An utterance by one person may mean the diametric opposite of the same utterance by another. Historians, lawyers and voters go to great efforts to differentiate these meanings and their relation, if any, to perceived reality; the task of archaeologists with regard to materials is in principle no different, although they face the added complication that direct links between things and words are almost always no longer tangible.

3 This view of human development has, in fact, a long and honorable place in archaeological thought, as, for example, expressed by Kenneth Oakley (1957) in his book *Man the Tool-maker*.

Two seminal theorists, both non-Marxians, writing at around the turn of the twentieth century, articulated the founding premises upon which this proposition could be made operative in the investigation of what Appadurai (1986) somewhat poetically has called 'the social life of things'. One, Georg Simmel, is sometimes referred to as the forgotten one of sociology's 'big four' (the others being Marx, Weber and Durkheim) and Beidelman (1989) admonishes anthropologists for their part in this neglect. Simmel noted, in *The Philosophy of Money* ([1907] 1978, 73), that value is not an inherent property of objects, but is a judgement made by subjects. In *The Philosophy of Value* he (1900) had previously stressed that in any instance of exchange:

> While the object itself is the thing in controversy – which means that the sacrifice [i.e., value] which it represents is being determined – its significance for both contracting parties appears much more as something outside of these parties and of the self-existent object than if the individual [acquirer or purveyor] thought of it only in its relation to himself.

What Simmel is saying here is that the value each party to an exchange places on an object is mediated by transcendent temporal, cultural and social caveats. For Simmel, then, as for Locke and Marx, the boundaries between persons and things are not rigidly separate; it is thus important to see the calculative dimension in all forms of exchange (Simmel [1907] 1978, 97–8). Simmel was interested primarily in the analysis of money, for him the most complex instrument of exchange; however, it is clear that his observations (particularly in *Value* as quoted above) may be applied to any conditions under which objects circulate in regimes of value in space and time, not only those specific to that of monetary capitalism. Appadurai (1986, 3) expands this to note that value is embodied in things that are exchanged and it is necessary to focus on the things themselves, in addition to the conditions of exchange, in order to appreciate the social judgements underlying that value, for the meanings of things are inscribed in their forms, uses and trajectories.

A corollary premise derives from Thorstein (1899), who, as a solid Spenserian evolutionist, would no doubt cringe to see his ideas applied in a pre-industrial context. Even so, his insight that prestigious objects are not merely reflections of their owners' status, but play a major role in bringing about that status is manifest in the biographies of many throughout recorded history who rose from humble origins to exalted station by arrogating to themselves the prestigious substances of their time (Weiner 1992, 35). It should take no more than a moment's reflection to grasp the salience of Thorstein's insight for earlier times.

As a consequence of these premises, it is clear that objects become invested with meaning through social interaction and are capable of accumulating histories (Gosden and Marshall 1999). Kopytoff (1986) provides an incisive critical component by drawing attention to the biographical aspect of things, which he notes is never irrelevant. The memory – of possessors and onlookers – of an object's association with past or present places, persons, events or other things imbues the material fabric of that object with the social judgements that give it value. That is to say, as did Weiner (1985), words and objects are not always mutually exclusive, for objects may have oral histories transmitted with their ownership. And the obverse is equally true: the meaning of an oral text – even a written one – is often instilled in specific objects (one need think no further than the role of flags in modern states or of beads in some religious devotions). Objects with particularly strong, or long, associations acquire the power to instill status in their possessors. Status items, thus, should best be regarded as objects whose principal use is rhetorical and social, as incarnate signs; and, since most are put to some sort of use, even if only as adornment or display, they should be further regarded as a register of consumption with a capacity to signal fairly complex social messages and a linkage in their consumption to specified persons (Appadurai 1986, 38).

Things

With these premises set forth, I turn now to the scope of Indo-Pacific commodity exchange with the southern African interior and to things in order to set the scene of activity.

About the turn of the eighth–ninth centuries, blue glass beads of a particular type called Zhizo appear in several sites in Zimbabwe and at the Tsodilo Hills site, Nqoma, in north-western Botswana 1,500 kilometres from the East African coast. The chemical composition of the glass from which these beads are made point to manufactories in what is now Iraq, Syria and possibly Indonesia–Malaysia as their source (Wood 2000; and Robertshaw et al. 2003).[4] The beads at Nqoma are accompanied by marine shells, conus and cowrie, some species of which are confined to the Indian Ocean. These luxury goods were brought to ports on the coast by traders in boats propelled by equatorial currents and monsoonal winds; from these ports they were transported inland. About 100 years later Zhizo beads increase in abundance and appear in a number of other sites, including Bosutswe in eastern Botswana; (Map 9.1) the greatest number occur at Nqoma and in the Limpopo basin, with typically only one or two at most other sites. Chickens (Southeast Asian domesticates) and Zebu-type humped cattle from India were also introduced at this time.[5]

4 Laser-ablation inductively-coupled mass-spectrometry (LA-ICP-MS) has been employed in these analyses.

5 Ceramic figurines at Schroda, in the Limpopo basin, and Serondela (Map 9.1) provide secure, positive evidence for the presence of these domesticates in the region from about 900 or earlier. At Nqoma, skeletal evidence in the form of bifurcate thoracic vertebrae is less secure; however, as Serondela is not far from Nqoma and its ceramics are stylistically associated with that site, we may infer the presence of humped cattle at Nqoma.

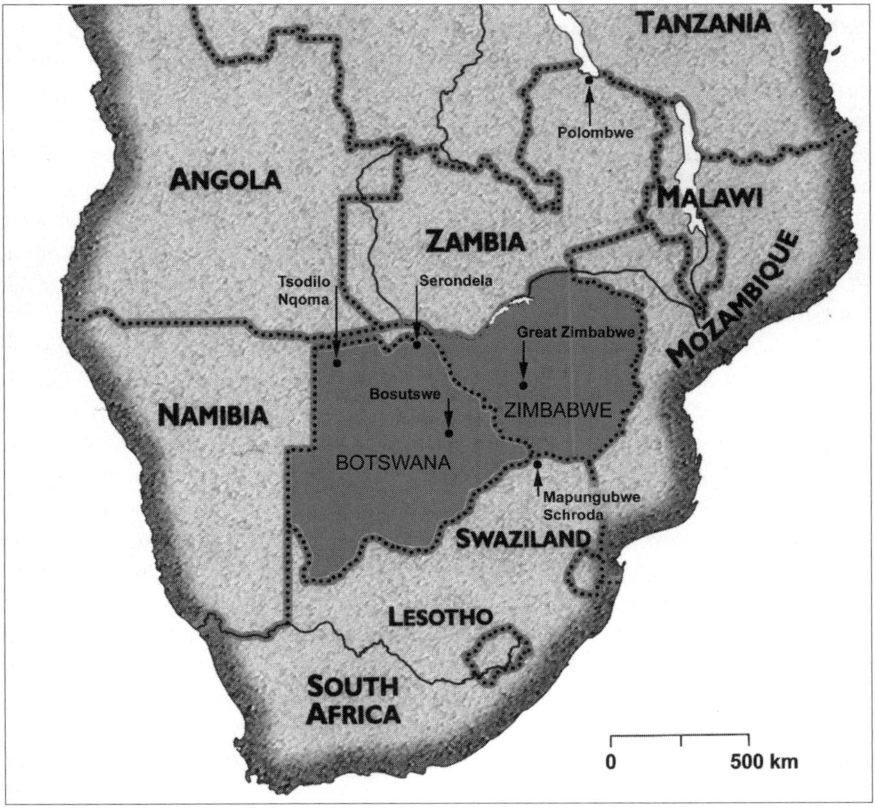

Map 9.1 Location of places mentioned in the text

Exports from the interior to the intra-ocean trade recorded in the early tenth century at the coast by the Arab traveller al-Masudi (died 956) include ivory, rhinoceros horn, tortoiseshell, leopard skins and gold (Freeman-Grenville 1962). At the time, any gold from the interior would have been found as surface nuggets in the Limpopo flood plain. The first use of such gold – as distinct from its possible earlier export – in the interior is found in mid-thirteenth century burials of elites at the hilltop site of Mapungubwe in this valley (Fouché 1937; Huffman 2000; and Miller 2001). Hard rock gold mining began on the Zimbabwe plateau shortly thereafter (Swan 1994; and Killick forthcoming), and its export brought considerable wealth to the builders of Great Zimbabwe until about 1420–1450 when the city was abandoned.

There is no gold at Tsodilo, but massive quantities of micaceous specularite were mined there at this time; this form of iron ore is poorly suited for smelting but when powdered is prized as a cosmetic which imparts a silvery sparkle to a person's skin and hair, as well as to clothing made of hides. Specularite is not recorded to have been a commodity in the intra-ocean trade, but that from Tsodilo was no doubt also coveted in the interior and was probably entirely consumed, or almost so, there; it would have in any case moved with other goods along internal pathways. Evidence for direct communication along these pathways is established by integrating analyses of pottery design motifs with those of the mineral composition of shards.[6] In this way, we have ascertained that Nqoma-style pots made at nearby clay sources were taken as far as Bosutswe, 600 kilometres away; we have also mapped an intricate network of pottery exchange throughout eastern and northern Botswana (Thebe et al. forthcoming; and Wilmsen et al. forthcoming).

Zhizo beads ceased to be made about 975 (Wood 2000). They were replaced by glass beads of different types in a variety of colours, mainly made in India but also in the Middle East and a few at al-Fustat (Fatimid Cairo). Vastly larger quantities were imported than before, but they were still concentrated at a very few sites, principally Mapungubwe and Great Zimbabwe and to a lesser extent Bosutswe in Botswana (Denbow et al. 2007). Adit mining for gold in eastern Botswana and Zimbabwe, some for local consumption but most for export to the intra-ocean trade, peaked between 1250 and 1330 in response to European, Indian and Muslim demand for the minting of coins (Sutton 1997; and Killick forthcoming). The consequent huge increase in local wealth was partly invested in the construction of towns with stone walling, first at Mapungubwe in about 1220 followed by Great Zimbabwe about 1300 where Arabian and Chinese ceramics and Indian cotton cloth were now added to the list of known luxury imports. The ubiquity of cotton cloth in recorded trade, however (due to cheap production costs, ease of transport, multivalent display attributes), suggests a much earlier date for its initial import, quite possibly by Nqoma people.

Whereas Nqoma, with a population of at most 100 persons, was a village, albeit the largest and most influential of its time and area, Mapungubwe with about 5,000 inhabitants was a fully developed town, and the much larger Great Zimbabwe is considered by some to have been a true city with possibly as many as 18,000 inhabitants (Huffman 1987; 1996).

At Nqoma, with no gold and far from coastal trading entrepôts, specularite ceased to be mined in significant quantity at about 1100, concomitant with the development at about this time of the major centres to the east which captured control of the coastal trade. Great Zimbabwe was abandoned by 1450, in part perhaps because of environmental degradation due to population pressure but mainly because the centre of gold trade moved to the Zambezi River, nearer the Swahili trading cities. In 1507, the Portuguese conquered these coastal cities and during the next quarter century took over all trade between Africa and Asia.

---

6 Minerals are identified by optical petrography and compared with those in clays collected from diverse geological contexts in the region. The environs in which individual pots were made can then be pinpointed.

Words

In episodes of Kapembwa origin mythology found in Ulungu at the southern tip of Lake Tanganyika in Zambia, Roy Willis (1999, 48–9) detects the structure of the social developments just portrayed, and notes that this myth occurs in similar forms over much of central and southern Africa. According to the myth, a primal pair descended spontaneously from a creative spirit and at first lived in darkness underground without any sense of self-awareness or of each other. After emerging into the light, they met and produced a series of children who initially lived 'for centuries' in a state of sexual promiscuity with their parents, lacking any form of custom or law. After the death of the primal pair their daughter, Mwenya Mukulu, departed to found a new country (Ulungu) to the east; enroute she encountered Kapembwa, a trickster/creator spirit who lived on a flat hilltop, Polombwe. Kapembwa arranged to marry Mwenya's daughter, Mangala, thus abolishing promiscuity and instituting social legitimacy at the core of which is chieftainship.

A similar myth centres on a rock, Ncuxgoridao (n#'u – food + g!o – vagina + ri – conjunctive + dàò – path: thus, 'path to vagina food' [Taylor (2000) glosses 'the path of sex']), at the foot of the Tsodilo Female Hill on a plateau of which lies Nqoma. This rock is said to resemble three vaginas, hence the name. The myth goes like this (Campbell n.d.):

> At the time when the earth was young, people were all youths; they did not grow old and were not born. One day, three girls went up the hill to collect water from a cave, Chokgam (Medicine Mouth). On their way home they met three boys who had been told by God to meet them. God told them that they must have sex so there would be life and death. They did not understand sex, so God shaped the rock and showed them what to do. The girls put the pots down and the three couples performed, thus the first children were born.

The temporality of life marked by birth in the one myth and death in the other introduces the concept of time and the founding of a country brings the concept of history into the cosmology of the region.

A parallel myth says that in the beginning the four Tsodilo Hills were people (Taylor 2000):

> The large Male Hill had two wives, and they were next to him. However, he liked the young second wife better than the other – the Female Hill was the second wife. The first wife became jealous and ran away, past the other woman (the third, Child hill) who was not married. She wanted to keep on running, but the others sent their servants to stop her, and she remained where she is, all alone.

Xau Nxwaa is the name of both the first wife who ran away and the Baby Hill which she became; the scatter of rocks north of this fourth hill is, in mixed Xani/

Zhucoasi, called Gxaakhoesi – poor persons, servants – that is the servants sent to stop Xau Nxwaa.

A cognate myth was recorded by Willis (1999, 52). Kapembwa had a first wife before he married the younger Mangala, whom he then preferred. One day this first wife failed to do what Kapembwa wanted and after an altercation with Mangala she ran away, never to return. She had, however, pulled off the crown of feathers given to Mangala by Kulungu and torn it up, throwing the pieces into the bush as she ran. In compensation for this insult, Kapembwa ceded the lake fish (transformed fragments of Mangala's crown) to the Lungu people and persuaded his brother-in-law, who lived on the plateau, to cause rain so that they could cultivate crops.

Space

In both myths, female associates of autochthonous males become vitalizing elements of the landscape, hence incorporating history with geographic space. We thus see in these myths both the establishment of a proper social order with a legitimate leader at its apex and the association of that order with the land in which it exists. The myth in its Kapembwa form is Bantu, the Ncuxgoridao form is Khoisan (Xanikhoe), underscoring Willis's observation of its wide geographical – and sociographical – spread in central-southern Africa; Frobenius recorded similar Shona myths. There is as well a deep temporal spread entailing flat plateaux of hilltops (Polombwe, Zimbabwe, Mapungubwe, Bosutswe, Nqoma) associated with elite leadership and supernatural power involving the control of rain.

Despite their differences in physical size, population numbers and position in the landscape all the sites mentioned share a number of quite specific characteristics. All are associated with flat plateaux hilltops on which elites established exclusive residence; at Mapungubwe and Great Zimbabwe the vast majority of people were commoners who lived on the surrounding plains. Preliminary work at Bosutswe suggests a similar pattern (Denbow and Miller 2007); and, although the necessary survey has not been done at Nqoma, the limitations of the hill make it certain that the same is true here. All these hills now have and have had for as long as memory recalls or records confirm an association with supernatural power involving, *inter alia*, snakes and the control of rain (Schoeman 2006). For example, Bosutswe, the abode of a large but invisible rain-snake, means 'The place toward which you must not point your finger' – for if you do you will die. The control of rain is the realm of the hereditary chief or king, who, in the time we are considering, was associated with hilltops and, where we can interpret the evidence, snakes and perhaps metalworking. Archaeological interpretation of certain structures at Great Zimbabwe as the seat of the mambo, the regional king, is confirmed by Shona/Venda oral histories, corroborated by early Portuguese reports; analogous structures at Mapungubwe are, by extension, the same (Huffman 1996). At Bosutswe at this time, there are no stone structures (they are present later) but caches of paraphernalia related to initiation rituals that normally take place at a chief's village, along with gold and bronze jewellery, mark it as such a location. Inferentially, Nqoma, which had been the richest southern African village in metal jewellery and imported glass beads and marine shells of its day (Miller 1996), was also the seat of an elite leader.

All these sites (except Bosutswe, for which there are no data) share another feature of elite privilege: cattle slaughtered at them were overwhelmingly in prime-age classes. These animals are the most desirable for food and they are also those of reproductive age; thus, their removal from the herd represents a double charge against its maintenance – because not only is the butchered animal itself removed from the herd but also, in the case of cows, that animal's reproductive capacity plus that of its unrealized offspring are removed. Such a charge can only be borne by someone in a position to deny others the same privilege so that the herd does not dwindle away. The contradiction is embedded in a Tswana praise poem (Schapera 1965, 115):

> When we go across to the chief's place, he sends away the oxen with large hoofs, with hoofs that fill the servants' bowls, so that a servant may eat. Molefi [the chief] doesn't slaughter big oxen, he slaughters young ones and pregnant cows, he slaughters animals in calf, so that old men may eat the foetuses.

Huffman (1996, 118–21) details Shona/Venda prescriptions for the distribution of parts of a slaughtered cow which he avers were in place in Great Zimbabwe times: choice parts go to elites, hooves and tail go to the herdsmen/servants. Clearly, this class discrepancy in access to categories of food is long established in the region (Denbow and Thebe 2006, for modern Tswana).

All these sites have a final characteristic in common: the restricted areas of the plateaux on which elite quarters are situated made it impossible for them to be self-sufficient, either in food or anything else. Indeed, the layout of the settlements left no space for growing crops or pasturing herds; the inhabitants were thus dependent for their subsistence on food produced on the plains below and had to ensure that supplies were available when needed. Clearly, then, these hilltops were not occupied for their production potential; rather they offered association with cosmological forces and the authority which that alliance entails. The elite status of the people living on them was thereby made manifest, thus enhancing their control over the means of production and distribution of all goods and services available to the community. At smaller sites on the level plain, servants, commoners, had charge of herds and agricultural fields, worked the mines and received few – usually none – of the exotic luxuries such as glass beads obtained in the intra-ocean exchange (Wilmsen 1989; and Calabrese 2005). These were home to relatively low numbers of persons (often on the order of an extended family) who also had little of the highly valued locally made iron and copper jewellery. An intermediary set of sites served as administrative nodes overseeing local resources; these normally had substantial metal inventories and small numbers of exotic goods.

The extent of land controlled by the centres varied greatly; that of Great Zimbabwe at its fifteenth century peak included all of present day Zimbabwe plus substantial parts of surrounding countries. That of comparatively small-scale Nqoma, 400 years earlier, extended somewhat more than 100 kilometeres westward in the sandveld but much less eastward across the Okavango Delta. This geography is established by the distribution of clay pots, now reduced to shards, decorated in the style of the respective centres. We should not, however, assume that these pots circulated in a purely functional capacity; rather their materiality was mediated by transcendent temporal and social qualifications. They were invested with meaning through social interaction and accumulated histories linking persons and families across class distinctions in space and time. Hendrickson (1986) has demonstrated that small, elaborately decorated bowls with a capacity of about half a litre, which could have functioned only as dishes for personal use, make up 80 per cent of the identifiable shard inventory recovered at Nqoma. Vessels of this kind, as opposed to common cooking and storage containers, acquire the power to instil status in their possessors; shards of only such vessels are found at peripheral sites. As presentations to headmen at cattle posts these bowls would have served as symbols of local authority and of actual or fictive kinship with the elite at Nqoma (Wilmsen 1989); this is the calculative dimension in their exchange. That is to say, in these pots the boundaries between persons and things are not rigidly separate. Another Tswana praise poem captures the sentiment (Alverson 1978, 126):

> Bowl of my father, when I have eaten from it my heart is glad, for it is the bowl of my parents, bowl for sweet gravy of the cow.

This is a class-based settlement system with geographical conventions reflecting an assumption of space organized around revered centres from which power – and law – radiates outward. During the centuries of our present concern, the most extreme form of this spatial organization is found in the Zimbabwe system in which, at the capital centre itself, the mambo and his ritual sister were secluded behind stone walls and bark cloth curtains at the top of Zimbabwe Hill; at secondary *dzimbahwe*, the local chief, a relative of the mambo, was similarly secluded on a smaller scale (Huffman 1996). Denbow (1983) describes a subsidiary three tiered system in that part of eastern Botswana including Bosutswe. At earlier Nqoma, hierarchies were no doubt simpler, probably bipolar and less formally structured.

To conclude, Zhizo beads and the many coloured ones that followed may have been inexpensive trinkets to eighth to fifteenth-century Indo-Pacific traders (Killick forthcoming), as they were to their nineteenth-century European counterparts (Wilmsen 2003). But Mwenya Mukulu was able to unseat the minor headman of the land that became Ulungu because she was 'brilliant … with beads on her head and anklets' (Willis 1999, 50); for her, the value embodied in those beads through the judgements of *her* social peers was great. The long distance movement of beads, marine shells and cloth entailed costs that made their possession at far interior places in itself a marker of sumptuary distinction regulated by the cost of acquisition. Considered in this way, social processes at work in temporally distant Nqoma, Bosutswe, Mapungubwe and Great Zimbabwe are more clearly recognizable. At each place, some members of society were able to channel value through their own hands while creating ideological structures for keeping it in the hands of their descendents, thereby rationalizing in their particular instances the incipient socio-economic stratification present in all societies. This would have entailed rules and strategies – what we call law.

The Regulation of Things in Space

We cannot know what specific form this law may have taken, but we can specify certain minimum components.

Rules Governing who may Possess/Own Specific Things

The myths recounted above reveal the structure of rights to possession found in many southern African communities when first observed by Europeans in the eighteenth and nineteenth centuries, and to a degree still in practice in some places today. Willis (1999, 50) sees the origin of this structure in an encounter some centuries ago between groups embodying two radically different forms of authority: one derived from descent from a deified ancestor, an authority legitimized by a supposedly unbroken line of descent through time (e.g., Mangala), and one derived from a parahuman entity or spirit identified with the land or territory, an authority in and over space (e.g., Kapembwa). Some myths, as indeed does the Kapembwa myth, suggest that the encounter was between incoming Bantu speakers bearing authority of lineage and autochthonous Khoisan speakers bearing authority of land. These myths, then, may preserve in metaphorical form the actual incursion during the early centuries of the first millennium of Bantu peoples into what had till then been Khoisan space.[7] In any case, the outcome has been a cluster of indigenous societies based on a complex and potentially unstable resolution of the inherent contradiction between the two concepts of authority and power: lineage and land (Mitchell 1956; Ranger 1973; Werbner 1977; Schoffeleers 1979; and Lan 1985). This resolved power is vested in a chief, who occupies a position of unique privilege and authority in the society over which he rules. As Schapera (1938, 62) said of Tswana *dikgosi* (chiefs), they are 'the symbol of tribal unity … at once, ruler, judge, maker and guardian of law, repository of wealth, priest and magician of the people'. In recorded time and in what is called the ethnographic present (i.e., past time in which recorded observations are thought to be cogent) all assets of a polity – land, cattle, mineral wealth, sumptuary goods – were the

7 The archaeological and linguistic evidence for this is voluminous. Vestiges of the ensuing relations of power and land are, or were until recently, still discernable in parts of Botswana.

property of its chief, who kept the conspicuous accoutrements of power for him- (occasionally her-) self.

Archaeological evidence coupled with slight but significant Portuguese records reveal a comparable constitution in the fourteenth to fifteenth-century Zimbabwe polity. The concentration of sumptuary goods (glass beads, marine shells, metal jewellery) at thirteenth-century Mapungubwe and Bosutswe (as well, their twelfth century predecessor K2) and ninth to eleventh-century Nqoma contrasted with the poverty in these goods at contemporary sites, along with evidence for the control of herds at Mapungubwe and Nqoma, allow us to infer a similar structure – although not the specifics of its construction – at these locations.

Rules Governing who may Inherit Specific Things

In southern Africa the contradiction between lineage and land is resolved by kinship. The chief is the eponymous 'father' of all his followers, his lineage is said to extend unbroken to the beginning of the polity. Of course, genealogical gaps have occurred which had to be filled by collaterals or fictives – as British royals have had to call in Dutch and German cousins to fill their gaps – but the ideology of continuity has been maintained. As well, concepts of differential wealth and land entitlements are embedded deeply in southern African languages, Khoisan (Barnard; Haake; Traill; and Wilmsen) as well as Bantu (Guthrie; and Heine). Often this differential is associated directly with chiefdomship; Bantu examples are: in 1824 Burchell (1953, 347) noted that the Tswana word *kgosi* (chief) also meant 'rich man'; and in 1886 Brincker (1964, 141) wrote that in addition to *Haüptling* (chief) Herero '*omuhona*' also meant '*einer, der viele Güter hat*' (wealthy person). The Zhu (Khoisan) word *xhaiha* is glossed by Snyman (1975, 129) as '*heer, rykaard, leier*' (master, wealthy person, leader) and derived from the verb *xhai* (*ryk wees* – to be wealthy). The contrasting concepts of poverty are, of course, necessarily also lexically marked in these languages. In order to maintain these economic–political distinctions, elite members of these societies have long preferred various forms of marriage between specified collaterals so that lines of inheritance remain continually intertwined; the rational is expressed in a Tswana proverb, 'Child of my maternal uncle marry me so that the herds may return to the kraal' (Schapera 1938, 128). The distribution of sumptuary goods and cattle remains in discrete precincts on hilltops coupled with deeply embedded linguistic markers of social difference points to analogous constraints on inheritance regulation at those sites. Huffman (1996) offers a detailed elaboration of this proposition for Great Zimbabwe based on Shona/Venda oral histories.

Rules Governing Movement/Transport of these Things

Huffman (2000, 27) has noted that control of the supply of imports such as glass beads and cotton cloth, and of their redistribution, appears to have been a central mechanism in the development of complex society in southern Africa. As well, historical records are unanimous in noting that a chief did not himself go for goods, rather they were brought to him by designated intermediaries. For Great Zimbabwe, oral accounts make it clear that a similar arrangement was the rule, and as Mapungubwe was its immediate predecessor we can safely deduce the same for that place. For Bosutswe and Nqoma, however, we must rely on archaeological evidence. A clay pot in which were more than 3,000 glass beads may provide a clue. This was found at Kgaswe, which in all other respects is like other small, probably cattle post, sites – notably in that no other beads were present. This is the only known hoard of its kind, with all other comparable masses of beads being from elite burials at Mapungubwe and Great Zimbabwe, and later from the royal precincts in the capital towns Mgungundluvo (1828–1839) and Ondini (1872–1879) of the powerful Zulu chiefs Dingane and Cetshwayo (Merwe et al. 1989, 101).[8] We may, therefore, conjecture that Kgaswe was not the intended final destination of the beads found there, but that they were enroute to a chief, probably at Bosutswe roughly 50 kilometres away, and were misplaced or abandoned for unknown reasons. This proposition is supported by analysis of pottery from the two areas which reveals that some pots at both have similar mineral compositions; this suggests that links did exist, but more work needs to be done to confirm this.

Rules Governing who may Handle them

In the ethnographic past, each subordinate tier of headmen down to household head was either filled by appropriately related kinsmen of a chief or persons brought to such status by genealogical manipulation. Huffman, in several works cited above, and Calabrese (2005) have extended this organizational principal to Mapungubwe and Great Zimbabwe, and Bosutswe appears also to conform to it (Denbow 1983). Kgaswe, then, may be seen as the seat of a minor local headman with ties to a chief, likely at Bosutswe, and responsibilities for overseeing the safe conduct of persons and things within his domain. Such a person would be authorized to handle sumptuary goods, but could not possess them for personal use. Eyewitness historical accounts reveal that the penalty for misuse of this authority could be death.

Rules Governing Processes of their Valuation

For oceanic merchants, a minimum value for goods, such as glass beads, landed at East Coast entrepôts was set by costs of production, transport, port taxes (multiple and high, according to Arab sources), loss (due to breakage, storms, theft and such) and a surplus sufficient to allow them to continue trade at the other nodes in their monsoonal cycle. Town merchants added another increment for their own profit. Thus, even in the eighth century the coastal trade must have been carried on

8 All of the 12,436 glass beads at Mgungundluvo and 8,848 (98 per cent) of the total of 9,042 beads at Ondini were recovered in the royal precinct.

in some commercial form, as Arab sources document for later centuries. Even if, as is most likely, in the interior where our sites are located, trade was less formal the basic cost of goods was set at the interface where imports, such as glass beads, were first exchanged for exports, such as ivory. On the other hand, early European traders (Andersson, Green, Chapman) were sometimes left holding worthless goods, particularly glass beads, because their stock did not include beads of desired colours or shapes and alternative sources of supply were available. Ultimately, however, interior peoples had limited control of trade because merchants could control the exchange value of the goods they offered (beads, shells, cloth and such), often at the level of what to them were 'trinkets' (Wilmsen 2003). Killick (forthcoming) stresses, furthermore, that if certain kinds of goods became essential to the maintenance of a social order (such as Mwenye's brilliance in beads), interior societies may have had to accept worsening terms of trade through time to assure themselves of a continued supply; merchants had complete control of the value of goods (above all ivory and gold) they would accept in exchange.

Yet more tenuously, demand for particular goods fluctuated in time and space, with fatal consequences for even firmly established, strong centres. When Limpopo gold enabled the fluorescence of Mapungubwe, the value of Nqoma's products was deflated and the site reduced to, at best, tributary status. Mapungubwe was abandoned when Great Zimbabwe captured the gold trade; the latter was itself displaced by competing centres when terms of trade were altered at the coast, and more importantly at global markets beyond. We are only now beginning to understand the dynamics of these transformations. Regulatory mechanisms, in the broadest sense laws, under which in prehistory things would have come under evaluative scrutiny have been neglected in this endeavor. To further this endeavor, we need to reinvigorate previously well reflected insights into general principles underlying the social construction of value in things.

References

Alverson, H. (1978) *Mind in the Heart of Darkness: Value and Self-identity among the Tswana of Southern Africa*. New Haven: Yale University Press.

Appadurai, A. (1986) 'Introduction' in A. Appadurai (ed.) *The Social Life of Things: Commodities in Cultural Perspective*. Cambridge: Cambridge University Press, pp. 3–63.

Beidelman, T. (1989) 'Agonistic Exchange: Homeric Reciprocity and the Heritage of Simmel and Mauss'. *Cultural Anthropology*, 4: 227–59.

Brincker, H. ([1886] 1964) *Wörterbuch und kurzgefasste Grammatik des Otji-Herero*. Ridgewood: Gregg Press.

Burchell, W. ([1824] 1953) *Travels in the Interior of Southern Africa*. London: Longman.

Calabrese, J. (2005) 'Ethnicity, Class, and Polity: The Emergence of Social and Political Complexity in the Shashe-Limpopo Valley of Southern Africa, AD 900–1300', PhD thesis, University of Witwatersrand.

Campbell, (no date) 'Notes on the Tsodilo Hills', MS in possession of author.

Denbow, J. (1983) 'Iron Age Economics: Herding, Wealth, and Politics along the Fringes of the Kalahari Desert during the Early Iron Age', PhD thesis, Indiana University.

Denbow, J. and Miller, D. (2007) 'Metal Working at Bosutswe', *Journal of African Archaeology*, 5: 271–313.

Denbow, J. and Thebe, P. (2006) *Culture and Customs of Botswana*. Westport: Greenwood Press.

Denbow, J., Smith, J., Atwood, K. and Miller, D. (2007) 'Archaeological Excavations at Bosutswe: Cultural Chronology, Paleo-ecology, and Economy', *Journal of Archaeological Science*, 35: 459–80.

Dietler, M. (1999) 'Review of C. Kramer (1997) "Pottery in Rajasthan: Ethnoarchaeology in two Indian Cities"'. *American Anthropologist*, 101: 194–95.

Dietler, M. (2001) 'Theorizing the Feast: Rituals of Consumption, Commensal Politics, and Power in an African Context' in M. Dietler and B. Hayden (eds) *Feasts: Archaeological and Ethnographic Perspectives on Food, Politics, and Power*. Washington: Smithsonian Institution Press, pp. 65–114.

Dumont, J.-P. (1980) *The Headman and I: Ambiguity and Ambivalence in the Fieldworking Experience*. Austin: University of Texas Press.

Fouché, L. (ed.) (1937) *Mapungubwe: Ancient Bantu Civilization on the Limpopo*. Cambridge: Cambridge University Press.

Freeman-Grenville, G. (1962) *The East African Coast*. Oxford: Oxford University Press.

Gosden, C. and Marshall, Y. (1999) 'The Cultural Biography of Objects'. *World Archaeology*, 31: 169–78.

Hendrickson, A. (1986) 'Early Iron Age Ceramics from Northern Botswana: The Evidence from Matlapaneng, Nqoma, and Divuyu'. MA thesis, New York University.

Hodder, I. (1982a) 'Theoretical Archaeology: A Reactionary View' in I. Hodder (ed.) *Symbolic and Structural Archaeology*. Cambridge: Cambridge University Press, pp. 1–15.

Hodder, I. (1982b) *The Present Past*. London: Batsford.

Huffman, T. (1987) *Symbols in Stone: Unraveling the Mystery of Great Zimbabwe*. Johannesburg: Witwatersrand University Press.

Huffman, T. (1996) *Snakes and Crocodiles: Power and Symbolism in Ancient Zimbabwe*. Johannesburg: Witwatersrand University Press.

Huffman, T. (2000) 'Mapungubwe and the Origins of the Zimbabwe Culture' in M. Leslie and T. Maggs (eds) *African Naissance: the Limpopo Valley 1,000 Years ago*. South African Archaeological Society Goodwin Series 8. Cape Town: South African Archaeological Society, pp. 14–27.

Killick, D. (forthcoming) 'Agency, Dependency and Long-distance Trade: East Africa and the Islamic World, ca 700–1500 CE' in S. Falconer and C. Redman (eds) *States and the Landscape*. Tucson: University of Arizona Press.

Kopytoff, I. (1986) 'The Cultural Biography of Things: Commoditization as Process' in A. Appadurai (ed.) *The Social Life of Things: Commodities in Cultural Perspective*. Cambridge: Cambridge University Press, pp. 64–94.

Lan, D. (1985) *Guns and Rain: Guerrillas and Spirit Mediums in Zimbabwe*. London: James Currey.

Locke, J. ([1690] 1980) *Second Treatise of Government*, Chapter 5, of Property, Section 27, edited with an introduction by C.B. Macpherson. Indianapolis: Hackett Publishing Company.

Marx, K. and Engels, F. ([1846] 1947) *The German Ideology*. New York: International Publishers.

Van der Merwe, N.J., Saitowitz, S., Thackeray, J., Hall, J.M. and Poggenpoel, C. (1989) 'Standardized Analyses of Glass Trade Beads from Mgungundlovu and Ondini, Nineteenth-century Zulu Capitals'. *South African Archaeological Bulletin*, 44: 98–104.

Miller, D. (1996) *The Tsodilo Jewellery: Metal Work from Northern Botswana*. Cape Town: UCT Press.

Miller, D. (2001) 'Metal Assemblages from Greefswald Areas K2, Mapungubwe Hill and Mapungubwe South Terrace'. *South African Archaeological Bulletin*, 56: 83–103.

Mitchell, J. (1956) *The Yao Village*. Manchester: Manchester University Press.

Oakley, K.P. (1957) *Man the Tool-maker*. Chicago: University of Chicago Press.

Ranger, T. (1973) 'Territorial Cults in the History of Central Africa'. *Journal of African History*, 14: 581–97.

Renfrew, C. (1972) *The Emergence of Civilization: The Cyclades and the Aegean in the Third Millennium BC*. London: Methuen.

Renfrew, C. (1978) 'Varna and the Emergence of Wealth in Prehistoric Europe' in A. Appadurai (ed.) *The Social Life of Things: Commodities in Cultural Perspective*. Cambridge: Cambridge University Press, pp. 141–68.

Robertshaw, P., Glascock, M., Wood, M. and Popelka, R. (2003) 'Chemical Analysis of Ancient African Glass Beads: A Very Preliminary Report'. *Journal of African Archaeology*, 1(1): 139–46.

Schapera, I. (1938) *Handbook of Tswana Law and Custom*. Oxford: Oxford University Press.

Schapera, I. (1965) *Praise Poems of Tswana Chiefs*. Oxford: Clarendon Press.

Schoeman, M. (2006) 'Clouding Power? Rain Control, Space, Landscapes, and Ideology in Shashe-Limpopo State Formation'. PhD thesis, University of Witwatersrand.

Schoffeleers, J. (1979) *Guardians of the Lan*. Gwelo: Mambo Press.

Simmel, G. (1900) *Philosophie des Wertes, in Gesamtausgabe, Bd. 6 Philosophie des Geldes (1900–1907)*. Frankfurt: Suhrkamp.

Simmel, G. ([1907] 1978) *The Philosophy of Money* (translated by T. Bottomore). London: Routledge and Kegan Paul.

Snyman, J. (1975) *Zul'hoasi Phonologie en Woordeboek*. Cape Town: Balkema.

Sutton, J. (1997) 'The African Lords of the Intercontinental Gold Trade before the Black Death: Al-Hasan Bin-Sulaiman of Kilwa and Mansa Musa of Mali'. *The Antiquaries Journal*, 77: 221–42.

Swan, L. (1994) *Early Gold Mining on the Zimbabwean Plateau*. Studies in Archaeology no. 9. Upsala: Societas Archaeologica Upsalensis.

Taylor, M. (2000) 'Place Name Map of the Tsodilo Hills'. MS in possession of the author.

Thebe, P., Wilmsen, E., Drake Rosenstein, D., Killick, D. and Denbow, J. (forthcoming) 'Diyana tsa mmopa: 2000 Years of Pottery and Potters in Botswana'. To be submitted to *Botswana Notes and Records*.

Thorstein, V. (1899) *The Theory of the Leisure Class*. New York: Mcmillan.

Weiner, A.B. (1985) 'Inalienable Wealth'. *American Ethnologist*, 12: 52–65.

Weiner, A.B. (1992) *Inalienable Possessions: The Paradox of Keeping while Giving*. Los Angeles: University of California Press.

Werbner, R. (1977) *Regional Cults*. London: Academic Press.

Willis, R. (1999) *Some Spirits Heal, others only Dance: A Journey into Human Selfhood in an African Village*. Oxford: Berg.

Wilmsen, E. (1989) *Land Filled with Flies: A Political Economy of the Kalahari*. Chicago: University of Chicago Press.

Wilmsen, E. (1994) *Pots and Power in the Pastoral Economy of Pre-colonial South Africa*. Research paper. Institute for Advanced Study and Research in the African Humanities, Northwestern University.

Wilmsen, E. (2003) 'For Trinkets such as Beads: A Revalorization of Khoisan Labor in Colonial Southern Africa' in T. Falola and C. Jennings (eds) *Sources and Methods in African History: Spoken, Written, Unearthed*. Rochester: University of Rochester Press, pp. 80–104.

Wilmsen, E. et al. (forthcoming) 'The Social Geography of Pottery in Botswana as Reconstructed by Optical Petrography', submitted to *Journal of African Archaeology*.

Wood, M. (2000) 'Making Connections: Relationships between the International Trade and Glass Beads from the Shashe-Limpopo Area' in M. Leslie and T. Maggs (eds) *African Naissance: The Limpopo Valley 1,000 Years ago*. Goodwin Series 8. Cape Town: South African Archaeological Society, pp. 78–90.

Chapter 10
Can There be Maps of Law?

Maarten Bavinck and Gordon R. Woodman

There has been discussion in recent years of the possibility of drawing maps of law, that is, of encapsulating in maps information about the scope of the functioning and social effects of law (Twining 2000, 136–73). The authors of this chapter have advanced opposed views on the subject. Gordon Woodman has argued the case for denying the possibility (Woodman 2003). Maarten Bavinck has challenged Woodman's arguments and claimed that there is a real possibility of useful mapping of law (Bavinck 2004). This joint chapter seeks to clarify and develop the arguments on both sides.

The question under discussion here, whether there can be *a map or maps of law*, is different and raises different issues from the question of whether it is illuminating to see *law as a map*. This chapter does not consider the latter question at length, although we mention it again near the end.

The Nature of the Issue

This is more than an argument about the most informative means of representing accurately a known set of facts – although it is an important merit of a good map that it presents a large amount of information in a manner easily and quickly understood. The notion of a map of law supposes that observed facts justify a conceptualization of law in a form which allows it to be plotted on a map. Our disagreement goes to this fundamental question as to the characteristics of law as an observed social phenomenon. Neither of us claims to advance a definitive analysis of the concept of law. But we believe that this debate can make a contribution to the understanding of this huge and important question. Comments related to this theoretical question constitute the main substance of the chapter.

We are also agreed on the recognition of a ubiquitous and 'deep' legal pluralism. We reject the ideological position of 'legal centralism', that 'law is and should be the law of the state, uniform for all persons, exclusive of all other law, and administered by a single set of state institutions' (Griffiths 1986, 3).[1] Consequently

1 It was claimed in 1995 by the author of this definition of legal centralism that the ideology it embodied had been defeated, that '[t]he new paradigm, as far as the social scientific study of law is concerned, is legal pluralism …', and that '[n]owadays, [this] point is generally accepted, or at least conceded without a struggle; anyone who does not is

we believe that any comprehensive account of the realm of law, such as might be contained in a map, must include not only state law but many instances of non-state law. We regard as law not only the law of the nation state, international law and the laws of regional institutions such as the European Union (the last two being varieties of 'non-state laws' which are almost universally accepted as law today), but also folk laws (or customary laws, indigenous laws – and there are various other names in common use – Woodman 1993, 263; and Benda-Beckmann, K. von 2001a) and religious laws which are generated and enforced in communities, which are often portions of state populations but which may extend across state boundaries.

The legal centralist view offered the possibility of a simple map of the legal world. On a flat sheet the boundaries between legal systems coincided with the boundaries of states' territories, and each state territory could be given a distinctive, evenly spread colour representing its law, which was uniformly, exclusively and totally applicable throughout its territory. Thus law was fully represented by the map of 'the countries of the world'. An example of such a map is that once designed by William Twining to depict the various classes of state laws of the world:

> I obtained a blank map of the whole world and used a palette of coloured chalks to characterise the legal systems of different countries. The map marked the borders of countries, that is nation-states and various forms of dependency … I might have used blue chalk for the common law (deliberately avoiding imperial pink), brown for civilian or Romanist systems, red for Socialist countries, yellow for Islamic Law, and green for customary or traditional law. Countries with 'plural' or mixed national legal systems were clumsily depicted by stripes in different colours (Twining 2000: 142).[2]

According to the more primitive, legal centralist view there were no insurmountable problems in mapping law. Private international law was not a problem because despite its name it was a branch of the law of each individual state. Public international law did not complicate the picture because it was not a part of it. Either it was 'improperly termed' law (Austin 1954, 11–12), or it governed solely the relations between states and so occupied uniformly the entirety of the world map. Regional institutions were denied legitimacy (as the more extreme Eurosceptics do the European Union today), treated as mere treaties, or, more recently, seen as exceptions.

The existence of state law pluralism, that is, the 'recognition' and enforcement by certain state laws of various customary laws, religious laws or both, was also not seen as complicating the picture unduly. According to the legal centralist view,

simply out of date and can safely be ignored' (Griffiths 1995, 210). It is doubtful, however, whether the new paradigm is so generally accepted as Griffiths asserts.

2 Twining had almost immediately serious doubts about this map (Twining 2000, 142–3) and he now rejects a number of the assumptions on which it was based (Twining 2000, 149–52).

these other laws acquired their legal character only when and because they were accorded recognition by state law, and that process made them simultaneously a part of state law. They were a cause of complexity within state laws, but not of legal pluralism involving the coexistence of different laws. (Vanderlinden 1971; Hooker 1975; and Griffiths 1986). This internal complexity has been referred to as legal pluralism 'in the weak sense' (Griffiths 1986). The analysis of this phenomenon by students of state law did not add complexity to the pattern of relations between different legal systems.

The factor which has led to complexity in this conception has been the rediscovery of non-state law by increasing numbers of modern legal theorists. Non-state law has long been known to legal anthropologists, and indeed was well known to lawyers in earlier periods before the modern development of the notion of state sovereignty led to its disregard. The recognition of other bodies of law has entailed an acceptance that the legal world is more multitudinous than legal centralism supposes. Different bodies of laws, each with its own independent source or sources of legitimacy, coexist. This new view challenged the theorist's powers of description.

The question is whether, with a greatly more complex and sophisticated view of law as a social phenomenon than that of legal centralism, it is still possible to depict it on a map. The next section presents a case against the possibility of mapping law. It is followed by a section seeking to rebut that case. After a brief response for the case against mapping, we seek in the final section to summarize our points of disagreement.

The Case against Maps of Law

This section puts Woodman's argument against the possibility of compiling maps of law from the social scientific perspective just indicated.

The Conceptualization of 'Laws'

It is necessary to consider first the concept of law which may be usefully adopted for the analysis of legal pluralism. In virtually all writings concerned with a synoptic view of legal pluralism it is assumed or asserted that the constituent elements of the legally pluralist world are different 'Laws' or 'legal systems'. For convenience these elements are referred to here as 'Laws', as one refers to the Law of England, the Law of the Navajo people of North America or the Law of Hinduism. It is generally assumed or asserted that Laws in this sense display certain visible characteristics. Thus, for example, Vanderlinden (1971) referred to 'legal mechanisms' (*mécanismes juridiques*) within a 'specific society' (*une société déterminée*) and Griffiths (1986) to 'legal orders' observed in a 'social field'. Such terms as legal mechanism and legal order suppose determinate social phenomena. The terms 'society' and 'field' might be taken to refer to the context or social setting within which a Law exists but which it does not necessarily fill. However, the implication is that one of the two or more Laws which are in coexistence in any given case is coterminous with the entire society or field. This implication is made explicit in Moore's paper (1978), which takes the case of a social field which 'is defined and its boundaries identified … by … the fact that it can generate rules and coerce or induce compliance to them' (Moore 1978, 57), although the members of this field also observe rules which are generated and enforced in a 'larger social matrix' of which it is a part (Moore 1978, 56).

The 'countries of the world' map of state Laws did not accommodate this legal pluralism. But an initial reaction to that might have been to argue that the pattern of Laws could still be represented on the map if minor additions were made. State Laws applicable throughout the territories of sovereign states could remain the base of the representation. Upon that base there could be placed patches, presumably in tinted but semi-transparent material, representing the societies or fields which were subject to non-state Laws as well as to their state Laws. These patches would be relatively small, and would nearly always be placed with their boundaries entirely within the boundaries of states: the non-state Laws were 'semi-autonomous social fields', subject to forces from outside their boundaries, whereas the state Laws were not.

The picture becomes more complex when it is seen that the groups which observe each non-state Law are frequently divided into smaller groups, each of which has its own Law for some categories of activity. Thus the branches of a Law concerning land tenure or family relations may be subject to special local norms on some forms of tenancy or some aspects of marriage relations respectively. Such a pattern may be seen as entailing a single Law with different 'levels' of norms (Pospisil 1971, 97–126). Perhaps if that pattern were taken into account, a map of legal pluralism would have an upper deck which would itself be a multilayered patchwork, each patch having a single Law forming its base, but above that one or more layers of ever-increasing numbers of every increasingly local Laws.

Even supposing that one continues to call what is now a three-dimensional creation a map, there are further objections suggesting that it still does not capture the complexity of the social facts. The representation just described may imply that the Law of the more comprehensive field is in some way 'superior' to the Laws operating only in subfields. 'Superior' here must mean more powerful or effective. The view would be that the more comprehensive Law effectively sets limits to the possible substance of the Laws with more restricted fields of observance. As an empirical fact capable of investigation, that cannot be assumed to be the case. Indeed, there is a good deal of evidence that people often prefer to observe the local Law even when it conflicts with the Law of wider scope. Another objection is that this system of legal levels, even if it sometimes exists, is far from universal (Griffiths 1986, 15–18).[3] As a result the map became, in Griffiths's

3 Pospisil has since stated that he has 'never tried to present a "model" of legal pluralism applicable cross culturally … What some … authors mistake for "my model",

words, 'a chaotic mess of competing, overlapping, constantly fluid groups, more or less inclusive … in a baffling variety of structural relationships to each other and to the state' (Griffiths 1986, 27).

Griffiths's reference here to 'fluid' groups seems to have arisen from the observation that groups could change their membership rapidly over time. Perhaps this element of change over time could have been catered for, if not eliminated, by making maps which represented snapshots at particular moments. Griffiths does not seem to find it impossible that a map, albeit chaotic and messy, could be drawn of legally pluralist situations at any particular moment. He gives a diagrammatic representation of Moore's view which might be taken as a formalized illustration of a possible map (Griffiths 1986, 35).

But we must ask: What then are Laws? This is not a demand for a definition of a research field. In selecting a research field factors such as the accessibility of people and events to the observer who has a limited time in the field, with limited research funding, can quite reasonably be taken into account. They are not relevant to the present purpose (Moore 1978). The argument against maps of law starts from the claim that, seen as an empirically investigated phenomenon, law (in general) consists of socially observed norms, and a Law, seen as a particular set of facts within the category of 'law', must be seen as *a particular body of observed norms*. This view will be contested in the next section of this chapter. A full attempt to justify it would require a book.

In the present section three claims are advanced. First, law (in general), and therefore each particular Law should be seen as composed of norms, or, in the terms of some modern writers, of rules and principles (Dworkin 1977; and Hart 1994). This view of law as norms does not exclude the study of disputing processes as a part of the study of law. Disputing processes are typically directed by and make use of norms. But they are only one part of law (for example, Abel 1973–1974; and Roberts 1979).

Second, norms are considered to 'exist' only if they are socially observed, not merely if they are, according to doctrinal reasoning from an initial presupposition, 'valid'. The view of law advanced in this section is an attempt to grasp laws as an aspect of the social world. This does not exclude the possibility that a decision as to the validity of a norm may in some social settings determine whether it is observed. The question of the relationship between the accepted processes of legal reasoning, belief in the validity of a norm, and existence of that norm as social fact (all of which are facts capable of empirical investigation) is complex, but need not be answered here.

Third, a Law is defined as a 'body' of norms, to avoid the assumption that a Law is some form of tightly coherent system. It is necessary to return to this point later.

---

which appears pyramidal and hierarchical, is nothing but a reflection of the Kapauku societal structure with its subgroups' (Pospisil 2001, 116).

The Problem of Internal Uniformity

The notion of mapping commonly supposes that evenly coloured patches may be placed on the map, even though on some maps there may be very many small patches and some of them may be on top of others. Mapping of law thus supposes that the entirety of a particular body of norms constituting a Law is observed uniformly throughout the population which accepts that Law. This would enable each Law to be represented by a constant, distinctive colour, even though their positioning on the map was untidy. In relation to this we may first consider the internal structure and form of Laws.

Uniformity of content of a Law is in practice often absent. Quite frequently the Law in relation to certain situations consists of different norms for one part of the population from those observed by another part of the population. For example, the entirety of the Akan-speaking population of West Africa observes many norms in common, including those according to which the significant grouping for landholding purposes is the matrilineal descent group. There are strong grounds for referring to an Akan customary law. However, the administration of land may be governed by different norms among different Akan groups. Among some it is exercised by communities represented by chiefs, who are typically the leaders of multi-lineage groupings. For others the norm states that this function is exercised by the single, extended lineage, not by a supralineage chief.[4] There are many further instances of particular 'variations' in Akan customary law within specific subgroups, just as there are widely varying dialects of the Akan language. Indeed, as with the language it is not possible in some instances to say that one norm or set of norms is the 'usual' or 'common' form and that another is a variant, although in other instances this may be said (see also Benda-Beckmann, F. von 2001, 125–6). These phenomena pose a problem as to the identity of a Law. In some cases a strong difference between two bodies of norms may lead the student to identify them as two different Laws, requiring two patches of different (although perhaps similar) colours to be placed on the map.

It is likely that many state laws exhibit this tendency to internal diversity, although this may be officially denied. In many state Laws there are officially radically different sets of norms for application to different categories of situations. Unofficially there are strong reasons for concluding that some judges persistently interpret and apply certain norms in a different way from others. Also unofficially, there may be judicial systems which discriminate in the sense that officials persistently apply different norms to a particular category of persons although this is not overtly endorsed in any declared norm. Such internal variations are likely to be overlooked, or their significance understated, if investigation is influenced by the legal centralist assumption of uniformity. That assumption encourages the 'common denominator synthesis' rather than the more reliable empirical method of

---

4 The sources for this and other statements about customary law in Ghana are referred to in Woodman (1996).

seeking generalizations built up from the study of many microstructures (Benda-Beckmann, F. von 2001).

Such differences are often so slight that to designate them as giving rise to different Laws would destroy the whole process of differentiating between separate Laws. So the only way to preserve the mapping process is to accept the existence of variations within a single Law. But it is unlikely that these can be satisfactorily shown on a map, and the problem remains as to the extent of the differences which will justify the categorization of people as observing different Laws.

The Problem of Internal Consistency

Related to this is a problem as to the conceptualization of a legal system. It is commonly supposed that the norms of any one 'system' refer to each other in various ways, are derived from a common source and are logically consistent with each other. There are no doubt many interconnections between legal norms, especially between those said to belong to the same 'system'. But derivation of all norms from a common source and logical consistency are not common. Even in state Laws, which adhere strongly to ideologies asserting these factors of coherence, there are frequently potentially conflicting sources of norms, such as those of legislation and precedent in common law systems. Many contain glaring conflicts between norms, although an effective judicial system usually finds some way to determine specific cases which embody those conflicts.[5] Instances of such inconsistencies may be readily found in non-state Laws, and sometimes are more openly recognized to exist there. In most Laws it is apparent that different sets of norms are derived from the political influence of particular interest groups and tend to advance their conflicting interests (Holleman 1949; and Comaroff and Roberts 1981). There is no reason to suppose that, in systems of customary law or in Western state Laws, the general population which observes a Law has any great difficulty in accepting mutually incompatible norms. Thus the notion that legal norms are organized into 'systems' is unsustainable. The neat packages which have supposedly been represented by spaces on the map now disintegrate.

---

5 In common law systems, a glance at any volume of law reports will show cases in which the courts are confronted with parties in conflict, each of whom appears to have a good case founded on established legal norms. Courts normally have a duty to reach a decision in such cases and it is never admitted that such cases cannot be determined according to pre-existing law. But a realistic analysis would suggest that the courts deciding such cases make new law. It is arguable that the manner of deciding such cases to which common law courts generally aspire is well explained in Dworkin (1977). The issue cannot be adequately argued here, but it may be noted that Dworkin's analysis claims that every developed legal system consists of principles as well as rules, and that the principles of one Law frequently conflict with each other.

The Problem of External Boundaries of a Law

The notion of a map of a plural legal world entails the notion that, however untidy the internal structure of a Law, at least it is clear where that Law ends and another begins. The state Law of Kenya, for example, is assumed to be observed by a population resident in a territory which extends (taking some sectors of the compass only for the purpose of example) up to the boundary with Tanzania, while on the other side of the boundary the state Law of Tanzania is observed. Similarly the Kenyan people who are Luo observe Luo customary law for some purposes, and they do not observe Kikuyu customary law, which is observed by the Kikuyu people. Thus Kenyan Law is delimited by the territorial boundary of Kenya. Luo Law is delimited by the territorial boundary around the Luo people.

To depict state Laws on a map of the world was supposed to be a simple matter of drawing lines on a miniature representation of the earth's surface. Now, it may be said, once one has not only ascertained the territorial boundaries of Kenya, but has also located all the Luo, one can begin to draw lines on a map of the legal world which is not limited to state Laws. This also may be claimed to be erroneous, for several reasons.

Many legal 'fields' are not territorially defined, but are the locus of so-called personal laws. The field of Luo Law is delimited by a categorization of people who do not all live in an ethnically homogeneous area. The population which observes a personal law may in some instances be physically widely dispersed within a much larger population of non-members. All references to 'localities' and to 'local law' or 'local communities' need now to be understood to be at least to some extent subject to this weakness. And the fact that a 'local law' may be more intensively observed in one particular geographical locality may increase the possibility of misunderstanding, because it can cause isolated instances of observance elsewhere to be overlooked. (Cotterrell 1997, 80–81, analysing types of 'communities' for the purposes of legal analysis, suggesting that many do not consist of persons within a defined geographical space.)

Another difficulty arises from the fact that, for nearly every social field, there is doubt as to whether certain individuals are members or not. It may be said that, once it is clear who is and who is not a Kenyan or a Luo, the field of application of Kenyan or Luo Law is clear. This common assumption is not correct. Even in the fields of state law there is room for exceptions. Kenya and Tanzania both apply rules of private international law according to which there are occasions when events on Kenyan territory, such as the distribution on death in Kenya of the property of a Tanzanian, are governed by Tanzanian law, and vice versa. In non-state law similar issues arise and have to be resolved when, for example, a Kikuyu marries a Luo.

The arguments just rehearsed concerned the complexity of the boundaries between patches which are to be placed side by side on the map. Each individual in this context is assumed to have as their personal Law either one Law or the other. An equal or greater problem arises from the many cases in which particular persons observe two Laws. These are cases in which the patches representing different laws overlap. The drawing of boundaries between such laws is clearly concerned with the mapping of legal pluralism. The most frequently discussed instances concern the boundary between a state Law and a non-state Law, although the same complexities can arise in separating two non-state Laws. This instance of coexistence between Laws may involve continuing conflict between Laws. In that case the dividing line or surface is determined by success for the time being in the conflict. But legal pluralism need not and, in most instances, does not involve conflict between the constituent Laws. It rather produces regular practices which allocate the determination of particular categories of issues to one Law, and of other categories to the other Law. It is not unusual, for example, for one Law to be is observed in matters relating to family matters but another Law in economic transactions between non-relatives.

All of these cases give rise to 'choice of law' problems, that is, problems in the determination of the Laws to be observed in particular cases. The parties to some transactions, such as agreements for employment, for example, may be able effectively to agree that their relationship arising from the transaction should be governed in some respects by a state Law and in others by a non-state Law. In regard to other transactions, such as marriage, the parties may have no effective option but to observe their personal Law. Again, one of the Laws may be dominant but not monopolistic, so that it may effectively determine the rules to be applied in deciding which Law governs. State Laws sometimes contain 'choice of law' rules, purporting to determine which Law is to govern a situation, and may then even claim to validate the non-state Laws by 'recognizing' them.[6] But such rules, like the remainder of a state Law, may or may not receive widespread observance.

It is also common for there to be, in an area of overlap between two Laws, no general practices resolving these issues of legal pluralism, so that events may be subject to varying norms as to the choice of law. For example, people engaging in transactions in urban areas may be able effectively to agree that their relationship should be governed in some respects by a particular state Law and in other respects by a non-state Law, but people engaging in analogous transactions in a rural area may be invariably governed by the non-state Law. Or events taking place and individuals living on the territorial periphery of the social field may not be governed by state law whereas events which take place and individuals who live in 'central' locations in circumstances otherwise identical, may be governed by state Law (See Benda-Beckmann, F. von 1999, 132, on the varying relations

6 This was the type of issue in *Wambui Otieno vs. Ougo and Siranga* (Cotran 1987, 331–45). There the state courts of Kenya controlled the outcome of the case and applied norms of Kenyan state law to determine whether the issue (the mode of burial of the deceased Luo man who had been married to a Kikuyu under the non-customary, received form of marriage) should be decided according to that part of Kenyan law which consisted of legislation and the norms of common law derived from England or that part of Kenyan law which consisted of the Kenyan state courts' representation of Luo customary law.

between state Law and local village Laws). Some individuals may for a variety of reasons live more of their lives according to one of the coexisting laws than do their immediate neighbours. It may even be possible for individuals or groups on the periphery of a field to begin to observe the law of a neighbouring field for some purposes. There is often a merging tendency at the edges of fields. It has been remarked that 'the interaction [between coexisting Laws] is more often like that between waves or clouds or rivulets than between hard, stable entities like rocks or billiard balls' (Twining 2006, 513).

The choice of law notion assumes the continued coexistence of two or more Laws. Over time, as many instances show, each may influence the development of the other. A period of mutual influence may eventually lead to a mixing of the Laws to such a degree that a new hybrid Law emerges to replace them. This also is difficult to depict on a map, or a series of maps at different points in time (see Benda-Beckmann, K. von 2006, 47, suggesting that 'the idea that the field of legal pluralism consists of clearly distinguishable legal systems is no longer and probably never was tenable', and demonstrating this with examples from Indonesia; Santos 2006, giving yet another demonstration of the complexity of situations of legal pluralism and the impossibility of drawing boundaries around distinct 'Laws').

The problem referred to here as that of the 'external boundaries of Laws' has repercussions in the lives of countless individuals and communities. Current concerns range from the struggles of individuals who feel imprisoned within communities and of others who feel a desperate desire for firm membership of a community to give them identity, and the 'safety of effortless secure belonging' (Margalit and Raz 1995, 86), to the stereotyping of crudely described communities with fixed membership on which racism, intercommunal war and genocide depend. The unravelling of the errors in this stereotyping shows the impossibility of depicting law even on highly complex maps.

The Case for Mapping: Laws Conceptualized as Norms Made and Enforced by Authorities

This section is Bavinck's response to the arguments of Woodman put in the previous section.

Summarizing the Argument hitherto

The argument presented against mapping hinges on a definition of law as 'a particular body of observed norms'. The emphasis is on the noun 'norms', which, according to common understanding, may be defined as 'a shared expectation of behaviour that connotes what is considered culturally desirable and appropriate' (Marshall 1998, 453). Similar to other aspects of culture, norms reside in the mind and are therefore quite intangible.

Norms attain reality in social life through the phenomenon of 'observance'. The latter term is not circumscribed, but suggests that people in their daily lives follow, or at least pay attention to, the norms in question. It is by acting out norms that in Woodman's view law enters and is distributed throughout the social world. Mapping, if it were to be possible, would visualize the manner in which the observance of Law is spread out geographically.

The collection of norms that makes up a particular Law is termed a 'body'. In choosing this metaphor, Woodman has made efforts 'to avoid the assumption that a Law is some form of tightly coherent system'. Although he agrees that there are 'many interconnections between legal norms', there are also too many inconsistencies to allow any Law to be described in terms of 'system' – a term which suggests functionality and order. 'Body' – presumably taken in the meaning of aggregate, and not as an organic entity – would allow more heterogeneity and contradiction, and is therefore more appropriate to the reality of observed Law.

This is the approach of an empiricist – someone fascinated by detail and variation, and distrustful of most generalization. The empiricist orientation displayed in the definition of law subsequently runs through the discussion of uniformity, consistency and boundaries, and informs the conclusion that living law is basically unmappable. After all, where law is internally untidy and diverse, inconsistent and characterized by a lack of clear boundaries, it can hardly be represented by visual means.

Introducing Authorities

The approach to law and legal pluralism advanced here differs from that just put, and is connected to the approach ventured by Max Weber in his seminal discussion of law in Volume I of *Economy and Society*. Weber defines law as follows:

> An order will be called … *law* if it is externally guaranteed by the probability that coercion (physical or psychological), to bring about conformity or avenge violation, will be applied by a *staff* of people holding themselves specially ready for that purpose (Weber 1954, 5, emphasis in the original).

This perspective contains several interesting features. Most significantly, Weber broadens the definition of law beyond rules and norms to include a category of people called 'staff', who are in charge of enforcement. Staff members impose the law on the relevant social field and act to protect it – they stand, as the term 'staff' implies, in the service of the normative system. Staff may be held to include judges, policemen and other members of bureaucracy, but also the members of a clan, ready to wreak blood vengeance (Weber 1954, 6). The latter is in line with Weber's non-ideological understanding of law.

There are, it may be claimed, advantages to exploring the definition of law in this direction. The benefits manifest themselves most clearly in what is termed law's social existence. Thus the definition of law advanced in the previous section emphasizes the phenomenon of *observance* – the adherence to law by its subjects. Weber's definition, on the other hand, draws attention to its *enforcement*. This is the realm where law is made and implemented.[7] Core concepts here are *influence* and *reach*. Influence is a measure of the imprint which authorities in charge of law make on society; reach is the geographical measure of influence.

Legal anthropologists have long since recognized the connection in society between law with other social dimensions, such as politics and management. Intermingling takes place first of all at the level of activity and rationale. Some authors (Moore 1977) thus point out some of the political purposes of court cases; contrarily, the legal implications of political activity can hardly be ignored. The generation, modification or confirmation of rules and norms is always the result of political action – a public process of consensus building. Similarly, many rules and norms possess management purposes, such as with regard to economic development (Benda-Beckmann, F. von 1989; and Benda-Beckmann, K. von 2001b) or the exploitation of natural resources (Spiertz and Wiber 1996). Some authors (Macaulay 1986), basing themselves on older anthropological traditions (Mair 1962), even discuss law in terms of government or administration.

Mixing of societal dimensions takes place in activities but also in the persons and agencies that are involved. Here we find a mingling of roles that in some societies have become more separated than in others. Thus the politician may in some instances act as judge or as manager, and the judge and the manager may dabble in politics without the activities or the roles being clearly distinguished. What unites these functions is the use of power and the wielding of public authority. Far beyond Weber's 'staff', who implements law, such authorities *make* law, in addition to enforcing it.[8]

Leopold Pospisil (1971, 43) recognizes the essential role of authorities for a 'viable' concept of law.[9] He writes:

> A decision, to be legally relevant, or in other words, to effect social control, must either be accepted as a solution by the parties to a dispute or, if they resist, be forced upon them. Such a decision, of necessity, is passed by an individual, or group of individuals, who can either persuade the litigant to comply or who possess power over enforcement agents or the group membership in general (Pospisil 1971, 44).

---

7 It could be argued that 'observance' is a form of 'making law' as well. However, it varies from the forms considered here in the fact that it generally takes place in the personal and not in the public domain.

8 In his discussion of political systems, Bailey (1969, 132) introduces authorities as 'umpires' or 'referees'. I prefer to extend the meaning of authorities to include those who formulate the rules of the game.

9 Whereas Pospisil first only uses the term authorities, he elsewhere (1971, 58) makes a distinction between authorities and leaders.

There is a clear echo here of Max Weber's emphasis on the role of 'staff' in the enforcement of law. Pospisil adds to his argument the fact that leadership is a universal phenomenon, and that there is therefore no logical reason to exclude it from the definition of law (Pospisil 1971, 50).

Continuing along these lines, one can imagine law as a spider plus web.[10] A web is effective only when the spider is in control; without an inhabitant it soon falls into disrepair. It is the combination that is particularly effective and long lasting. Spiders make webs and repair them; like many public authorities, they depend on their weaving for a livelihood. Webs consist of individual threads, connected in some way or another.[11] They may be in different stages of development or disrepair, fully woven and shining in the sun or made up of only a thread or two. Alas, some webs have been deserted by their owners, with a few hapless victims swinging in the wind, testifying to their earlier dexterity.

The analogy of spider plus web is helpful in making yet another point. Spiders are strategic thinkers: they fabricate webs in locations where they are deemed to yield dividend. Each web, however, covers only one spot in the forest area. Likewise there are many applications of law in the social universe, and it is difficult to speak in general terms about law. Rather, it is useful to consider one web – or one kind of web – at a time. In my ethnographic work (Bavinck 2001; 2003; 2005), for instance, I consider the 'spiders' occupying one particular corner of the metaphorical forest, namely the species dealing specifically with marine fisheries in Tamil Nadu, India. As in other forests, there are more spiders here with overlapping and duplicating webs. Together, they have fabricated, and continue to fabricate, a state of legal pluralism.

We may return once more to the argument, made above, that law is intimately connected to other social domains, such as politics, economics and management. The implication hereof is that legal systems are replicated in political, economic and managerial systems, and, moreover, that these systems are sometimes almost the same. So are the authorities at their core, many of whom combine various functions. The legal pluralism we are at care to study, is therefore paralleled by states of political, economic and managerial pluralism.

The inclusion of authorities in the definition of law has important implications for the evaluation of normative incoherence, which – it will be remembered – is one of the major reasons given above against the conceptualization of legal systems. The conclusion proposed here is much less harsh. Authorities, in the perception suggested, act to tie the normative body together – they perform an integrative function that remains invisible to the scholar focusing on norms. Moreover, law being a process (Moore 1978), we may assume that legal systems are in continuous flux and development and that what is not there today, may well

10 The analogy of spider plus web of course goes wrong when the observers of law are identified with the spider's victims.

11 See Benda-Beckmann, F. von (2002, 62–4) for a discussion of the possible nature of interdependence and connection in legal systems.

come into existence tomorrow. Like spiders, authorities are busy mending gaps and bridging contradictions.

Rather than speculating about the existence of coherent rule systems, one might therefore inquire into the existence of authorities interested in, and capable of, developing and enforcing law. Just like it makes more sense, when one aims at achieving insight into the dynamics of insect life, to count spiders than spider webs, it is more useful to take authorities as an index of living law than normative bodies. Their functioning, it is contended, deserves more scholarly attention.

Legal Systems as Ideal Types

The second step that helps us to address the predicaments identified by Woodman is a shift in the analytical mode. Remember that Woodman's critique of the concept of legal system leans on the difficulties of identifying coherence in the observation of law as it takes place *empirically,* as well as of defining the differences between one legal system and another. For all those who have studied law in the field, these points are of course well taken. One may wonder, however, whether another conceptual reading is possible. My suggestion in this regard is to consider law and legal systems as *ideal types*.

Max Weber coined the term 'ideal type' as a conceptual tool to facilitate comparisons between societal phenomena. As Gerth and Mills (1948, 59–60) point out, Weber 'felt that social scientists had the choice of using logically controlled and unambiguous conceptions, which are thus more removed from historical reality, or of using less precise concepts, which are more closely geared to the empirical world'. Because of his interest in worldwide comparisons, he chose to consider 'pure cases', constructed as ideal types.

The Dutch methodologist Vercruijsse (1970, 136) describes ideal types as follows:

> The true meaning of an ideal type is not only that one leaves out the coincidental and selects the relevant [...] It includes the adding of essential elements, yes, even the practice of exaggeration. In this way, an ideal type attains the character of a utopia; in other words, it consists of a composition of characteristics, that does not – or only rarely so – exist in reality.

It is important to realize that, despite their exaggerated nature, ideal types have a sound base in reality. Rather than replicating the details of each particular manifestation of a societal phenomenon, however, ideal types 'serve as guides in a filing system' (Rheinstein 1954, xxxviii) – they are distilled images, constructed for analytical purposes. As such, they are more than generalizations.

The term 'ideal type' does not appear much in writings on legal pluralism. Similar analytical concerns, however, emerge time and again. Thus, in an article on law's reproduction, Benda-Beckmann, F. von (2001, 121) speaks of the need for 'generalizing statements' to fill the landscape of law. Two years later he makes another step, by advancing the possibility of creating 'typologies of different ideal-typical legal forms' (2002, 50), with regular morphological dimensions. Like ideal types, such typologies are a step removed from reality – 'one cannot expect that empirical phenomena would fit into analytical categories in a one-to-one manner … [E]mpirical data will not always fall squarely and exclusively within one analytical domain'.

It is argued that it is useful to consider legal systems, and their constituent elements, such as authorities, as ideal types and not as one-to-one representations of reality. This helps us to identify and study key features, actors and processes, and also to make comparisons between one setting and the next. It assists, in other words, not to get bogged down in a plenitude of localized facts, and to proceed with the scientific task of analysis. As Weber describes the function of ideal types:

> The ideal typical concept will help to develop our skill in imputation in *research:* it *is* no 'hypothesis' but it offers guidance to the construction of hypotheses. It is *not* a *description* of reality but it aims to give unambiguous means of expression to such a description (Weber 1949, 89, emphasis in the original).

For the Possibility of Depicting Law through Maps

The last sentence of the above quote – ideal types give 'unambiguous means of expression' – takes us to the third and last part of the argument, on the possibilities of depicting law. It points out that ideal types are, besides tools of analysis, also a form of representation, a way of depicting essential features of reality.

The authors of an authoritative handbook on mapping (Robinson et al. 1995, 18) liken cartography 'to a drama played by two actors, the map maker and map user, with two stage properties, the map and the data domain (all potential information that might be put on a map)'. This rich sentence suggests first of all that maps – that make up only one category in an overall set of depictions – are the coagulations of a communication process between makers and users. Worded differently: map makers have a message to put across, and will try to do so in a manner which the user is likely to appreciate.[12] Second, the term 'drama' in this quote implies that the cartographic process is not a simple, one-time conversion of data, but a longer drawn and even suspenseful activity. Outsiders generally do not appreciate the fact that a cartographic process involves many stages. The authors quoted above emphasize the importance of the various steps as 'a series of information transformations, each of which has the power to alter the appearance of the final product …' (ibid., 18).

'Drama', 'process', 'message', 'choice' – these terms challenge the common understanding of cartography as an exact and relatively straightforward science. As Santos (1987, 282) points out, however, 'the main structural feature of maps is that

12 Whether the message actually does come across or is transformed in the perception of users is a question we leave aside in this chapter.

in order to fulfil their function they inevitably distort reality'. Distortion, Santos argues, takes place through three 'specific mechanisms' that are intrinsic to the map making process: scale, projection and symbolization. Santos is referring mainly to orientation maps, and the typology of distortions can be added to, certainly when thematic maps are also taken into consideration. More generally, one could note that distortion is a result of the process called cartographic generalization. This includes classification, simplification and exaggeration (Robinson et al. 1995, 458).

It will be clear that in Santos's perception, distortion – or the deviation that occurs between map and reality – is not the result of wilful deceit. Rather, it follows from the exercise of function. Distortions are an involuntary side effect of the fact that cartographers, in order to be effective, must define their purpose. Here there is no difference from the academic, who relies on language to make his point. As one cartographer points out: 'A map must [...] be a simile or metaphor if it is to tell us what we need to know. A map has as much right to be *figurative* as spoken or written language has; it too is a language' (Greenhood 1964, x; emphasis in the original).

It has been said several times now: '[T]he look of a map depends largely on its intended use'. Because of this condition, there exists 'an almost unlimited variety of maps' (Robinson et al. 1995, 11). In order to produce this diversity, cartographers have at their disposal an array of instruments that vastly surpass the understanding of Woodman, who limits himself to the description of fields and boundaries. Using colours, shapes, patterns, lines and arrows; through accentuation and leaving out, cartographers strive to convey many messages, at different levels of abstractness and generalization. Why not the understandings of law?

Some scholars have actually ventured into this field. F. von Benda-Beckmann (1999, 144–5) thus presents a set of maps detailing:

- Settlement and land use patterns in one part of the Moluccas.
- The legal status of land according to adat law.
- The legal status of land according to village adat.

I myself have imagined the varying normative systems applying to marine fisheries in Tamil Nadu as overlays on a map of inshore resources (Bavinck 1998). This is one way of mapping law.

In line with this chapter's emphasis on authorities and their role in law, one can envisage another kind of map. Herein, the influence and reach of authorities, and their version of law, stand centre stage. First of all, one may map the influence of the state, as it is spatially distributed. In Tamil Nadu fisheries (Bavinck 2003), the state's influence reigns supreme in the capital city, and is reflected with some strength in the various district headquarters. But in the villages, the state's power is far less. Here the village headmen and *panchayats* wield a sceptre, deciding on the affairs of fisheries according to their understanding of prerogatives and rules. The influence of these authorities, however, scarcely reaches beyond the village boundaries. On a map, therefore, this would show up as a string of sparkling beads. Finally, I would colour in the influence of the newcomers in fisheries: the professional associations of modern fishers, based in harbour towns along the coast. Their influence is foremost in the harbour towns themselves, but stretches out over the full reach of their fishing activity.

Having mapped, in an ideal typical way, the reach of the various legal systems, one can draw attention to the areas of overlap. This is where conflicts over the exploitation of resources take place, and where more than one legal system holds influence. This is where 'forum shopping' takes place, and where authorities battle for their hold over matters and subjects.

A Rejoinder to the Case for Mapping

This section is Woodman's response to the arguments of Bavinck, insofar as it seems necessary to add to Woodman's argument in the first section.

The question in issue regarding the conceptualization of law is whether there is a concept of law which designates a class of facts apt to be represented on a map of law. Bavinck's argument is that Weber's concept of law as an order enforced by an authority consisting of a staff with this enforcement function defines a type of object which can be represented on maps. This, he argues, overcomes Woodman's claim that a Law must be seen as a body of norms observed by a given population, which cannot be so represented.

A standard definition of a map states that it is a 'graphic representation of spatial relationships and spatial forms' (Robinson et al. 1995; see also Robinson and Petchenik 1976, 15–16). Thus if instances of a class of objects are to be shown on maps, each instance must exist in space in a form which can be graphically represented. The objects may be countries, geographically distinct areas, social practices or any other objects, provided that they can be spatially delineated. Maps are generally concerned with the presentation of large amounts of information about spatial relations and forms rather than conceptual analysis. It is doubtful whether a definition of law in terms of authority enables maps of law to be drawn.

In the first place such a definition does not encompass all the phenomena which we would usually wish to include in the term 'law'. Weber wrote that he proposed his definition only for the purposes of his particular discussion (which did not include the compilation of maps). He accepted that it might be useful to define law differently for other purposes (Weber 1954, 6; 1968, 34). The limits to the value of his definition are well illustrated a few lines later in Weber's text, when he writes that '[i]n terms of the present terminology [it] would be correct' to deny that international law could be called law (Weber 1954, 6; 1968, 35). At the time Weber wrote the norms of international law were not enforced by a staff of officials, but there would have been serious objections to the suggestion that international law was to be excluded from any comprehensive study of the laws of the world, or of any part of the world (see also Woodman 1998).

Indeed, it is questionable whether a definition in terms of authority even encompasses satisfactorily all cases of state law. Societies are too complex to rely on an official list of law enforcers, as Weber recognizes when he refers to 'the clan, as an agency of blood revenge and of the prosecution of feuds' (Weber 1954, 6; 1968, 35) as an enforcement body. He mentions a series of other laws, such as those enforced by 'brotherly admonition' in religious sects, and the rules of German student fraternities about convivial drinking and singing (Weber 1954, 6; 1968, 35). It is not easy to identify a 'staff' in such cases. In the case of state law there is often some person or body of persons (a 'staff') who claim to be the sole source of law-making, or law enforcement, or both. But such claims cannot be accepted as necessarily empirically correct. A defect of this definition is that, by directing all attention towards enforcement, it reduces the possibility of a realistic empirical assessment of the motivation behind the observance of norms. As Bavinck rightly says, maps are necessarily selective in the facts they record. But selectivity does not extend to the positing of 'facts' which do not exist.

Second this concept of law fails to identify objects which are sufficiently clearly delineated to be depicted on a map. The difficulty here is much the same as that identified above in the concept of law as a body of observed norms. It was suggested that it is not possible in the real world to draw lines around the populations or territories which can be said to observe one body of norms rather than another. Bavinck's proposal for drawing maps of law identified by authority suggests that the lines depicting the space of each Law would delineate the 'influence and reach' of its authority. This would appear to be subject to almost exactly the same set of criticisms.

Bavinck seeks to anticipate these objections by presenting the concept of law enforced by authority as an ideal type. This defence would not have been available to Weber. It seems unlikely that he intended his definition of law to be an ideal type; but, regardless of that, it is certain that he did not propose to compile maps of law. His device of the ideal type, like the notion of authority, has great potential for assisting an understanding of various aspects of law, especially its histories. But for the purpose of mapping law the ideal type is misleading. Weber's ideal type was a conceptual construction, not an attempt to summarize empirical fact. He referred to 'the danger that the ideal type and reality will be confused with one another' (Weber 1949, 101). Commentators have frequently acknowledged this. Thus it has been said that 'a distinguishing characteristic of ideal type concepts is that they have no instances' (Papineau 1976, 137; see also Weinert 1997, explicitly taking the same view while disputing some of Papineau's other arguments). Yet maps are of their essence concerned with presenting 'instances'.

It is arguable that some restricted aspects of legal processes may be depicted by maps, although these are likely to be more in the nature of tables arranged to look like maps. Wood's *Maps of World Financial Law*, for example, compiled for the use of legal practitioners, sets out certain features of states' Laws on financial regulation (Wood 2005). The book is an impressive display of expert knowledge, but the author states at the outset that he seeks to record only 'the legal rules … i.e. the law on the books, hard law'. He does not attempt to include 'the impact of those rules in practice', nor to measure 'compliance by the courts and administrative authorities with the rules and the degree of enforcement' (Wood 2005, 13). His maps are little more than tables, in which the information about each state's financial law, provided through colour coding, is given in a box representing the territory of the state on a map of the countries of the world. The location of each box serves only to remind the reader of the location of the state on the world's surface. At various points in the book the series of maps gives way to tables.[13]

None of this is intended to deny that maps may be helpful in providing information which may assist an understanding of the causes or effects of particular parts of the law. Thus F. von Benda-Beckmann employs maps to show the settlement upon and use of land in a district, and the legal status of land according to different coexisting laws (Benda-Beckmann, F. von 1999, 144–5, referred to above by Bavinck). These provide useful information about the facts of land use and about claims asserted in different Laws. They do not claim to be, and they are not maps of law.

It is not intended to deny that other forms of representation may be helpful to an understanding of legal situations. Metaphors and similes of law are used by various writers. Bavinck writes that the influence of village headmen and *panchayats* in Tamil Nadu 'scarcely reaches beyond the village boundaries' and so 'on a map … would show up as a string of sparkling beads'. This appears to be a helpful simile. But a picture of a string of beads is not a map. The same can be said of the Bavinck's simile of the spider's web, and of the simile of a river developed by F. von Benda-Beckmann to represent the mingling of different Laws is a population (Benda-Beckmann, F. von 2001, 119–21, taken from Merry 1997). But these word pictures are not 'graphic representations of spatial relationships and spatial forms'. A map itself may be a visual metaphor; not all visual metaphors are maps. The presentation of a map is a process of communication, intended to transmit a message, as Bavinck says. But the texts on cartography recognize that the message which is the object of this particular form of communication is always about spatial forms and relations.

Similarly a geography of law, discussed by some scholars including the editors of this volume, is not the same as a map of law. Franz von Benda-Beckmann has rightly argued that a study of the total 'landscape' of law in a region, producing empirical generalizations, requires the collection of data which cover the whole variety of the region (Benda-Beckmann, F. von 2001). Whereas Bavinck is concerned that we should not 'get bogged down in a plenitude of localized facts', Franz von Benda-Beckmann sees a large body of micro information as necessary

13 The notion that tables and diagrams can be called 'maps' appears occasionally in the literature of various disciplines other than geography (see for example, Honderich 1995, 927–44). This usage loses the value of having a distinctive term for the products of cartography.

to a full account of what he calls a geography of law. However, his conclusion concerning the variety of law in a region is that this cannot be mapped: 'In order to make such variety visible we need a time-oriented *geography of law rather than cartography of law*' (Benda-Beckmann, F. von 2001, 129, emphasis added).

A similar observation may be made of Twining's generally approving comment on Woodman's earlier paper on this issue, concluding with an example thus:

> [I]f we agree that Shari'a travels with every devout Muslim, a good map of Islamic diasporas can at least give a general indication of where Islamic law is likely to exist at a given time as an institutionalized social practice. We need to guard against overusing spatial metaphors, but there is still scope for legal geography (Twining 2006, 509, footnotes omitted, referring to Woodman 2003).

A 'map' of diasporas, presumably consisting largely of a map of the world, with arrows placed upon it and with notes about such matters as historical periods and political developments, would, on this view, provide useful background information. It would not indicate where, when or to what extent Islamic law was observed or enforced, only where it was 'likely' to be observed. This would be legal geography assisted by a map, but not a map of law.

Finally we should also recall the distinction between a map or maps of law, and the view of law as a map.[14] The latter was Santos's concern in his stimulating discussion, cited by Bavinck, in which he argued that law, like a map, necessarily distorts reality in its compilers' choices of scale, projection and symbols (Santos 2002, 417–38). Santos does not propose to draw maps of law.

Conclusion

The cases for and against maps of law, as presented above, depends on contrary positions on three issues. Regarding the identity, or definition, of law, Woodman emphasizes the aspect of norms and their observance, whereas Bavinck stresses the role of authorities in defining and enforcing law. The former position highlights aspects such as boundaries and tidiness, whereas the latter concentrates on nodes and reach. This results in different positions with regard to mapability.

The second issue is empiricism versus generalization, or, more specifically, the value of ideal types. Woodman tends to take an empiricist position, paying special attention to variations and contradictions as they occur at the level of the rank and file, who are the observers of Laws. Having opposed the ideal type of legal centralism, he is more wary of generalizations, which are by definition somewhat removed from social reality. Bavinck, on the other hand, argues that ideal types

14 Woodman is indebted to Franz von Benda-Beckmann for this neat expression of an important distinction, put in a discussion of Woodman (2003).

are useful instruments to distil and study key aspects of law, and compare between one setting and the next.

Finally, the authors differ on the shape maps of law may take. Woodman takes a classical view, emphasizing the difficulties involved in creating a proper representation of the untidiness of the observance of Laws. Bavinck, on the other hand, argues that maps reflect the purpose of the maker; the pursuit of purpose always means generalizing and leaving out. He suggests that once the message has been determined, there is a range of cartographic instruments to make use of.

References

Abel, R.L. (1973–1974) 'A Comparative Theory of Dispute Institutions in Society'. *Law and Society Review*, 8: 217–342.

Austin, J. (1954) *The Province of Jurisprudence Determined* (H.L.A. Hart (ed.) first published 1832). London: Weidenfeld and Nicolson.

Bailey, F.G. (1969) *Stratagems and Spoils. A Social Anthropology of Politics*. Oxford: Basil Blackwell.

Bavinck, M. (1998) '"A Matter of Maintaining Peace". State Accommodation to Subordinate Legal Systems: The Case of Fisheries along the Coromandel Coast of Tamil Nadu, India'. *Journal of Legal Pluralism*, 40: 151–70.

Bavinck, M. (2001) *Marine Resource Management. Conflict and Regulation in the Fisheries of the Coromandel Coast*. New Delhi: Sage.

Bavinck, M. (2003) 'The Spatially Splintered State: Myths and Realities in the Regulation of Marine Fisheries in Tamil Nadu, India'. *Development and Change*, 34: 633–58.

Bavinck, M. (2004) 'How to Start Mapping Law – A Rejoinder to Woodman'. Paper given at the XIVth International Conference of the Commission on Folk Law and Legal Pluralism. Fredericton, New Brunswick, 26–29 August 2004.

Bavinck, M. (2005) 'Understanding Fisheries Conflicts in the South – A Legal Pluralist Perspective'. *Society and Natural Resources*, 18(9): 805–20.

Benda-Beckmann, F. von (1989) 'Scapegoat and Magic Charm: Law in Development Theory and Practice'. *Journal of Legal Pluralism*, 28: 129–48.

Benda-Beckmann, F. von (1999) 'Multiple Legal Constructions of Socio-economic Spaces: Resource Management and Conflict in the Central Moluccas' in M. Roesler and T. Wendl (eds) *Frontiers and Borderlands: Anthropological Perspectives*. Frankfurt: Lang, pp. 131–58.

Benda-Beckmann, F. von (2001) 'On the Reproduction of Law: Micro and Macro in the Time-Space Geography of Law' in W. Fikentscher (ed.) *Begegnung und Konflikt – eine kulturanthropologische Bestandsaufnahme*. Munich: C.H. Beck, pp. 119–31.

Benda-Beckmann, F. von (2002) 'Who's Afraid of Legal Pluralism?'. *Journal of Legal Pluralism*, 47: 37–82.

Benda-Beckmann, K. von (2001a) 'Folk, Indigenous, and Customary Law' in N.J. Smelser and P.B. Baltes (eds.) *International Encyclopedia of the Social and Behavioral Sciences*, Vol. 8. Amsterdam: Elsevier, pp. 5705–708.

Benda-Beckmann, K. von (2001b)'Transnational Dimensions of Legal Pluralism' in W. Fikentscher (ed.) *Begegnung und Konflikt – eine kulturanthropologische Bestandsaufnahme*. Munich: C.H. Beck, pp. 33–48.

Benda-Beckmann, K. von (2006) 'The Contexts of Law' in E. Baerends and H. Vijers (eds) *Griffiti: Articles in Honour of John Griffiths*. Groningen, pp. 45–65.

Comaroff, J.L. and Roberts, S. (1981) *Rules and Processes: The Cultural Logic of Dispute in an African Context*. Chicago and London: University of Chicago Press.

Cotran, E. (1987) *Casebook on Kenya Customary Law*. Abingdon, Nairobi: Professional Books, Nairobi University Press.

Cotterrell, R. (1997) 'A Legal Concept of Community'. *Canadian Journal of Law and Society/Revue Canadienne de Droit et Société*, 12: 75–91.

Dworkin, R. (1977) *Taking Rights Seriously*. Cambridge, Mass: Harvard University Press.

Gerth, H.H. and Mills, C.W. (1948) *From Max Weber: Essays in Sociology*. London: Routledge and Kegan Paul.

Greenhood, D. (1964) *Mapping*. University of Chicago Press: Chicago. [Previously published as *Down to Earth: Mapping for Everybody*, 1944. New York: Holiday House.]

Griffiths, J. (1986) 'What is Legal Pluralism?' *Journal of Legal Pluralism*, 24: 1–55.

Griffiths, J. (1995) 'Legal Pluralism and the Theory of Legislation – With Special Reference to the Regulation of Euthanasia' in H. Petersen and H. Zahle (eds) *Legal Polycentricity: Consequences of Pluralism in Law*. Aldershot: Dartmouth, pp. 201–34.

Hart, H.L.A. (1994) *The Concept of Law*, 2nd edn. Oxford: Clarendon Press.

Holleman, J.F. (1949) 'An Anthropological Approach to Bantu Law (with Special Reference to Shona Law)'. *Rhodes-Livingstone Journal*, 10: 51–64.

Honderich, T. (1995) *The Oxford Companion to Philosophy*. Oxford: Oxford University Press.

Hooker, M.B. (1975) *Legal Pluralism: An Introduction to Colonial and Neo-colonial Laws*. Oxford: Clarendon Press.

Macaulay, S. (1986) 'Private Government' in L. Lipson and S. Wheeler (eds) *Law and the Social Sciences*. New York: Russel Sage Foundation, pp. 445–517.

Mair, L. (1962) *Primitive Government*. Penguin Books: Middlesex.

Margalit, A. and Raz, J. (1995) 'National Self-determination' in W. Kymlicka (ed.) *The Rights of Minority Cultures*. Oxford: Oxford University Press.

Marshall, G. ([1994] 1998) *Oxford Dictionary of Sociology*. Oxford: Oxford University Press.

Merry, S.E. (1997) 'Legal Pluralism and Transnational Culture: The Ka Ho'okolokolonui Kanaka Maoli Tribunal' in R.A. Wilson (ed.) *Human Rights, Culture and Context*. London: Pluto Press, pp. 28–48.

Moore, S.F. (1977) 'Individual Interests and Organisational Structures: Dispute Settlements as "Events of Articulation"' in I. Hamnett (ed.) *Social Anthropology and Law*. New York: Academic Press, pp 159–88.

Moore, S.F. (1978) 'Law and Social Change: The Semi-autonomous Social Field as an Appropriate Subject of Study' in S.F. Moore *Law as Process: An Anthropological Approach*. London: Routledge and Kegan Paul, pp. 54–81. [Reprinted from (1973) *Law and Society Review*, 7: 719–46.]

Papineau, D. (1976) 'Ideal Types and Empirical Theories'. *British Journal for the Philosophy of Science*, 27: 137–46.

Pospisil, L. (1971) *Anthropology of Law. A Comparative Theory*. New York: Harper and Row.

Pospisil, L. (2001) 'Corrections of a Reappraisal of Leopold Pospisil'. *Journal of Legal Pluralism*, 46: 115–20.

Rheinstein, M. (1954) 'Introduction' in M. Weber *Max Weber on Law in Economy and Society*. Cambridge: Harvard University Press, pp. xxv–lxxi.

Roberts, S. (1979) *Order and Dispute: An Introduction to Legal Anthropology*. Harmondsworth: Penguin.

Robinson, A.H. and Petchenik, B.B. (1976) *The Nature of Maps: Essays Toward Understanding Maps and Mapping*. Chicago: University of Chicago Press.

Robinson, A.H., Morrison, J.L., Muehrcke, P.C., Kimerling, A.J. and Guptill, S.C. (1995) *Elements of Cartography*, 6th edn. [1st edn. 1953]. New York: John Wiley and Sons Inc.

Santos, B. de Sousa (1987) 'Law: A Map of Misreading. Toward a Postmodern Conception of Law'. *Journal of Law and Society*, 14: 279–302.

Santos, B. de Sousa (2002) *Toward a New Legal Common Sense: Law, Globalization, and Emancipation*, 2nd edn. London: Butterworths.

Santos, B. de Sousa (2006) 'The Heterogeneous State and Legal Pluralism in Mozambique'. *Law and Society Review*, 40: 39–75.

Spiertz, J. and Wiber, M.G. (eds) (1996) *The Role of Law in Natural Resource Management*. VUGA Uitgeverij: 's-Gravenhage.

Twining, W.L. (2000) *Globalisation and Legal Theory*. London: Butterworths.

Twining, W.L. (2006) 'Diffusion and Globalization Discourse'. *Harvard International Law Journal*, 47: 507–15.

Vanderlinden, J. (1971) 'Le Pluralism Juridique: Essai de Synthèse' in J. Gilissen (ed.) *Le Pluralisme Juridique*. Brussels: L'Université Bruxelles, pp. 19–56.

Vercruijsse, E.V.W. (1970) *Het Ontwerpen van een Sociologisch Onderzoek. Uitgangspunten Enrichtlijnen*. Assen: Van Gorcum.

Weber, M. (1949) '"Objectivity" in Social Science and Social Policy' in *Max Weber on the Methodology of the Social Sciences*, Translated and Edited by E.A. Shils and H.A. Finch. Illinois: Free Press of Glencoe, pp. 50–112.

Weber, M. (1954) *Max Weber on Law in Economy and Society* (edited with introduction and annotations by M. Rheinstein, translation by E. Shils and M. Rheinstein). Cambridge: Harvard University Press.

Weber, M. (1968) *Economy and Society: An Outline of Interpretative Sociology* (translated by E. Fischoff et al. and edited by G. Roth and C. Wittich). New York: Bedminster Press.

Weinert, F. (1997) 'Weber's Ideal Types as Models in the Social Sciences' in A. O'Hear (ed.) *Verstehen and Humane Understanding*. Cambridge: Cambridge University Press, pp. 73–93.

Wood, P.R. (2005) *Maps of World Financial Law*, 5th edn. London: Allen and Overy LLP.

Woodman, G.R. (1993) 'Folk Law' in A.-J. Arnaud (ed.) *Dictionnaire Encyclopédique de Théorie et de Sociologie du Droit* (2nd edn). Paris: Librairie Générale de Droit et de Jurisprudence, pp. 262–65.

Woodman, G.R. (1996) *Customary Land Law in the Ghanaian Courts*. Accra: Ghana Universities Press.

Woodman, G.R. (1998) 'Droit Comparé Général' (translated by M. Veneau) in W. Capeller and T. Kitmura (eds) *Une Introduction aux Cultures Juridiques non Occidentales*. Brussels: Bruylant, pp. 117–50.

Woodman, G.R. (2003) 'Why There Can be no Map of Law' in R. Pradhan (ed.) *Legal Pluralism and Unofficial Law in Social, Economic and Political Development. Papers of the XIIIth International Congress of the Commission on Folk Law and Legal Pluralism, 7–10 April 2002, Chiang Mai, Thailand*, Vol. III. Kathmandu: International Centre for the Study of Nature, Environment and Culture (ICNEC) pp. 383–92.

Index